RUN LIKE CRAZY

Tristan Miller worked his way through a number of career paths, including bartending and film production, before settling in ad sales at a commercial radio station radio. A divorce had him on the ropes, and he took to running to get back on track. He landed a plum job as an account manager at Google. When the Global Financial Crisis forced the closure of Tristan's regional office, he decided to take control of his own future, risking everything by running around the world. The gamble paid off, and Tristan has an entirely new career as an inspirational public speaker. He lives in Melbourne with his fiancée, Rebecca, and still runs in remarkable parts of the world as often as possible.

runlikecrazy.com

Tristan Miller

RUN LIKE CRAZY

52 MARATHONS
52 WEEKS 42 COUNTRIES

how running changed my life

MICHAEL JOSEPH
an imprint of
PENGUIN BOOKS

MICHAEL JOSEPH

Published by the Penguin Group
Penguin Group (Australia)
250 Camberwell Road, Camberwell, Victoria 3124, Australia
(a division of Pearson Australia Group Pty Ltd)
Penguin Group (USA) Inc.
375 Hudson Street, New York, New York 10014, USA
Penguin Group (Canada)
90 Eglinton Avenue East, Suite 700, Toronto, Canada ON M4P 2Y3
(a division of Pearson Penguin Canada Inc.)
Penguin Books Ltd
80 Strand, London WC2R 0RL England
Penguin Ireland
25 St Stephen's Green, Dublin 2, Ireland
(a division of Penguin Books Ltd)
Penguin Books India Pvt Ltd
11 Community Centre, Panchsheel Park, New Delhi – 110 017, India
Penguin Group (NZ)
67 Apollo Drive, Rosedale, North Shore 0632, New Zealand
(a division of Pearson New Zealand Ltd)
Penguin Books (South Africa) (Pty) Ltd
24 Sturdee Avenue, Rosebank, Johannesburg 2196, South Africa

Penguin Books Ltd, Registered Offices: 80 Strand, London WC2R 0RL, England

First published by Penguin Group (Australia), 2012

10 9 8 7 6 5 4 3 2 1

Text and photographs copyright © Tristan Miller 2012

The moral right of the author has been asserted

Design by Adam Laszczuk © Penguin Group (Australia)
Cover photograph by Eddie Jim © Fairfax Syndication
Typeset in Sabon by Penguin Group (Australia)
Printed and bound in Australia by McPherson's Printing Group, Maryborough, Victoria

National Library of Australia
Cataloguing-in-Publication data:

Miller, Tristan.
Run like crazy / Tristan Miller.
9781921901034 (pbk.)
Miller, Tristan.
Runners (Sports) – Australia – Biography.
Male long-distance runners – Australia – Biography.
Running – Psychological aspects
Self-actualization (Psychology)

796.42092

penguin.com.au

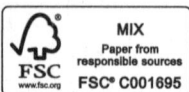

MIX
Paper from
responsible sources
FSC
www.fsc.org   FSC® C001695

CONTENTS

My year of adventure included thousands of great
moments, memorable mishaps and amazing people,
and not all of them could be included in the book.
Although a few names and experiences disappeared
in the editing, not one single person I met throughout
that year has been forgotten. You all made this story
happen and I can never repay you enough for your
friendship and support. Whether we shared a meal,
a roof or a run, you affected my journey and
changed the way I look at the world.
Thank you. For everything.

THE BURNING BUSH

I'm not special . . . I just want to put that out there right away. I'm enthusiastic, I'm mildly amusing, but I'm an ordinary guy. I'm not a natural leader, but I don't follow blindly in the footsteps of others either. I can be a little self-righteous, but I'm not arrogant. I drink too much when I drink and I think too much when I have a lot of time to myself.

I'm not particularly sporty. My parents split when I was three and we didn't have a father around to teach us ball sports. I've got two older sisters, Rebecca and Alexis, and a brother, Chris, who's just a year older. Our stepdad, Jim, gave us a love of motorbikes, but he didn't much care for sport. Chris taught himself how to kick and play cricket well enough to get by at school. I wasn't a sports outcast; I just admitted that I wasn't much good at it. In team sports you need to anticipate the play, have a feel for where the ball will end up. I don't have those skills. I can't see more than a step ahead, so I couldn't plan my movements among other players. I still joined in, but I didn't really get it.

But I could run. I remember in the few races I won at school, when I was 13 or 14 years old, that I loved the last 150 metres. I would wait until we were heading into the last turn and fly home, powering from third or fourth place to the front. As I'd pound right by the guy in the lead, I would hear his sigh of resignation and know I had it in the bag.

I got older and slower. I often came in the top 10, but only when a small percentage of guys were competing – the reality was that the competition wasn't stiff. I was a long way behind the fellas who won.

I'm not all that smart. I like to say I'm clever, though. My IQ is fine and I'm a rational thinker, but I didn't stand out in class or at university. I did go to one of the highest ranked boys high schools in Victoria, and I'd like to think the smarts of the guys around me might have rubbed off.

What I've found is that I think laterally a lot of the time. I'm always trying to think of ways around a problem, rather than solving the problem directly. I waste time figuring out the process or the reason behind things. For instance, if the vacuum cleaner breaks, I pull it apart and fix it, rather than buy a new one. I usually break it further in the process, but I like the idea of being handy or finding a solution. Then again, maybe I'm just a tight-arse.

I hate it when people tell me I can't do things. My way is often a little left-field, but I like to know that it won't work before I'm keen to hear others' opinions. This is one of the many traits that's got me into trouble over the years and although I believe it's endearing to a few, I have no doubt it's downright annoying for most.

So like I said, I'm not special. I don't have a better body or a bigger heart than yours. I don't have years of training and I haven't been a runner all my life. I'm just a guy who's a little clever and likes to do things differently. And I really, *really* like to have fun.

But I did always think I'd do something special. I dreamt about it, imagining that one day I'd be in a bus and the brakes would fail and it'd be down to me to use all my ingenuity to slow it down, while everyone else was panicking and screaming . . . Perhaps I sometimes confuse movies with dreams. Nonetheless, I just knew that an opportunity would one day present itself and that I needed to be ready for it.

Every boy wants to be a hero. We live that idea as children, running about with tea-towels attached to our necks as capes. 'Dishwashing

Man' doesn't have the same ring to it as it did when I was a kid. I could wash 100 dishes in around 10 minutes – which is pretty impressive at eight years old – but it's not something I could boast about at school. The opportunities to be heroic diminish as we get older. You can be chivalrous and impressive, but being heroic is at a whole different level and requires you to go out of your comfort zone. And therein lies the problem. Not many of us like being outside our comfort zone. Running into a burning building isn't very comfortable. Volunteering in third-world countries is particularly uncomfortable. Going to war for your country or a cause is downright scary. Hard work is, well, hard.

Heroes do all of this as a matter of course and thus they will inevitably become champions of the people.

In general, we want to continue to do the things we know how to do, instead of learning or experiencing something fresh. It's learning and being outside the space we know that leads us to greatness. It leads to better understanding. It thrusts us away from sameness. It gives you wings and provides the insight necessary to judge a situation and decide that the time to be a 'hero' has arrived.

It took me a while to stumble onto my Hero Time. I thought a special moment would arrive some day, but quite a few of those moments rushed past me without my noticing. My first inkling that it might be my Hero Time came when I was trying to put my life together after a divorce.

My marriage to Sarah came to an unexpected end in 2004. At the time, I really didn't know how to react, as all my plans had been intrinsically linked to our fate as a couple: we'd been together for 10 years, since I was 18. We'd constantly spoken about what was right and wrong with my decision making. I always wanted to gamble with our futures, whereas Sarah had a more conservative view on how life should play out. Inevitably I was wrong a lot of the time, and it must have been very tiring for her to put out the fires I started. That she loved me for so long is a testament to her patience and ability to see past my bravado and foolish behaviour. The outcomes weren't always ideal, but I was busy making mistakes in my twenties, trying to understand what worked and what didn't. It was right up there with kids sticking mud in their mouths, learning that dirt doesn't taste too good. As Albert Einstein said, 'Anyone who has never made a mistake has never tried anything new.'

Suffice to say, Sarah didn't share my view and the time came when she realised she needed someone a little more stable in her life. I couldn't hold it against her. We parted as friends and I still love her.

A newly single guy with a nice car, a property and a good sales job in radio, I tried to figure out what I should do next. I found out very quickly that the dating rule book had changed quite dramatically since I'd last been single. It turned out that I was useless with women and even worse on the drink.

I wondered how things had all gone so very wrong and took to drinking on weeknights to get my head around it. I spent months after my divorce drinking myself into oblivion, figuring that I could fix myself by just blotting out the distress.

Unfortunately when you fail in your personal life, it's hard to keep it separate from your professional one. I was a salesman at 3AW Talkback Radio, and I did okay. When I was struggling with depression, though, I wasn't doing as well. A few times I broke down in very quiet tears at my desk, hiding under the partitioned walls. I just sat there and looked at the wall outside my window and tried to tell myself that everything would be fine, that time would heal all wounds. But, I learnt, time isn't enough. Time only softens the blows and fades the memory. Time takes the edge off pain, but it doesn't mean you forget it and it doesn't fix you. It's only half the solution.

A guy I worked with at 3AW gave me the other half. If I trace all the greatness of the last six years to just one moment in time, it's when

Rob Gilbert asked me to go for a run with him.

I hadn't really talked about my divorce at work, but Rob noticed I was struggling. He asked if I'd like to run with him on the weekend and have a talk. Rob's a very busy guy who juggles a huge portfolio, a gorgeous wife and two lovely sons, Tommy and Alexander. Alexander has cystic fibrosis. Rob had run 10 Melbourne Marathons, and he used his running as a period of meditation every day. He was prepared to break that meditation and listen to my problems on a Saturday morning, so I couldn't very well say no. I was worried I wouldn't be able to run too far, but Rob promised we'd go easy: we set out on a cruisy one-hour tour of Melbourne on foot.

I think we only ran about 10 kilometres in that first effort, which was still further than I'd ever run before. I discussed how I was going at work and Rob gave me a few tips on how to turn things around, but eventually the story of my failed marriage came up and we talked it through. Rob told me about the hurdles in his own life and the way he'd managed to stay focused and transcend the odds. He talked about physical activity as a good place to start in getting my headspace settled, and encouraged me to meet with him again the following week. He also made me realise that, on my current trajectory, I was in danger of becoming a cliché – a drunken ex-husband who had sunk his career as well. Rob encouraged me to look for a brighter path.

We started to meet regularly and I began to feel better about myself. I was working a second job in a nightclub and, in fact, I stopped drinking after work so I could meet Rob for our Saturday session. Every time we went for a run on a Saturday morning, I would have the rest of the day ahead of me, sans hangover. My weekends became automatically longer and more fulfilling.

As time went on, I added a Sunday run too. Rob mentioned the Melbourne Marathon to me and I laughed, responding that I wasn't really cut out for distance running. That'd take planning, determination, courage, focus, plus the mental and physical strength of the gods themselves. I wasn't blessed with any of these traits in large proportions, so covering 42.2 kilometres seemed beyond me.

I signed up for a half marathon instead, and was overjoyed when I got across the finish line. I hurt in places I hadn't known existed, but I realised that the biggest test was in committing to the start line – once I'd got going, the race essentially took care of itself. It became an important lesson. In the post-race bliss I told Rob I wanted to join him in the Melbourne Marathon a few months later. Rob laughed, saying he had already organised an entry for me. He knew I'd eventually come round.

My running efforts increased over the subsequent months and I began to run during the week as well. I was getting up earlier and eating better food. I was switching on in the morning and feeling vibrant for the whole day, rather than struggling to get to work on time and nodding off after lunch. My sales figures increased and my engagement with clients and within the business improved exponentially. I looked healthier, felt stronger and found a point of focus in my personal life – a marathon.

The old Melbourne Marathon route was from Frankston to the CBD. Frankston itself feels like a fair distance to drive from the city, so the idea of running all that way set off anxiety spells. But when we toed the line with a couple of thousand runners in 2005, I was determined to follow through. Rob was calm, tempering my nerves, but he also voiced what had been reverberating in my head: 'A big challenge lies ahead, but you've come here prepared, so you'll be all right.'

We pushed off on that blustery morning and Rob didn't let me get too caught up in the excitement, making sure I didn't surge off with the seasoned runners in the first hundred metres. By 10 kilometres in, I was still pretty frisky. Rob stuck to his race plan and beat out the distance – 'Still a long way, mate; settle down. We'll get there if we stick to the strategy.'

By 30 kilometres I was cooked. I was walking through drink

stations and having to run hard to catch up to Rob. I knew that I was slowing him down and he wouldn't be on track for a sub-four-hour marathon for much longer, so I had to let him go.

'Just keep going, mate. Find a way to keep moving and you'll get there,' Rob encouraged me as we said farewell.

It took everything I had to keep moving. I looked at a crossroads in Elwood and realised that it was the road I'd take to drive home. The finish line was 10 kms away, but home was only a few kilometres to my right. There was a horrible moment when I considered how easy it would be to sneak off and find a tram up that street. I wondered if I could even just have a rest and come back later to finish it off. I considered what other people would think of me and realised that I didn't really care. Then I weighed up the most important opinion: what would I think of me? I wanted, more than anything else, to be able to respect myself. If I gave up now, I might just start giving up on everything in my life. I'd already given up on my marriage. I'd nearly given up on my career. I'd certainly given up on many childhood hopes and dreams. Now I had a chance to right those wrongs. I decided, from now on, I would never give up. So I looked past the intersection to the road ahead and vowed to struggle on until the end, however it turned out.

I looked for the 1-km markers and kept moving, running a bit, walking a bit, until I came through St Kilda and realised that at my current rate it would take me over an hour to cover the last 6 kilometres. I wanted the end to come so I could stop, and the only fix I could think of was to get it over with as quickly as possible. It was time to run through the pain, the cramps, the friction that caused my nipples to bleed. It was time to believe that I could raise myself up and accomplish this goal. It was Hero Time. 'Lift, Tristan,' I commanded myself. 'C'mon, buddy, you can do this. You were built for this. You too can be a hero, if you just LIIIIIIIIIFT!'

And I did. I was running again and the kilometre markers just fell away. I pushed and grunted and wheezed, dragging my sorry old body along the road. 'Liiiiiiiift,' I repeated, trying to stoke the small fire I'd lit in my heart. 'Beliieeeve,' I breathed out as I forced myself forwards.

And I got there. I all but fell over the line after 4 hours 19 minutes of running. It's not a magical first marathon time, but considering how bad I felt, it was definitely a win for me. But the best part was that I'd achieved the impossible. I'd managed to run a marathon.

I gave Rob a hug. He'd beaten me by 15 minutes and looked as tired as I felt. I thanked him for all his advice and belief in me. It was a moment like no other and I'll remember it forever. It was the first time I'd really felt like a champion. The first time I'd truly believed in myself, without cause to question or reason to lie. I'd defeated those horrible feelings of failure that had dogged me since my divorce. I'd risen above the minor setbacks in life and carved out my own slice.

I was a hero and it felt really good.

The experience helped me to realise the importance of goal setting. I'd loosely set goals in my professional life, but never in my personal life. And they operated in tandem. So as I became fatigued at work, if things weren't going well, I'd get frustrated at home too. I realised if I gave myself a goal and laid out a plan to achieve it, then I'd create an easy daily victory that would offset any stresses I was having at work. If I went for a run in the morning, I'd start the day with a win. If I ran particularly fast, getting closer to my desired goal, then I was on top of the world before I'd even stepped into the office.

I started to look at everything I did in terms of that marathon. If I set a start point for every goal I wanted to achieve, broke down the steps involved in getting there, anticipating the problems or 'walls' that might get in the way, then I was on my way to knocking off yet another task. It's often said that 'Life is a marathon, not a sprint'. I would take that a step further and say that life and every year within life, every month, every week, each day and every task mirrors a marathon. It starts, you get it right for a while, a few things go to crap, you find solutions, then you stride onwards again . . . You are pestered by fears of failure and inspired by ideas of success. You struggle to control what you can and you look for markers that signify your progress. Eventually, you get to the finish line, full of pride at your accomplishment, hoping that someone will hang a medal around your neck for your stunning performance. Usually the lessons from the journey are far more satisfying than the achievement itself, the finish line not looking much like you anticipated, but, hell, it's still worth a celebration!

Thought-provoking stuff, I know . . .

I took this all to heart and started to knock out tasks like it was going out of fashion. I went out of my comfort zone as often as possible, both physically and professionally. I didn't always get it right, but I was learning something new every day. I was becoming more like the image I'd always had of myself. I was finally filling my skin.

I travelled more, heading to Germany for the Berlin Love Parade – 1.2 million people dancing in the streets of that amazing city. I went to Tokyo and met a beautiful Japanese girl, Mayumi, enjoying a long-distance relationship for a couple of years. I had a crack at a triathlon. I decided to get out of radio, and investigated what other type of advertising I could switch to – and digital looked pretty good.

I applied for a job at the biggest company I could think of – Google – and was immediately told by my peers and the recruitment agencies that I had no chance of getting the gig. They had a small office in Melbourne, so I reasoned someone must be working there. I decided I needed to back myself even if no one else would. Eight interviews and six months later, I landed an account manager's job with them.

I had a steep learning curve at Google but I was inspired by the technology and the company's forward thinking. It was where I met some of the most exciting and interesting people I have ever known. I made lifelong friends and experienced extraordinary moments. Life was good. My new plan was working.

Up to this point I'd been running a marathon a year, except in 2007, when I only ran a couple of half marathons. At the insistence of a good friend, I joined Tribal, a triathlon and running group, at the same time I started at Google, January 2008. I had avoided joining a club, thinking that their runners would be a little too focused and competitive for me. But when I joined Tribal, I found a group of people with varied abilities and a huge appetite for laughter and fun. It made me want to show up three or four days a week, and gave me a reason to get out of bed at 5:30 a.m. on cold winter mornings. I figured if these clowns could get up to run in frigid temperatures and still laugh their butts off, then I wanted to join the party. By the end of that year, I was running faster and stronger than I ever had before.

After knocking off that year's Melbourne Marathon, a few of us looked to something bigger. One of the guys, Chippa, had already completed the prestigious Comrades 89-km ultra-marathon in South Africa – twice. The way he spoke of the experience made the hairs on my neck stand up. Comrades is the largest ultra-marathon by participation in the world and the race literally stops the nation. It has a 12-hour limit, though the winners can finish in around 5:20. Comrades is nearly as old as the Boston Marathon, beginning in 1921, and has a really friendly community vibe. I was hooked.

In March 2009, I ran the Canberra Marathon for a second time. They had a 50-km challenge and our whole group performed very well. I ran 4:03 and felt like I could have run forever. The key thing here was not the race, however, but the goodie bag that came at registration. This was, as per usual, full of crappy promo gear and advertising, but included something that would change everything. *Distance Running* magazine is produced by AIMS (Association of International Marathons) and is chock-full of race results, short reviews and glossy ads for international marathons. At the centrefold, though, is where I found the gold: a calendar of all the AIMS-registered marathons, half marathons and ultras from around the globe. The list included some absolute rippers, including Berlin, the Great Wall and Reykjavik. But what was most exciting was the way the races were listed. Each weekend, every week, had as many as six races listed in different parts of the world.

I sat staring at this list for about 10 minutes while conversation continued around me. It occurred to me I could travel to some truly stunning destinations – Copenhagen maybe, followed by Moscow, then Edinburgh and a quick trip to Kigali, finishing in Phuket – and run a marathon in each place.

I brought up the idea with my running buddies, Kevlar and Loz. (Yep, everyone's got a nickname – mine is T-Bone or Bone. It's a long story so let's just say it's a moniker for my more reckless side.) During the long hours spent training, we'd often wonder how we could be making the most of our time. Now, I sat in the back of Kev and Loz's car and pitched the idea of running around the world, while perhaps filming product reviews and race experiences at the same time.

'How many races?' asked Kev.

'Fifty-two,' I responded.

'One a week?!'

'Yep,' I stated, while I gulped down a whisper of fear.

'Sounds pretty crazy. Man, if I didn't have a business, I'd love to take on a challenge like that!' Kev said, while calculating the possibilities. His wife, Loz, was not so enamoured with the running part, but loved the notion of travelling the world for a year.

I had a lot of discussions about the idea from then on, slowly destroying the calendar I'd pulled out of the *Distance Running* mag, as I worked through different permutations of destinations and races. 'But look where you could get to!' I kept saying, wondering how the hell I could make such a journey work.

The opportunity was handed to me at the beginning of April 2009. A tidal wave was sweeping across the world – the Global Financial

Crisis. It had been in full swing since the end of 2008, but I still thought I'd be safe. Then the announcement came. Google would not be keeping the Melbourne office and I'd get a small payout. It took me a day or so to see this as an opening, but once I recognised it, the angels started to sing and the light from above began to shine. I had no responsibilities, except a mortgage and my little cat, Hugo. Being a cat, Hugo chose not to remember who I was unless I was patting him or feeding him, so really the mortgage was the most pressing issue.

I focused on the first step – Comrades, held in May. I needed to get to Africa. I figured the rest of the story would unfold from there.

I'd been training for the Comrades ultra-marathon for a number of months. It would be my first real ultra, a gruelling 89.3-km race renowned for its spirit-breaking hills. Plus it'd be my first time in Africa, a whole new continent, with wild animals that I'd only ever glimpsed in zoos. I had no idea what would be in store for me by running in another country, let alone running so far in a single race.

As it turned out, Comrades was one of my life's defining experiences. The run itself travels from Pietermaritzburg to Durban and vice versa on alternate years. It's hard to believe the level of support thrown to you by onlookers as you run the long road to Durban. It's by no means a lonely stretch, as the other participants know you're an international runner by the colour of your bib. They're quick to sidle up and welcome you to South Africa and the race that holds so much pride for them.

Something special happened to me during that race. I was so caught up in the joy of running in a foreign country that the pain I was inflicting on my body lost most of its bite. I couldn't help but remind myself with each painful step that I had planned and trained to be in this very position. Each time my foot hit the road, I remembered I was touching Africa, so the pain became a privilege and the kilometres melted away.

As I entered the stadium to roars from the packed bleachers, I felt like every yell and each clap was directed straight at me. Having run 89 kms to get there, I savoured each metre of that final 300, finishing in 9:18.23.

I had made it. And all of my friends from Tribal – Cougar, Kev, Chippa, Ali, Loz and Robyn – made it too. We were always going to make it. A couple of weeks with my buddies touring to Botswana and Zambia opened my eyes even further. I saw baby elephants falling about in the mud, under the watchful eyes of beasts that were twice the size of our trucks. I watched as lion cubs crept out of hiding to gorge themselves in the chest cavity of a buffalo. I was gobsmacked through-out my African adventure. I realised how little I'd seen throughout my life, and made a pact that I would continue to travel.

My dream of running 52 marathons in 52 weeks around the world really took off on that trip. I decided that it was completely possible, and, even better, I was in an amazing position to try it. What was stop-ping me from getting out there and just making it happen?

That resolve ebbed and flowed once I returned to Australia. One Fri-day I got an unexpected job offer, and it tested my determination; I was given until Monday to decide. That weekend I thought long and hard about what I wanted. If I took the job, I could continue to pay my mortgage and follow my career path, wherever that might lead.

But something else had been bubbling in the back of my mind, that old deep desire to do something great. I wanted to be a hero and although I didn't have an enemy to rise up and vanquish, I could battle the oldest foe of all, the one common to all humankind: fear.

Because of fear we run from the unknown, we don't attempt things outside our experience and fear means that most of us fall far short of our potential. It's the number of times you say, 'One day, I'd like to try skydiving', but never pick up the phone and schedule the day of reckoning. Yet, if you do, you know you'll be full of pride, energised by your ability to take your life in your own hands. You know the experience will be with you forever, having faced your fears to fly like a bird across the sky.

I decided this was the catalyst. I'd set out to defeat my fear.

On Monday I called back the recruiter and said thanks, but no thanks – I had a new project that I wanted to throw myself into.

By then it was July 2009. I called a real estate agent and asked them to sell my apartment. I announced to my friends that I was going to take the following year off to see the world. The responses were mixed. I think most people didn't really believe what I was pitching. I was named 'Male Runner of the Year 2009' at the Tribal awards night, a gong given to me largely because I'd improved dramatically that year. I gave a short drunken speech and ended it by telling everyone of my plans. There was some clapping but a lot more awkward staring. My buddy, Cougar, shook his head and offered, 'Well, you've told *every-one* now . . . You better bloody do it!'

And, I guess, that was that. I began planning the journey, day and night. I'd spend hours online, trying to figure out the most exciting routes. I constantly spun the Google Earth virtual globe around on my computer and looked at where I most wanted to visit. I made a few spreadsheets, cutting and pasting the alternatives, trying to make it work. I locked down the 'Five Majors' first: Berlin, Boston, Chicago, London and New York. They were undoubtedly exciting prospects, but there were also other spectacular cities I wanted to visit – Rome, Tokyo, Paris, St Petersburg, Athens – so I pinned those down too. Between these dates, I considered the Great Wall Marathon, races in Hungary, Israel, Egypt, India. Places I wanted to return to were added to the list – Cape Town, Prague, Verona and Loch Ness. I even found a way to work in some big festivals that I'd always wanted to see: Roskilde Music Festival in Denmark, the Running of the Bulls in Spain.

My only prerequisite for going to these festivals was that I'd also have to fit in a race that same week. Crazy, but possible. Then there were the stretch goals, places that were expensive to visit or difficult to access – Iceland, Easter Island, Mongolia, Rwanda, Cuba, Antarctica – but if I could get there, I swore I would.

While the calendar took shape, I drew up my list of rules.

1. Every race had to be a verified marathon – 42.195 kilometres, or 26.2 miles or more.
2. Each one needed to be recognised by an athletic body or have a history of more than 10 participants.
3. If I decided to do a 100-kilometre ultra (Mongolia), then it only counted as one race.
4. If I needed more time to get to a race (i.e. a 10-day program), then I had to make up the missing marathon by doubling up with Saturday and Sunday marathons.
5. All races needed to be completed between and including the first and last weeks of 2010: 52 marathons in 52 weeks.
6. If possible, each consecutive race had to be in a different country.
7. As many different countries as possible should be included.

That was about it. It seemed simple, but when you considered the amount of travel involved and the extra stress I'd be facing from doubling up marathons, then you could imagine the doubts that started creeping through my mind. I tried to create a schedule that wasn't limited by cost, but this was obviously a very real hurdle. I did my sums and realised that I would need more than $70 000 to see through this plan. It also seemed clear that I would need help, or support, so I began to consider taking someone with me.

The Daz is one of the most lovable people you'd ever meet. The Dazzler, christened Darren John Foss, is from Oamaru, New Zealand.

I first met him in 2003 while working behind the bar at the famous Esplanade Hotel in St Kilda, Melbourne. He bounced straight into the bar, fresh off the boat from New Zealand and I could tell straight-away we were going to get along. He was goofy, laughed at everything, and would work hard all night before heading to nightclubs to dance his butt off till dawn or beyond. Back then, I found myself hitting the clubs with him pretty regularly, when really I should have been going home to my wife. I found his enthusiasm for life totally infectious, especially because I was struggling.

Darren would hit a club and own it in 30 minutes. He'd smooth-talk the bouncers, befriend the bartenders, shake it up with a few girls, then get up on a speaker or podium and play imaginary tennis across the room with random dancers. Everyone loved him and we became as close as brothers. I'd do anything to see him laugh – although to be fair, that didn't take much.

Late one drunken night Darren suddenly became serious. He said he had a secret he wanted to talk about. I wasn't used to this side of him, so I quickly tried to pull myself together. He told me of his last few years in New Zealand. His mother had passed away when he was 11, a slow, painful death from breast cancer. It had devastated his family and he missed his mother terribly. A few years later, while he was playing high-level tennis at the Sports Institute of Otago, he'd been diagnosed with non-Hodgkin lymphoma. His family was horri-fied and with the death of Daz's mother still raw in their minds, they were unable to support him very well.

He was lucky that he had a strong network of amazing friends who spent hours with him while he battled it out. Daz fought against the disease as it destroyed his immune system. He was in a very bad way for a long time, but his spirit won out. Once he'd recovered, Daz vowed to live every moment of every day to the fullest. He was going to live for the now, just in case tomorrow brought back the cancer.

I was shocked by his story, but it certainly explained a few things.

It also put my own experience into perspective. I truly can't imagine how abandoned he must have felt. Darren showed me that it was worth making the most of life.

Not long after this, a friend of Daz's took her life. It hit him hard, but gave him a moment of clarity. Daz had always planned to use Australia as a stepping stone to the rest of the world and so he took off to Europe. I followed his adventures eagerly, reading his emails and enjoying the occasional phone call. He lived in Manchester, London and Barcelona and had all sorts of crazy mishaps.

In his own way, Daz had given me a kick in the butt, showing me it was not too late to immerse myself in the world. When I was working out the details of the madcap marathon journey and running through the list of people I could take with me, Daz was my first choice. He was carefree enough to want to come, he was loads of fun to be around and he would basically let me lead the expedition – meaning we probably wouldn't butt heads over too many things.

What I hadn't anticipated was Daz saying no. He had only been home from Europe for six months and he was just beginning to get enough tennis-coaching work to live comfortably. I understood he wanted to build a business, but I begged him to wait 12 more months and come on an all-expenses-paid trip around the world. But Daz wasn't all that keen. He didn't want to run marathons and he didn't have much experience in shooting video, which was one of my requirements. By now I already had it in my head that Darren would be perfect, so I bugged him about it till he acquiesced. The last push came when his adopted grandma contracted cancer and it gave him a scare. He realised one of life's great adventures was right in front of him, and he decided once again to take advantage of the opportunity.

I had made countless lists of possible destinations and detailed the steps involved in achieving my goals, but I knew that success would hinge on a few very important factors. There was a danger of not making it through the first month. I'd have to complete six marathons in a month and I'd only done six in my five-year running career. Risky . . . but possible. And if I got it right, I'd have a marathon in hand to waste later in the year if I needed it.

The villains here were Sickness and Injury. There could be no way I'd get through the entire year without facing both of these spectres. I'd have to make a decision early on about whether to wrap myself in cotton wool and remain conservative in everything I did outside of running and travelling. This is the absolute antithesis of all of my instincts and a terrible way to squander the gift of seeing the world. I decided I'd be a hybrid of super-athlete and classic backpacker – I'd run like blazes when I got to the marathons, but I'd drink and dance when I had the chance. If I was going to spend all my money on a world tour, then the least I could do was enjoy the hell out of it!

If I met up with Sickness, I'd buy as many local drugs as possible to kill the bug. If Injury loomed, I'd slow down in a race and rest as much as possible between events.

My biggest threat, though, was fear. Fear leads to more systemic problems like depression and anxiety. If I was going to spend the year being scared of losing my gear, missing my flights or hurting myself, then I might as well stay home. I worked these losses into my budget and confronted Murphy's Law: everything that could go wrong would most definitely go wrong. I accepted it. Embraced it. And forgot it. The world can be a scary place if you let it. Once I embraced the impending inevitable disasters, I found myself without much fear left.

I wasn't so afraid of failure any more. In fact, I only would have considered the venture a total failure if I hadn't made it to that first start line in Zurich. To get there and start the adventure would be the biggest triumph of my life. But there were some issues to iron out before that. I needed help. Daz coming along was one thing, but I needed dollars and some help with PR.

I set up a blog to tell my story. Everyone said I was crazy, so I decided that's what I'd call the website: RunLikeCrazy. I set up a Facebook page and a YouTube channel too. I didn't know which would work best, but I thought I could add to those outlets without too much trouble.

Another friend, Nick McCormack, volunteered to be my PR manager and to drum up some sponsorship for me. We hoped that one of the corporate conversations would generate some money, but after a few months it didn't look too promising.

Nick was true to his word, though – he sincerely wanted to help. He started sending media alerts to the major newspapers and event organisers in each country we were headed to, running the media release through Google Translate in the hope that each country could glean enough information to want to contact us.

Nick also introduced me to his lovely girlfriend, Kirsten. At the time she was working at Areeba, a web company, and we brokered a deal for them to sponsor me. The Areeba guys were good enough to give my website a complete makeover, also promising me any tech assistance I might need throughout the year.

RunLikeCrazy. I loved the name and just needed a logo to go with it. I'm a big believer in good branding, having learnt its power from my father, who is a bit of a marketing guru, Bob Miller. Travis from Areeba put a logo together in his spare time and did a spectacular job. I wanted the emblem to epitomise strength and fear. I was going to run with the bulls, a mental thing to do in itself, so it seemed fitting that the bull was represented in the logo. The final image was a red bull, look-ing fierce and wild, emerging from a black circle, which represented the globe. It had the perfect feel. I loved it and proudly plastered it onto my clothes and website. It felt like I'd created something special.

If you're going to run around the world, spend loads of money, get exposure and tell your story, it's a great chance to raise some money and awareness for a worthy cause.

I connected with UNICEF. They help children who are victims of disasters, natural or otherwise, by quickly moving in to distribute clean drinking water and food, while encouraging children to get back into school as their world is rebuilt around them. I believe that lack of education is the biggest hurdle the modern world faces. With every school day a kid misses, opportunities disappear. As an Australian, I mostly take for granted the education gifted to me by my parents and government. At least raising money for a group like UNICEF made me feel like I was channelling my energy in the right direction.

The year 2010 turned out to be an outstanding one to take on my challenge, as it was the 2500th anniversary of the Battle of Marathon. I had planned to run the Athens Marathon, which celebrates the humble beginnings of the world's most renowned test of endurance, and its story resonated with me.

In 490 BC, the Persians launched an attack on Athens, aimed at subjugating Greece. The Persian king, Darius the Great, mustered an army of 150 000 men and landed them near the Greek town of Marathon. As their enemies collected on the beach, the Athenians pulled together their own army to defend the city-state. They were unable to secure immediate help from their allies, the Spartans, and could only rely on the neighbouring Plataeans to lend their support with 1000 men. This meant the Athenian army had only a total of 11 000 men to fight off a force more than 10 times their strength.

After holding the Persians on the beach for five days, the Athenians saw their chance. When the Persian cavalry left the battlefield, they attacked. The Greeks were well equipped and fought the poorly armoured Persians with such ferocity that their enemies turned and fled to their ships. The battle was said to have resulted in 6400 Persian dead, with only light losses to the Greeks – 192 Athenians and

11 Plataeans fell. The Persian fleet attempted another landing, so the Greek army marched to defend their native beaches once more.

Ahead of their returning army, the Greeks sent a runner to Athens to tell of their victory, but also to warn of a counter-attack. The brave messenger, Pheidippides, ran the 40 kilometres from the battlefield, in full armour and in spite of injuries received during the fight, to bring this extraordinary news to the people of Athens. As the message spilt from his lips, he fell to the ground, exhausted, and immediately died. His was a grand reflection of the heroism of the Athenian army, which had won a first and decisive victory over the mighty Persians.

Nearly 2400 years later, the Greeks decided to create a modern version of the Olympics, to herald the glory of their people. They included a race that mirrored the path of Pheidippides, celebrating his heroism and that of the Athenians who stood against the Persian hordes.

In 1896 the first run occurred as part of the Games, but the distance we use today, 42.195 kms (26.2 miles), wasn't made official until the Paris Olympics of 1924. In the meantime, marathon running around the world began to proliferate, creating such institutions as the Boston Marathon (which began in 1897), Slovakia's Košice Marathon, London (formerly the Polytechnic) Marathon and even famous ultra-marathons like the prestigious Comrades of South Africa.

This distance-running phenomenon has produced many heroes over the last century, but its brave beginnings 2500 years ago are what give it such poetry today. It captures the imagination of more and more weekend warriors every year, people who are preparing themselves for their first or their 100th attempt at this glorious challenge.

I am one of those it has inspired. The idea of becoming a hero on the track, if not in my personal life, resonated so strongly that I rose to the challenge again and again. I found something very powerful in the deed. I found a sense of self-awareness that I had struggled with up to that point. I certainly haven't saved a city like Athens in the process, but the race itself must be given the credit of saving me.

GETTING READY

Once I sold my flat, I had to get ready to be constantly on the move for a year. The better the plan, the more likely fate would favour me and allow me to overcome the inevitable obstacles. To leave myself less exposed financially, I decided to only book flights and accommodation two to three months out, sometimes less.

Darren's role would be threefold:

1. Take as many photos and videos as possible. The more content, the more interesting the story would be for followers and the more saleable the concept to sponsors.
2. Book accommodation, taking into account proximity to race, free internet, clean beds, potential fun, cheap but not cheapest.
3. Prepare an ice bath post-marathon and do all the thinking for the 12 hours that followed a race, because my brain would go to mush.

These tasks sound easy, but my expectations were high. I saw filming as his most important job; it would be the one he found most challenging.

I put together a budget in August 2009, allowing an average $500 per flight (some would be $60, others would be $2000), $40 per day for food, $50 per day for accommodation. Along with race entries, shoes, clothes, cameras, computers and other web-related tech expenses, I figured I could get through the whole year by myself with around $75 000. To take Daz, it would cost more like $135 000.

Once I'd sold my house and paid a number of outstanding debts – including credit cards and a personal loan – I had around $70 000 to work with. I figured I'd just make this last for as long as I could, in the hope I'd pick up some sponsors along the way. I tried not to let the lack of sufficient funds freak me out. I had approximately 10 grand in stocks and a car that I'd leave in Australia, and I was prepared to sell these later if I needed to – if I was still running.

I decided on standard 15-kg backpacks. Most of the space was taken up by running gear, including shorts, singlets, a pair of runners (I started out with well-cushioned Nike Equalons), a supply of Gatorade powder, along with some carbohydrate gels (GUs). I had a 'fuel belt' too, for my drink bottles, GUs and camera.

My Garmin 310XT sports watch was GPS enabled and Garmin have a great online repository, so you can view your race stats and a map of the run. I had a couple of false starts with my cameras but I settled on the small handheld Canon IXUS 200IS, with a fast shutter action and a great image stabiliser.

Before I left, I went to see a nutritionist, Alison Walsh, for advice. One of her most interesting discoveries was my wonky hydration. Essentially I was consuming around half the daily water intake of most people. I rarely sweat, even during a three- or four-hour run, but when I get extremely hot, I sweat profusely and then rapidly lose energy. In normal people, perspiration evaporates from the skin, cooling them down; it's the body's way of regulating its own temperature. I had unintentionally trained my cooling system to remain switched off until my body overheated, then it would kick in too late, leaving me in a critical state of fatigue.

I tried to slowly increase my intake of liquid, but ended up nearly peeing my pants during numerous marathons. I found it too difficult to change my habits, so after a while, I just let my body do its thing.

Alison advised me about nutrition too. I would seek out pasta in most places, along with protein-rich vegetables. I vowed to avoid crappy white-bread sandwiches and not get carried away with the in-flight meals. I'd make a point of avoiding meals altogether if only heavily processed food was available.

In marathon training you work on your weaknesses and hone your strengths, all the while mentally preparing for the struggles that lie ahead, usually after the halfway mark. A marathon is the ultimate 'best-laid plan', because it's one that's up against the highest odds of failure. In a race, especially one that takes three hours or more to complete, there are too many variables to account for: try nutrition, weather and trail conditions for starters. I'd be adding jet lag on top of all that.

That said, around 20 minutes into a marathon, after I've warmed up, I can almost always tell how the day will turn out, judging by my energy levels and the course I'm running on. I'll know what my splits (the average time per kilometre) will be and I can rework my plan in response. I'll always try to go as fast possible, so when I feel good I'll set the target high. If I feel bad, I'll figure out a way to just keep running until it's over. You just never know what will happen. But that is the challenge of the marathon: to get out there and see.

One thing I didn't have to investigate was how to run marathons in other countries. You can enter the Rome, Tokyo or Kigali marathons, and the registration process, bib pick-up, start time and race etiquette is basically the same. You don't need a lick of the local language to figure it out, although it helps to have Google Translate on hand if you're entering online.

When you enter a marathon, you get the following:
- A race bib, with a start time. Some races are so big that you're slotted into a 'starting wave' based on your anticipated finish time.

- A map for the upcoming race, so you know where to start and where you're going.
- An invite to a pre-race 'pasta party', where you can meet other runners and consume loads of energising carbs.
- A T-shirt, which you'll wear while you train for your next race.
- The right to RunLikeCrazy through your chosen city!

During a race, common sense generally prevails, but there are some **Dos** and **Don'ts**:

- **Do** bring your own toilet paper to an event. Their stocks are guaranteed to run out.
- **Don't** wait until five minutes before the race to let your nerves force you into a toilet queue. Be early!
- **Do** use a tree, if you're a male, unless you're in Japan.
- **Don't** pick up the first water or Gatorade at a drink station and stop to drink it – you're likely to cause a pile-up!
- **Do** be brave and try something new on a foreign refreshment table – I found out that flat Coke is awesome, but salted gherkins are not so much fun.
- **Don't** throw your cup in the middle of the road; look for a collection box.
- **Do** encourage others to keep going, even if it's difficult to talk.
- **Don't** try to carry anyone, figuratively or literally. It's their journey, for better or worse.
- **Do** thank supporters. They've given their time to applaud your heroics.
- **Don't** stop. **Don't** give up until you're at the end.

1
ZURICH MARATHON
1 January, Zurich, Switzerland
3:42.32

On 27 December 2009, Darren and I boarded a Singapore Airlines flight to Zurich. Some family and friends came to the airport to bid us farewell. My mum, Cherryann, was a bit teary, but she knew this was one of the biggest moments of my life so she was incredibly proud too. My eldest sister, Rebecca, was excited, but I knew she was also jealous: she loves adventure and travel. 'See you in New York!' she said as she hugged me. The New York Marathon was in November; I just grinned at her, silently hoping I would make it that far.

Earlier in the day, I'd stood in the morning sun while giving an interview to a Melbourne TV station. Christmas had passed and they were looking for stories to fill the slow period up to New Year's. I was so nervous about the TV appearance that my thigh started shaking uncontrollably. I don't think it came over on camera, but I felt like that leg was going to bounce away. On top of that, I was boasting about my 'amazing' running ability, which would have me travelling the whole world, smashing out a marathon every week, when really I wasn't even sure how the first one would go.

I'd been recovering from an adductor injury. After I'd strained this muscle in my thigh, I went through a lengthy course of rehab. With the help of my mate Kevlar, who was also my physio, I managed to come good. Kevlar gave me lots of time and showed great patience (even when I wasn't listening to him), helping me get on track for the year ahead.

'Wow, this is incredible,' said the presenter. 'How do you think you'll manage it?'

'I'm going to take it one race at a time,' I boldly stated. 'I'm just going to get out there and have a go!'

It was a very Aussie thing to say and seemed to placate the interviewers. I'm not sure how many Aussies really do have a go, but we say it a lot, so there must be an element of truth to it. In actual fact, I was relatively new to the whole game.

Once we got to Zurich, I was well and truly out of my comfort zone. I'd left 30°C days in Melbourne and arrived in the middle of one of Europe's coldest winters on record. Daz and I were rugged up but hadn't packed any big jackets, as they would have taken up too much space in our packs.

My other sister, Alexis, was coming over from her home in London to cheer me on for race number one – it'd take place on New Year's Eve. The race was due to start at midnight: the first minute of the first day of 2010. On the way to the starting place that icy-cold night, I was filled me with trepidation, but this was soon overwhelmed by an unearthly feeling. *I'd actually made it.*

At the sports hall where the start line was, the Swiss were pretty well wrapped up. Everyone was wearing plenty of layers, including track jackets, beanies and gloves. I was a little less prepared; I'd just donned my SKINS compression gear with a RunLikeCrazy T-shirt over the top.

I talked to myself throughout the countdown. 'This is your time, my friend. Think strong and believe in yourself.'

Then we were off . . .

A few brave souls clustered near the start of the race and at various checkpoints along the way to cheer us on. The course follows a trail along the Limmat River, which runs through Zurich. From the sports hall we headed to the river, then we began a long 10-km loop, with the last loop finishing up back at the hall.

Most runners wore head torches. But there was a full moon and although a lot of fog was about, plenty of natural light guided our way. Actually, I wouldn't have wanted a torch anyway: you end up focusing on that one spot of light and lose sense of where you are. I mean, I was running along a Swiss river in the middle of the night on New Year's Eve, for Pete's sake! Fireworks were going off every few seconds on the horizon. That was a scene you wanted to remember.

I felt good for the entire run. My adductor strain gave me a couple of pinches, tightening up a few times through the distance. I slowed to a walk at the drink stations and that loosened it up.

The last lap just felt good. I had left a lovely Italian bloke behind on lap three. He'd told me how he needed running to keep him focused and fit for his two baby sons. The eldest was now so quick that chasing him was all the training my new friend needed. As I left him in the mist and charged on to finish my first run, I was alone, unable to see more than 20 metres in front and nothing behind. I was on my own in the Swiss night, with only about 6 kms to go. Right then, I realised, was the moment I'd been hoping for – the moment of clarity. Here I was really running around the world. My little dream was an actual adventure! I started storming home, passing struggling runners in their own worlds of pain, and wishing them a 'Guten Morgen'.

I turned off and ran into the hall. I spotted Alexis cheering for me and Daz with the camera going. I completed it in 3:42.32. No PB (personal best), but it felt great. They even had awards for the fastest athlete from each country, so being the only Australian, I cleaned up. Daz knocked off his 10 kms in 55.51, a top effort. He even got a gong for being the fastest Kiwi!

Marathon 1, tick.

The buzz dropped away quickly. By the time we got to Berlin, I knew we were screwed. We'd missed our flight to Tel Aviv. We were set to spend my 33rd birthday, 3 January, in Israel, which would leave a few days before we needed to travel to Lake Tiberias for my next marathon. But the gods had intervened and we were now stuck in Berlin.

The thought of being stuck in the snow for my birthday was a letdown. I'd imagined sitting on a beach, watching the sun go down on a tumultuous year, and getting ready for the greatest adventure of my life. Now we'd be staying at the wrong hostel, in the wrong part of town, in the wrong country. But I still had Daz and we were determined to have a good time.

Berlin is renowned for its pub crawls, and we immediately signed up. Within a couple of hours we were drunk and Daz was taking his homework quite seriously. Before we left Australia, a very creative friend of ours, known only as 'the Jones', had concocted a list of 52 misadventures that Daz needed to complete throughout our tour. Most of them were quite silly, but that was the point, and many would expose Daz to the risk of arrest or retribution.

The task in Berlin was to start a snowball fight. Daz went for it, picking up a rather large chunk of ice and hurling it at the head of a fellow pub-crawler. There was a moment of silence, followed – thankfully – by some wild laughter and then a barrage of return fire. The most poignant moment was when Daz spilt an entire beer on his crotch in the process of negotiating a peace settlement. How Darren went home with a girl that night while reeking of beer is beyond me, but such is his magical presence.

I woke up the next day with a hangover and without a Daz. He showed up later and we tried to remember the finer details of the night. We both had a good time there was no doubt, so it had been a successful birthday.

I was happy to leave the cold when Tuesday finally rolled around. The Berlin Marathon, in September, meant I'd return to make the most of this spectacular city.

We boarded the Tui Fly plane and headed south-east.

2
TIBERIAS INTERNATIONAL MARATHON
7 January, Tiberias, Israel

3:52.35

I really didn't know what to expect in Israel. I half thought I'd get frisked at the airport and maybe even dragged into a side room to answer 100 questions under spotlight, reducing me to tears and making me confess to liking daisies on a summer's day . . .

Of course, I soon found out that the passport check at Tel Aviv Airport was no more difficult than anywhere else. We got a couple of buses into town and noticed straightaway how many soldiers there were around. They weren't all on duty; in fact most of them seemed to just be heading to or from work in their fatigues. I was more than a little distracted by the groups of women walking past with weapons hanging over their shoulders. It was kinda hot actually . . .

We spent a night in town before heading out to Lake Tiberias for race number two.

Tiberias itself is quite small, and has the feel of an old resort town, like Cowes near Melbourne, or Brighton in England. Some Tel Aviv guys we'd met said there was no reason to be there, unless you're Christian or you like running, but they all agreed it was a pretty place for a visit.

The night before the marathon and after I'd picked up my race number, we went to the pasta party – a pre-race carbo-loading event – in the Golden Tulip Hotel, a nice spot on the edge of the lake. The pasta was plentiful and they had loads of bread and salad. I hadn't eaten properly all day, so I really made the most of it.

We met a few people, including Duby, a man who'd suffered a stroke the year before and through sheer determination had trained to do his first marathon – what a hero! We also had a couple of really easygoing guys in our room. As we all had marathon experience, it was nice to be able to talk about strategy and not focus too much on whether we could go the distance. In the morning, though, we still had nerves about what the day was going to bring.

Daz and I got down there with plenty of time, carrying our back-packs to stash at the Golden Tulip. We were a bit of a sight really; you don't normally have runners show up to an event with their lives on their backs. After a toilet stop and then a good-luck hug from Daz, I went out on one of the main streets to the start line and joined the throng.

The countdown revved everyone up and as 9 a.m. struck, the crowd of runners surged forwards to begin their journey. I tried to find a rhythm, sticking to the left so I could wave to Daz and the camera. It wasn't long before I was weaving, looking to get past the slower-paced groups. I was aiming for 3:30, and settled on running with Julian, a South African I'd met at the Comrades marathon the year before. You couldn't have missed this guy: he had long, flowing hair, a dark tan and was built like he ran through walls as a warm-up. We compared notes – it was definitely going to be a hot one, so conserving energy was important.

I don't sweat much. Alison Walsh, my nutritionist in Melbourne, had told me that without enough fluid in my body, my system couldn't afford to sweat until it was totally overheating. One of the things I was determined to do was take her advice and drink more, so that my body would have some fluid to sweat out to help cool down my muscles. The first drink stop didn't appear for a while, and when it did, they were handing out whole bottles of water. I downed half and trucked along to the next, doing the same there. Normally I'd leave drinking till later, but it was toasty and, unusually, I was sweating like I was in a steam room.

I hadn't even reached the 15-km mark when a man came bolting past me in the opposite direction. Apparently the leader had hit halfway at a little over 59 minutes, which was a course record. From Tiberias, the course winds around the lake before returning the same way back into town, so you get to see who is ahead and how they are feeling. It's good when you see your mates, but a little disheartening when the leader is so far ahead.

Along the way, I picked up more about the history of the area. Apart from our proximity to the Sea of Galilee, where it's said Jesus started his ministry, we were running below the famed Golan Heights, a cliff face that was the scene of some pretty horrific fighting between the Syrians and the Israelis. So here I was running along the sites of scripture and bloodshed.

All of a sudden I was at the halfway point and lagging off my pace. It was time to step it up. I cruised back along the lake, knowing that my pain point would come somewhere between 26 and 36 kms. I always hit a wall in that space for a few clicks, so I knew just to hunker down and tick off the kilometres. But, it didn't really happen: I hit 30 kms feeling pretty good and actually started to speed up, catching the 3:45 pacer who had passed me. A pacer's job is to run slightly ahead of a group of competitors, providing a moving target to help them achieve specific finishing times – think of the fake bunny they have greyhounds chase at the track. I knew that as long as I could get to 35 kms, I'd be pumped up by the impending finish, so I guzzled plenty of water at each stop and kept moving.

I hit the 35-km mark without too much concern and to keep my sugar levels up I downed another GU – a carbohydrate gel that gives you a quick power boost. But then it all went wrong . . . 36 kms was where I found that wall. It was like someone had hooked up a couple of truck tyres to my ankles. I went through the list of everything I had done and could do to fix this. Maybe I'd not had enough GUs, maybe not enough electrolytes. I'd been pretty good about drinking. Perhaps it was just from the travel and the marathon six days ago.

Whatever it was, I knew that all I could do was keep moving. I walked a little, ran some more, aiming for the next marker and running till I passed it. I started playing seesaw with a guy in an orange top. He'd run past me and then slow to a walk for a few hundred metres. Then I'd run past him and only make it a little farther along. After exchanging positions a few times, I got a tap on the shoulder and a nod of the head as he passed me – 'Come on, buddy, let's get there together.' We ran along together for a while, but it didn't last. It's the fleeting friendship, but while you're there it helps you forget you've got to get home alone.

I sucked it up while passing the 41-km mark. I dumped a whole bottle of water over my head and tried to shake off the fatigue. I wasn't going to let myself crawl across that line, so it was time to grit my teeth. I found a little kick so that I came in looking less like the crippled runner I'd been only 3 kms earlier. There's something about a finish line that'll always give you a shot in the butt.

We didn't stick around in Tiberias, because once you've run 42 kms there, you've seen most of what it's got to offer. So at 7 p.m. on Thursday, we were back at a hostel in Tel Aviv. Now, anywhere else in the world, you'd just hit the sack and wait for Friday night. But Israel's holy day is Saturday, and their weekend begins on Friday. And try telling Daz that he has to stay home on the weekend. Ain't gonna happen, my friends.

We went to a few bars in Florentine, an area hidden away in the south of Tel Aviv. You wouldn't stumble on it. If you're not local, you stand out like a sore thumb too. We tried a few places and I struggled to stay chipper as the day's efforts took their toll.

As it cruised past midnight, all of a sudden the street was packed with people. Apparently no one goes out till late; they head home first to eat and rest after a long week at work. Unfortunately, I'd peaked too early. I said my goodbyes and left Daz to it.

Next day, I woke up and Daz's bed was empty. Maybe he had continued the adventure and went looking for fun? Maybe he'd met someone special, who was now cooking him breakfast? There were many possibilities, and as Daz's phone was dead, I thought I'd do some work and give him time to show. He rocked up about 3 p.m. Apparently he'd hit some clubs, then met a beautiful woman who'd insisted on having him come home to play checkers. Daz was such a gentleman he couldn't refuse.

A couple of days later we went to Jerusalem and stayed at a backpackers' hostel near the Damascus gate of the Old City. We went for a walk before it got dark and stumbled across the place where Jesus is said to have been put on trial, sentenced to death and loaded onto his cross. We followed some of his unfortunate journey through the city before entering a huge open area full of tourists, mostly religious and orthodox Jews, who kept going up to a wall and touching it while praying. I asked a woman what the place was. She answered that it was the Western Wall, otherwise known as the Wailing Wall and possibly the most holy place in Judaism. I felt like an ignorant fool.

Walking back towards the hostel, we took some random turns and ended up in an enormous church where Christians were kissing a stone on the floor and lining up to get into a small chapel at the top end of the cathedral. I sensed that this was a very important place (though somewhat dark and ominous) and finally got the courage to risk making a tit of myself again by asking a gent where we were. It turned out to be the Holy Sepulchre, where Jesus was crucified and then buried. Strike two to the clown brigade.

The next day we caught up with Duby, the marathon runner who'd had a stroke, and he gave us a tour of the Old City. It was extraordinary to get a sense of the area's historical significance. These streets had been walked for thousands of years and we were in the birthplace of three major religions. Many of the sites had significance to two religions, if not all three. It put Jesus' story – being a teacher and philosopher who died because his beliefs were not in line with others' – in a context I could now understand. All of these tales and histories were interwoven.

And then something happened . . .

I realised that these stories were like marathons. Each has a start, a middle and an end, albeit never final. When one marathon ends, another will start, sometimes on the same track, sometimes on a completely different one, but each runner will make their own story, create their own history. Each runner will see something on that track that he'll tell his friends about in the hope that they understand what he has gained from the experience. But the next runner will retell the story with a new lesson. What's important is that each story is given its own credibility, without judgement. Each runner has earnt his right to tell his tale. Hopefully, as I travelled to places like Jerusalem, I'd have the chance to listen to all these stories and learn something special from each one.

3

MUMBAI MARATHON

17 January, Mumbai, India

3:58.44

We arrived at Dubai airport in the early afternoon. A mate from school was living there, working in the auto industry, and he'd invited me to stay if I was ever coming through.

Adam Peake was a welcome sight when we spied him at the airport. He's a big dude, standing at around 6 foot 4. He'd been living in 'Dubbers' for about three years and was an old hand at dealing with the heat and the desert. Oddly, so much of Dubai is now glass and steel that you have to actually go looking for the desert. I can't imagine what the area must have looked like 30 years before. It is now very livable, with office and residential towers of impressive size and glamour. The beaches are gorgeous and the shopping centres are beyond ridiculous. Adam was living up near the famous Palm Jumeirah, the man-made islands that protrude into the sea. His apartment was on the mainland and it was like staying in any luxury beach accommodation in the world – clean new pool downstairs and views of the beach below. This was a huge step up for me and Daz, after staying in hostels.

Adam had two flatmates, both beautiful English girls who were working in radio and finance. I noticed Daz's jaw drop twice – I just gave Adam a sideways glance and waited till later before saying, 'Damn, mate, life here is pretty good. Top job, amazing apartment and a harem of beautiful women!' He just laughed, but I immediately dubbed him the Sultan of Dubai.

Daz and I'd had a very short, very relaxing stay, but it was time to go back to the airport.

I still don't feel like I can say I saw India. Daz and I went to Mumbai for five days and the city is such an assault on the senses, it can't possibly reflect the whole country. What it does give you is a taste of overcrowding, extreme poverty, heat and humidity, brilliant colours, stifling pollution and an immense love of cricket!

Daz had found us a decent hotel in Churchgate, an area full of hotels and businesses frequented by foreigners. I was concerned that we'd either end up in a dive that was too far from the action, or a hotel that cost a fortune but didn't offer more than a bed in a box. But Daz's research was good and we were so close to the race start line that we were on the track.

I didn't recognise how hard it would be to keep control over my diet until we were in India. So there I was in a country that offered some of the most impressive food in the world, and I was too ill at ease to try much of it. This was the first time I had really faced the dilemma of whether to make the most of a place as a tourist or an athlete. I certainly didn't want to eat food from the street vendors, but I'd also been warned about eating meals as innocuous sounding as salads – the vegies may have been rinsed in unclean tap water. I decided to stick to packaged food and have a few select dishes in decent-looking restaurants. Daz was keen to try different things, so he was going to be the canary down the mine. If Darren ate and looked happy, I was clear to eat it too. If Daz ate it and turned interesting shades of green before making a butt-clenching dash for a toilet, then I would probably avoid the dish.

Mumbai is quite a dirty city. I think they just clean one building at a time, so it takes about a century to get around to cleaning the first again. It's deceptive, though, because when you get inside some of these places, they're really clean, ornate and lovely. The Indians obviously prefer to show off to their guests and friends, rather than the outside world.

The Mumbai Marathon itself was touted as the biggest race in Asia and had long sold out when I tried to enter. It was only through the good graces of a friend in Melbourne who knew someone who knew someone at the company sponsoring the event that I got an entry. They all liked my story and wanted to help. I didn't have full confirmation until a few weeks before we got there, but I'd put my faith in the adventure and booked our flights, including expensive visas. I figured, at worst, that we would get a taste of India and then I'd still complete enough races in January to be on track. Inclusion in the run meant I would be a race ahead of schedule in the very first month.

I had never really rated Indians as being particularly sporty – besides their cricketing prowess, of course – so I was interested to see what kind of people were participating. The thing is, distance running is a practice that is usually taken up in two contexts: either (a) you're from a country that has a sporting culture because it's wealthy enough to afford the sports-related infrastructure, or (b) you're from a country that has learnt to use running to rise up from poverty, like in Kenya, Ethiopia, Jamaica. I wondered why there were not more elite athletes coming out of a country with 1.3 billion people, especially when the marathon world-record holder of the nineties age category is an Indian by the name of Fauja Singh (six hours at age 93), and the world-record holder for the youngest marathon runner in 2006 was the little tiger Budhia Singh, a 4-year-old 65-km ultra runner.

At the expo, lots of men and women of all ages were collecting their race bibs. I certainly didn't see loads of serious Indian runners picking up their gear. There were plenty of participants, just not guys I'd wager cash on running a super-quick marathon.

While I was getting my bib, Daz was out with Kerry, a Kiwi mate who was backpacking around India and just happened to be in

Mumbai. He's a big guy with a Bigger smile and an even BIGGER laugh, a lawyer who lives in a farming community back in NZ. Another one of Daz's challenges was to drive a taxi in a foreign country, so he and Kerry had accosted some poor cab driver and asked if they could steal his car for a bit. God knows what they actually said to him, but they ended up getting in the cab and reversing up and down the street. Both of them were laughing so hard while trying to get in the car that I think the cab driver got a little spooked at what was about to happen to his livelihood.

If you can't walk across the road without being nearly hit by five taxis/buses/mopeds, then how do you clear 42 kms' worth of track in one of the most congested cities in the world for Asia's largest marathon? Mumbai's streets were about to be taken over by 37 000 people in the full marathon, half marathon and 15-km races. The start times were staggered, with the marathon kicking off at 7.40 a.m., but that was still a lot of people to organise to run through a city of 14 million people.

In the morning I walked out of the hotel and was shocked to find the streets empty. There were no cars in the typically bustling roads, and only supporters lined the streets as I jogged toward the start. Daz stayed up near the hotel, at a corner where the track turned towards the bay, a strip called Chowpatty.

As I got closer to the starting point, the crowd thickened, so I jumped through a gap and found myself near the start line, but I instantly noticed that something was wrong. There were only about 30 runners there, and they all looked fast. Like, Kenyan fast. I seemed to be hanging with the elite runners and as I looked around for the rest of the entrants, I was surprised to find there just wasn't anyone else about. With only about a minute before the race was due to start, a number of 'regular' runners made their way up a side road and stepped in behind the elites. There wasn't a lot of ceremony; the gun just went off and then people were running. I figured that the runners coming up behind were the rest of the greater group and they just weren't in a rush, so I got myself over the start line and headed into round three.

Apart from the elites, the rest of the runners seemed, well, not cut out for that kind of punishment. They were wearing all sorts of gear. Some wore runners, others street shoes, and I spotted leather boots, cricket shoes and even bare feet. They were in assorted tracksuits, work shirts, tennis gear and jeans too. I ran along trying to work out where the bulk of the 37 000 were.

Within 10 minutes I hit the first turn and saw Daz on the side of the road. Next to him was a group of locals in matching whites, all holding up sheets of paper with letters. The red letters spelt out a nickname I went by back home – T B O N E. Daz had acquired a local fan club for me! I wondered if he'd been able to explain the origins of that name to the locals – we barely remembered how I'd come by it in the first place. Just one of those drunken things that caught on, I reckon.

Daz was holding the camera, trying not to lose his shit at how funny it was. I ran down the road chuckling. Not far along there was a U-turn and I followed the water back to Darren's position. This time he had another group and they were holding up the letters E N O B T. Less than 5 kms in and I was already all over the place from laughing so hard.

I was faring better than others, though, with some competitors slowing to a walk after just 3 kms. They'd either been running too fast to begin with, or their race plan was to run in short bursts for 42 kms.

I ran along the bay until I came to a turn some 3 kms later that took me into a city area. I started seeing more runners on the other side of the road, but it seemed these were the half marathoners, who must have started an hour before me, because they were passing 15 kms. Very confusing.

Coming up on the 10-km mark, I kept my eyes peeled for a toilet sign. I'd done pretty well in eating the right things over the past few days, but it was inevitable that Harry Potter would show up with the goblet of fire. I spotted the booths coming down a hill and barrelled straight in. I lost about four minutes, but it was worth it.

As I ran further through town, I realised there was no chance that this many people could have passed me at the beginning of the run. I was doing a pretty decent clip and you tend to recognise who you've passed and who's new in front of you. I just couldn't figure it out. But I took solace in the fact that, whatever had happened, I was passing people all the time – a big confidence booster.

I ran through a section of town that was bustling with foot traffic and rows of motorbikes, cabs and buses being held back by a mere chain. As the wave of runners I was in went past, the cops dropped the chain. Crazed Mumbaikar drivers surged forwards and flew across the track, trying not to hit each other. As the next wave of runners came up, the chain was raised again. Mumbai was becoming restless with this invasion of their streets.

I ran onto a freeway. On one side some very tired-looking souls were picking up washed-up rubbish and assessing its usability. On the other side was a hillside with a slum sprawled across it. I presumed that the people on the shore belonged to that slum. It hit me I was one of the lucky few, in a city of so many poor, running a foot race for my amusement, while these guys sifted through the wreckage for something to help them survive. It was a humbling thought.

Looming ahead along the freeway was a long suspension bridge, the Rajiv Gandhi Sea Link, looking reasonably new and solid. In the distance was the city that I'd come from. I'd travelled from the ritzy part of town where most tourists spend their time, through the suburbs and into the slums. I was startled by the contrast.

Banners lined the bridge advertising the marathon, featuring pictures of the marginalised groups that would benefit from the marathon's fundraising. The ads read, 'I will win this marathon' and showed blind men, children from impoverished families and AIDS sufferers. The ads aligned the long battle of the marathon with the lonely struggle of so many Mumbaikars. As I reached the other side of the long sea link, I felt like I'd seen a little piece of their struggle. I would never truly understand it, and hopefully I will never know it, but I could see it.

After the halfway mark, I ran back through the city and the fans were waning. My fellow runners too were struggling. I approached one guy and asked him how he was going. He said he was okay, but he was looking forward to getting to the end. I asked him what time he'd started. He said 6:45 a.m. I asked if that was a special marathon time, like for a team event, and he replied no, it was the time everyone started. I told him I kicked off at 7:40 and he laughed and said that I didn't look much like an elite runner.

WHAMMO!

I'd started an hour later than I needed to for potentially the hottest marathon I'd do. I seemed to have passed about 1000 other runners, but these were all the five-hour marathoners.

I pushed myself through the city and as I crested a hill, I could see a commotion at one of the drink stands. Volunteers were grabbing at a whole lot of little kids running this way and that. The street kids had robbed the water stop at the 34-km mark! I needed a drink, but I guess they needed it more. They were laughing as they ran off and the cops were half-heartedly trying to stop them. No one seemed to care that much, but the runners behind me were going to see it differently.

At 35 kms I was waiting for the wall. I was struggling to keep pace for a sub-four-hour marathon, but as I looked at my watch, I realised I could still do it. I'd had an extra GU and plenty of Gatorade. It was potential suicide to step up the pace now, with the heat and so many marathons ahead of me, but my quads were still driving forwards. If last week's run was anything to go by, this is where it would potentially all go wrong, but I decided to go for it.

Then, as I ran over another small hill through the city streets, a little guy popped up next to me. He couldn't have been more than 18 years old, and we fell into step. I tried to talk to him, but he just smiled and said something I couldn't understand. I told him my name and he said, 'Six kilometres, 6 kilometres.' I said, 'Okay, Gary it is then. Yes, Gary, we have only 34 minutes to get there. Are you thinking what I'm thinking?' I'm pretty sure he wasn't, but he kept smiling and running next to me, so we pushed on together.

Gary and I powered on and when I stopped to grab a drink, he stopped too, when he slowed to grab one further along, I found myself looking back, trying not to leave him behind. This was dangerous; in the later stages of the race you really need to focus on getting yourself home. You can't stop for anyone. But he was up next to me again pretty quickly and we kept ploughing along. As we ran side by side, I think the spectators took a liking to us, because they were shouting loudly and cheering the two of us on. I realised that this was a bit of a statement: I was a comparatively bulky white guy, running next to one of the slim local boys. To anyone on the side of the track, we looked like teammates. And right then, that's exactly what we were.

I kept checking my watch, and time was running out. We passed the 41-km mark and I looked over to Gazza and said, 'Mate, we're too close to the line here; we need to go under five minutes. You got anything left?' He just looked back and said, 'One kilometre, 1 kilometre.' I grinned. 'That's right, old mate. Let's get this done.' And as I dropped a gear and increased the pace, I could feel him push on harder too.

As we ran towards the end, the crowd at the sides was going ballistic. We kept passing runners who looked ready to faint, and stayed in step, coming up to the finish line with only a minute to spare – 3:58.44!

I was pumped! Daz was there and he'd roped another group of fellas to do the T-Bone sign right on the finish line for me. I thanked Gaz for his stellar performance. He said his name was Laxmann and he'd enjoyed running with me. 'Well, Gary Laxmann,' I said, 'you're a champ and it was an honour to run with you too!'

I was pretty stuffed after that. All I wanted to do was lie down.

We headed back to the hotel but Mumbai had one more crazy trick up its sleeve. As we reached the road that had been part of the last kilometre of the track, it hit 12:30 p.m. And that was it. The cops removed all the barriers and allowed the cars, buses and motorbikes back into the street. But there were still runners coming. The taxis veered all around them trying not to hit anyone, honking madly. The Mumbai Marathon was over and the city wanted its roads back.

What a mad and exciting place. I was so happy I'd come. I wish I'd started earlier, but maybe my experience would not have been so full.

4

DUBAI MARATHON

22 January, Dubai, United Arab Emirates

3:35.15

The next day we bounced back to Dubai for my fourth marathon in just three weeks. I was getting slower with every race and I was already concerned that this was due to my body breaking down.

We caught up with a friend of my brother's and over an excellent dinner, Nick asked me why I was doing this. I struggled to give an answer to a guy I'd know since I was a teenager. 'I just wanted to do something different, mate,' I said, trying to get it straight in my mind. Thinking about how tired I was from the last two races, I wasn't sure I really knew the answer at that moment.

I'd been invited to attend a press conference by the PR firm that was looking after the Dubai Marathon, with the star of the show being the world champion, Haile Gebrselassie. Haile, in typical fashion, was gracious and friendly, and everyone sat in awe of him. When the reporters asked if he would win, he responded that he would do his best.

'Will you break your own world record of 2:03.59?'

'Well, I'd like to, but first I'd like to run my best and see what happens. A marathon is 42 kilometres and takes over two hours, so just like any good football match, a lot can happen in that time. I will go out there and do my best and if that means I win, then that's great. If it means I break my own world record, then that is even better!'

He said it with such ease. The odds of breaking a world record three years in a row must have been quite slim, but he was prepared to

45

give it all he had. He kept dragging the conversation back to a singular message. 'Everyone should run more,' he stated. 'If you run more you will be more happy – like me!' I found myself grinning and nodding.

Run more and you will be more happy.

Run more, more happy.

I couldn't help but feel that in those words was a message for me.

The PR rep was acting as MC and he decided to throw a little grenade into the room.

'Haile,' he said, 'would you care to comment on the fact that we have a runner here who is attempting to run 52 marathons in 52 weeks, racing all over the world? Please stand up, Tristan.'

Haile looked at me incredulously and laughed. 'I can't believe it! You will run and fly and run and fly. I wouldn't even try that; it's too much. It's magic, if you can do it. Good luck!'

I stood there shaking. The world champion, my running idol, was staring at me and telling me my plan was magic.

'You're my hero, Haile!' I stammered. 'I'm just honoured to share the same track as you.' Everyone laughed and I quickly sat down. I felt like a donkey, but nothing could take the smile from my face. When I was given the opportunity to get a photo with Haile, I was in danger of being arrested as I tried to bear-hug him. I was floating on a cloud for the rest of the day.

That was Wednesday. As with Israel, the Emirates' weekend runs from Friday to Saturday, with Saturday being the Sabbath. The race was on Friday morning, beginning well before dawn.

I was probably a little too pumped about the run in Dubai. I went for a run in the evening and overdid it. Being eager to run like a champion after seeing Haile, I sped along at an average of 4.45 per km. After 16 kms, I felt my calves tighten right up. I decided I'd done enough and hopped in a cab home.

Of course, that stressed me out a little, but tight calves were nothing new and I did a little self-massage when I got back to the Sultan's. By Thursday arvo, I felt okay again and took the opportunity to go sightseeing. We went shopping at the Mall of the Emirates, the massive joint with the ski slope in it – what ridiculously awesome excess to stick that thing in the desert!

That night we went out with our expat friends. I left about 11 p.m., while Daz stayed with the others to party. I managed a few hours' sleep, but was more nervy than usual, waking up at 5 a.m. Poor Daz, I woke him up too, and he'd only got to bed at half-three.

We got down there with little time to spare.

The siren went off, sounding the beginning, and a cheer went up, but they cried out for one reason only – Haile Gebrselassie had begun his quest to smash another world record. Moments later, I crossed the line and followed in his footsteps. Spine-tingling stuff!

The runners seemed to be mostly Anglo expats. There were plenty of spectators on the sides of the road, the families of these middleaged white-collar workers out to support their wives, husbands or friends. In stark contrast to this were the large groups of uniformed Indian or Asian workers on their way to the hotels and entertainment venues that lined the nearby beach. They stopped and waved while waiting to cross the road. As we were running, those keeping Dubai's service industry going were heading to perhaps their sixth or seventh day of work in a row so they could send remittances back to their families in far-off countries. I'm not going to pretend to understand the dynamics of Dubai's community, but I've rarely seen a more obvious socio-economic divide. It all seemed to work fine, but it was clear who was running the show, who was there to advance their career and who was doing all the grunt work to keep the wheels turning. I was told that some of the workers there only earn $75 (Australian) per week. They work really long hours in an expensive city, so all that for $75 . . . well, I just couldn't figure it out.

I came up on 11.5 kms after an hour of running. The one-hour mark meant that Haile would be rounding the turn to head back my way very soon.

The sun had risen by my 15-km mark but there was a cool breeze coming off from the nearby sea and I felt pretty fresh. Then I noticed up ahead that runners were veering to the side of the track.

He was coming!

I pulled out my camera and ran to the left, just as a procession of police motorbikes and cars powered down the road in front of the race leaders. I flicked on the camera, pointed it in the general direction, but didn't look to see what I was recording. I had to see this with my own eyes. Emerging through the fleet of vehicles were two majestic runners. They were both African, but I only zoned in on one.

'GO HAAAAAAAAAIIIIILEEEEEEEEE!'

Haile was absolutely flying. I looked at my watch: 1:24, with a few kilometres to the 30-km mark. Taking into account that I started a couple of minutes later, I figured he was on track. I was running an international marathon and the world's greatest distance champion was running just metres away from me, looking as though he might smash a world record.

Feeling pumped again, I jetted along for a while, wondering how I'd go after halfway. I was a long way off what I was hoping for. I always aimed to make halfway at 1:50 or better, because that meant I could cruise and look to lose a few minutes in the back half and still go under 3:45. Being on a fast track and in the footsteps of greatness, I wanted to go under 3:40 for this one. So when I passed the 21-km mark at 1:56, looking down the barrel of a four-hour marathon, I was annoyed at myself for letting the time get away.

I made the turn to head home moments later and as I looked at the long stretch of road ahead of me, something snapped. *Bugger this*, I thought. I'd been sitting on five-minute kms and even up to 5.30s too often in the last few races. Some quick calculations told me that

I'd need 4.45-minute kms to drag the time back towards a 3:45 finish. Plenty of people were at the turnaround and I'm sure someone yelled out my name. It was a little thing, but it urged me on.

I stepped it up and scanned my body. Everything was in its right place and my calves weren't hurting. I wasn't feeling lethargic and I'd been consistently downing my own strong mix of Gatorade. I threw back a GU and hoped that the two I had left would be enough. As soon as the new pace was set, I started passing people. As I saw their pained faces, I judged that I was looking pretty good in comparison. I pushed a little faster to see how I'd go.

I felt great! I ran past a few spectators and they cheered heartily. I powered past runner after runner and didn't feel tired at all. I thought about how much harder Haile had worked on this very track just an hour and a half earlier. He'd be done by now, but I could still proudly run in his wake. Maybe he'd won, maybe he'd broken the world record; either way I was running on the same path as a supreme running machine.

Towards the 30-km mark, I'd picked up loads of time and was close to a 3:45 finish. 'Hang on,' I said to myself. 'What's important here? Getting a comfortable 3:45 and being able to back it up on Sunday, or pushing too hard for your own personal glory and risking your body?'

I thought about my sister, Rebecca, the eldest of my three siblings, whose birthday it was that day. I'm the youngest, but the tallest of our brood, so I kid around by calling the girls my 'little' sisters. Rebecca is anything but little, though, and I don't mean body-wise. She's fit, healthy and is one of the most powerful characters I know. She's so determined to get things done that she only sleeps four hours a night, power-walking in the morning, hitting the gym, ploughing through a long workday and seeing her friends in the evening. She does it all, doesn't complain and, I swear, her appetite for life just keeps on growing.

So, I thought, what would Bekko tell me to do at a time like this? 'You feel good?' she'd ask. Yeah, I feel good. 'Does the risk outweigh the return?' Ahh, well, maybe . . . 'If you feel good and the risk is worth it, then you know what I'd do . . .' she'd announce quite frankly. 'GO FOR IT!'

'This one's for you, little sister!' I said out loud, as I passed the 32-km mark at about 2:51. 'Happy birthday!'

The plan was to stick to 4.30-minute kms with fast spurts to make up for lost time during drink breaks. I was passing a lot of people now and bystanders were giving me funny looks. One guy even said, 'This dude is flying; he's going to sprint home!' It felt great to make those demands of my body, having it respond without question. It's rare that you feel that type of control so late in a race. I hadn't had to hurdle the wall this time; I just powered up so much that I punched right through it.

The only thing that had begun to worry me was my old adductor strain. I could feel it tighten, but it didn't feel as bad as it had in the past. I thought about what my good mate Pat Allen had done when he tried to help me. He's a manipulator who moves the tendons around bones, looking for a point of release. He'd told me I had mild osteo pubis, which triggered a variety of problems. To fix it, he'd stuck his fingers right into my groin and grabbed the tendons around my pubic bone, flicking them about. It'd hurt like hell but at the time had really helped. So without slowing down, I jammed my fingers into the right side of my groin and found my pubic bone. I held my fingers there while I ran and let the movement of my stride slowly work the area free. It was probably not what any therapist would have recommended and, to be fair, it's possibly pretty stupid and not something I'd do regularly . . . but it worked. It still hurt like I was stabbing myself in the crotch, but the muscles eventually began to loosen.

I felt that rush of power that allows you to separate your brain from the pain in your body. It spurred me on and I pushed harder. I looked at my watch and saw that I was looking at 3:37. This was a moment of experiencing the 'runner's high' we all dream of. I felt unstoppable.

Forty-one kms came past and the crowd had thickened. As I came around the final bend, the people on the side of the track were going crazy. I looked at the line and gave it everything I had. I found something deep in me that let me sprint when all I should have been able to do was fall down, and crossed in 3:35.15.

I'd run a 17-minute negative split (that is, running the first half slower than the second), finishing the latter half of the marathon in 99 minutes. Daz wasn't expecting me, so hadn't even got his camera out. He was in the stands with the Sultan and some friends. I came up into the stands for high-fives all round.

Haile hadn't broken his world record, but he had won the race, even with a back strain. He finished in 2:06.09. It was such an honour to be on that same piece of road, and something I will never forget.

After the race I got a little rest. Then we ended up back at a beach bar. We were flying out that same night, so there wasn't going to be a lot of opportunity to celebrate properly. Anyway, post-marathon, adding alcohol to your system is probably the worst thing you can do, as it increases the inflammation in your muscles. People were dancing, celebrating the day's victory, and I stood there with a grin.

I was happy to still be on track, but I'd pushed myself hard and within a couple of hours, I was a wreck. The idea of getting on a flight that night, flying to the Canary Islands via Qatar and London, and running again in 36 hours on the Spanish island, Gran Canaria . . . let's just say I considered pulling the pin.

More pain and the possibility of epic failure were just two days away.

5

GRAN CANARIA MARATÓN
24 January, Las Palmas, Canary Islands, Spain
3:18.09 PB

What happened in Las Palmas is beyond my comprehension.

My adductor injury had reared its ugly head again. The last time it happened, I was limping for weeks. This time, it wasn't quite so bad. I figured some time spent in the sea, wearing compression pants while flying, plus an effort to keep the area raised and 18 hours cramped on a plane might help . . . Or maybe not that last bit. I really didn't have much choice, though.

We had a stopover planned in London and it was a chance to catch up with my sister Alexis, so we headed to Shepherds Bush, where she runs a place called the Happiness Centre, a health and wellbeing hub. When we arrived, I was pretty testy and tired, but luckily, my sister was there to give me a hug and make me feel better. On top of this, she had organised some time with Tim, one of the centre's osteopaths.

Tim worked on my calves and my adductor to free up the muscles, telling me that the strain was coming from a mismatch between the amount of blood (carrying oxygen) that was being pumped from my heart and that required by my muscles. This meant my muscles were working harder than they were accustomed to. He said that as my heart got stronger, it should cope better with the demand, but that would take time to increase and might never reach the level I'd like it to. Tim kept it simple and said that the key was to find a balance between the amount of oxygen needed by my legs and the amount my system was delivering. If things were beginning to strain, I'd know it was time to slow down. He assured me that, although my calf muscles and adductor were tight, he'd felt worse and they were about where you'd expect them to be after the amount of punishment I'd dished out. In fact, he thought I was good to go for another marathon.

Well, that was a huge relief. As most marathoners know, the game is won or lost in your head. Your body is a machine that will do exactly what it's told to until something breaks. I was getting worried that a breakdown was on the cards, but now my confidence had returned. If you enter a race worrying about finishing, chances are you won't finish, or at least it will be an ordeal to get there. If you believe you can do it at the start line, then it's just a matter of how long it will take you.

I was ready to back myself again. Just one more flight to go.

After we landed in Las Palmas, a cabbie took us to our couch for the night. We'd hooked up a place to stay via CouchSurfing.org. The idea is that if you have a spare bed or couch, you allow people to come to stay, then when you're ready to travel, someone else will open up their home to you. It's a 'pay it forward' scheme. It's a little utopian, but seems to work very well. We were staying with a lovely Spanish girl named Rebeca. As this was our first CS experience, we weren't sure what to expect, but Rebeca had a lovely apartment near the sea. She even took us out to dinner with a friend.

Eating in Spain was tricky. The food was magnificent, but often quite rich and generally tapas style. So when I asked if they had pasta, I got a polite 'No'. Any rice? 'Ah, no.' I explained that I really needed carbs and vegetables, and lots of them, and what came out was kind of potato salad with vegetables and tuna. Perfect! I hadn't eaten since breakfast and I was tired and dizzy. I scoffed the plate in moments but soon I was hitting a very large wall. It was already 11 p.m. and I had to be out the door by 7 a.m. to get my bib before the race. So I left Daz with the girls and headed home.

It seemed as if no sooner had I walked in the door and put my head on the pillow, than my alarm was crowing at me. I was still fully clothed and trying to remember where I was. I climbed down the stairs, assessing my body as I went: tired, sure, but there was no real pain in my legs. Daz was already awake. He told me that a friend of Rebeca's would pick us up in 15 minutes, saving us from finding the line ourselves, so I scrambled about to get my things and we were out the door.

We bundled into Omar's car and got moving. Daz had met him last night, and it was nice to have a friendly face at that time of the morning. He was volunteering for the race too, so knew exactly where to go.

After so much moving around, I really hadn't taken time to mentally prepare for this race. Once we had picked up my racing bib, Daz went for a wander, so I found a little café near the start line. I enjoyed a slice of tortilla, essentially a huge potato omelette, which came with bread and *café con leche* (coffee and milk). It was a breakfast of champions and I felt loads better for eating it. Until one fella with a marathon bib lit up a cigar next to me. By now Daz was back and I looked at him incredulously. 'Ha! *Loco*,' said Daz.

By the time we emerged from the café, the previously quiet street was packed with runners. The half and full marathons would start at the same time. There was a real buzz at this start line and I felt like I could forget the races I'd already done and just focus on the excitement of this one. The weather was probably 18°C and overcast, and there were no expectations on me to get a particular time. I just wanted to get through uninjured.

At 9 a.m. the gun went off with a roar from runners and spectators alike. I started near the front and moved out with some committed-looking runners. They were all wearing local club shirts and triathlon jerseys. We set under five-minute kms almost immediately. I felt okay, so I just stayed with them. We made a few turns and were on the port quite quickly.

Las Palmas sits on a sandy ridge that connects the main landmass of Gran Canaria and the little 'island' just off its coast. It has been built up and the city has the protected port on one side of the ridge and a beach area on the other, which faces north. The course essentially crisscrosses the city in two 21-km loops. It's a great spectator track because you can be near the start and walk one street over and see your runner three or four times.

I ran through town, noting the architectural mix – there were buildings at least a century old, in the midst of lots of '50s and '60s-style structures. Actually, I was going a lot faster than I anticipated. I was at the 16-km mark and feeling pretty strong. My adductor was not bothering me and my heart rate was good. I was on a 4.45-per-km pace. I figured I'd just sit on this speed till I hit halfway and then see how I felt. There were plenty of drink stops and I alternated between Powerade and water at each stop. I had accidentally left my Gatorade powder in Dubai, so only had water in my belt bottle. If I was to keep this pace and not cramp, I'd need to keep up the electrolytes.

I looked at my watch and saw I was racing towards a 1:40 half. That pace took me close to personal-best territory, which had never been in the plan. But I looked at my Garmin again and did the calcs over and over. If I stuck to this pace, I'd be able to blow up in the final kilometres and post a 3:30 finish. As I came into the halfway chute, I looked for Daz, wanting to tell him that I was running well and that he'd have to look for me somewhere after 12:20 p.m. But he was nowhere to be seen . . . I figured he'd turn up sooner or later.

I couldn't figure out why I felt so good. I was getting tired, but I was definitely running better than I had in months. An idea began to roll through my mind. I'd read a book not too long ago called *Born to Run,* by an American named Chris McDougall. He writes a lot about these crazy Mexican runners, the Tarahumara Indians, who run like the wind and have done so for thousands of years. In the book Chris tries to figure out why they are so good, and one of the reasons he comes up with is that the Tarahumara run with an innocence that is akin to playing. They do it for fun, and aren't focused too intently on winning.

Maybe that infectious feeling of running for fun was what had taken hold of me. I was playing a game, ticking off the kilometres, seeing if I could stick to my pace. I whooped as I passed some more spectators and they cheered at me. I patted another guy on the back as I passed him and he smiled weakly, but managed a 'Vamos', too. I wasn't waning, in fact I was now tracking at 4.30 per km.

I wished I'd had a phone to call Daz. I just wanted to let him know I was running hot! I didn't have far to go till the end, though. He'd either be there or not. I was still passing other competitors and I just looked ahead and kept trying to run them down. These were serious runners too, punching out very respectable times, so it was pretty exciting to pass them.

I rounded the last corner and stepped on the gas for the final 200 metres. I ran into the chute and heard the announcer saying my name. Then I saw Daz and the girls on the other side of the finish line, cheering. I crossed as the announcer was repeating my website's name: 'RunLikeCrazy.com!' I had just beaten my own best time by five whole minutes, at 3:18.09.

I went to the massage area and was pleased to discover a huge tent set up with ice baths and massage tables. I sat in the ice bath for a while and shared some stories with a few other runners. Three of them had just completed their first marathon and all had finished under 3:30, a huge effort for race number one. They all looked like they couldn't move and one guy was lowered into the pool, shaking uncontrollably. But they were all content, satisfied, happy. As was I. I got out after five minutes and found one of the masseurs working that day. I told him my story, and he said he was surprised my legs weren't tight, like everyone else's he'd treated.

I didn't know how my body had recovered from the last marathon. I did the right things, I guess, within the parameters set by travel and time.

Rebeca took us to lunch later that day with a number of her friends.

It was a feast and I ate as much as possible. I'd had such an amazing day and this was the perfect way to celebrate. After lunch we spoke with a TV crew and they took lots of really arty shots of me looking out to sea. It must have looked pretty cool, because the next day a lovely older woman came up to me in the street and chanted, '*Maratón, maratón, maratón!* Well done!' Apparently she'd seen me on TV and she was excited about our journey . . . at least, that's all Daz and I could figure from her Spanish.

Maratón times five. Magical.

6

INTERNATIONAL MARATHON OF MARRAKECH

31 January, Marrakech, Morocco

3:37.35

We got to Madrid on Tuesday afternoon. I hadn't been there for many years, not since I was 21 and travelling with a friend. It's a big city, cleaner than I remembered, and it's easy to get around on the Metro. After we stowed our gear at the hostel and had a sandwich, I decided to go for a walk. It began to snow. Madrid is pretty high above sea level, so this wasn't a big surprise. What was surprising was how magical it was to walk through a city like that with little snowflakes falling down around you. It's nice to be in a city you've visited before and feel like it's the first time again.

I was in a good mood and must have looked it because some kids came up to me and showed me a note on an A4 envelope. It said they were collecting for deaf and blind kids on behalf of UNICEF. I was wearing a UNICEF jumper and they made the connection, saying I must sign their petition. 'Sure,' I said. There were five of them around me, all talking at once and I just signed the paper and didn't think much about it. I felt like helping, as I was having a nice day and they seemed like nice kids. They asked me for money, so I pulled out a tenner, thinking it was a bit much on my budget.

They said, 'Others give 20 or 40!' I told them I was travelling and I needed the money myself. As soon as they realised that they would not get more, they were off without so much as a goodbye, on to the next tourist. *Hang about*, I thought. The kids were not carrying any official ID or even being escorted by an adult. They were just stealing money from tourists!

I thought about going after them, but it was too late. It wasn't a lot, but I felt like such a fool for handing it over so easily, without question. It was only €10, but that was a night's accommodation.

The next morning we had plenty of time to get to the airport, but once we were down in the Metro, the trains were packed for peak hour. On one of the three trains we had to get, Daz and I got separated in different carriages. I kept my backpack on because we only had three stops to go. People were jammed in around me and at the next stop three guys got in next to me. They kept trying to squeeze past me. I apologised, vainly attempting to take up less space. I was a bit off balance and it was all I could do to hold myself up, but with smiles on their faces, they kept trying to move past me. 'Wait,' I said. They replied in Spanish and kept pushing impatiently. The train finally stopped and everyone poured out, including me, so I could let these guys get to wherever they so desperately needed to go. I got back in and we went on to the next stop.

Daz and I were making good time getting to the airport, but I wanted to check anyway, so I reached for my phone. Nothing. I checked my pockets three times. I looked at Daz. I realised very quickly what had happened. 'My phone's gone.' Those three Spanish guys had played me. As much as it pissed me off that I'd been robbed, I had to admit it was my own fault for having my phone in my back pocket. I made myself an easy target. Sooner or later I was going to lose stuff or have it stolen; it was to be expected. I was just hoping it would be in a few months, not in January. *Idiot!*

We flew to Morocco. The airport is right next to the city, so it didn't take us long to get to the main square, or *souk*, which means 'market'. Daz grabbed a map and we tried to work out where our hotel was. I looked at the print-out I had from Google Maps.

A little guy missing his front teeth came up and asked where we were staying. I told him and he said, 'I show you.' I told him we'd be okay – I figured we should try to get our bearings and work out where to go ourselves. It was confusing, though, and we soon gave in to him. He said, 'I am good map, you follow.' And we did, through the market, down some winding streets and further in the warren that is the Medina of Marrakech.

The further we got from the market, the more concerned I was that we were being led into a trap. The little guy, who we named Danny, started asking for directions, which made me more worried, but we ended up down a narrow street and in front of a door, with 'Riad Puchka' above it. We never would have found it on our own. For his help we gave Danny 20 dirham. Mustafa, our host, opened the door and beckoned us in, while Danny argued with Mustafa, asking for money from him too, saying he'd recommended the riad. Mustafa told Danny we already had a booking and shooed him away. Apparently everything had a price here in Marrakech.

The difference between being in the street and inside a house was absolutely extraordinary. It wasn't a pretty area but once you opened the door . . . paradise! The riad had a beautifully tiled garden inside, with an open-air courtyard in the middle, dominated by a wading pool. It was a real hidden treasure, an oasis in among the busy, dirty streets.

We went into town to look for a good place to eat. We picked a winner, and both enjoyed sumptuous meals, Daz having chicken and vegetable tagine, while I chowed down on meat and vegetable cous-cous. Daz wanted to walk around the square, but I decided to head back for a nap. I didn't feel I'd get lost so easily now. I stopped at a store and grabbed a bottle of water and a chocolate bar. A kid of no more than 15 came over and started speaking to me in French, the country's second language, behind Arabic. He recognised that I didn't understand him and switched to English.

'Where are you from, my friend?'

I replied that I was from Australia and got the obligatory 'Gooday, maaaate!' Yep, you got me, man.

'Hey, where are you going to? You look lost.' No buddy, I'm fine, just heading back to my hotel.

'Where you staying?' Riad Puchka.

'I'll show you the way, follow me.' No, mate, I'm fine, I know where it is.

'Follow me, follow me.'

Ahmed walked about 30 metres ahead of me, as I headed down the street to my hotel. I knew where it was, but he led the way at any rate, turning into alleys every 50 metres or so. I was shaking my head, knowing that he would ask me for money for showing me to the door I was already headed to. As I rounded the final corner, there was Ahmed, right in front of the door to my riad. I stopped and burst out laughing. He was facing the other way and had his pants pulled down, showing me his bare butt.

'*What the hell?*' I exclaimed.

'Come on,' said Ahmed, 'touch it!'

'Ah, no, mate, I'm good,' I responded, still laughing.

'Touch it, touch it,' he repeated urgently, waggling his arse at me.

'Thanks, man, but, really, I'm not interested,' I said while heading to the door, pressing the buzzer frantically.

Someone above yelled out and Ahmed looked up but seemed unperturbed. He pulled up his pants (thankfully!) and turned to me saying, 'You give me money.'

'Look, champ, I'm not giving you any money, okay? So just let it go,' I said, laughing at the ridiculousness of the situation. I hit the buzzer again and Ahmed grabbed my arm with one hand and punched me in the shoulder.

'You give me money!'

I would normally react angrily if someone attacked me like that, but he was just a kid. I pushed him away, still laughing, as the guy above yelled out again. This time Ahmed looked up and said something back, then took off up the street.

'Crazy,' yelled the guy from the rooftop. I looked up and nodded.

'Very crazy!'

The Marrakech marathon was in two days' time. But this tour was about seeing the world as much as it was about running. With this in mind, we hit a club attached to the casino. We discovered pretty quickly that we were out of our depth, particularly cost-wise. I'm not going to pretend I had a great night, but with loads of money and a love of glamorous (read: full of crap) clubs, I'm sure you could have a blast there.

The next day we both felt a bit ill, even though we'd drunk relatively little. Daz started throwing up and then found himself sitting on the toilet on and off for most of the day. I felt sick, but not even close to that bad. It was disappointing to have Saturday in a new place as a write-off, so I ended up sitting above the busy *souk* by myself with a surprisingly good bowl of spaghetti bolognaise and a book.

The following morning – race day – I woke up feeling apprehensive. I didn't feel sick, just not well. Since cracking my PB in Gran Canaria a week before, I hadn't run at all. I'd tried to give my body time to recover from the beating I'd dished out, but maybe that had been a mistake. Even though I was walking plenty, with about 20 kgs strapped to my back, I hadn't been running to see how my body had recovered from the stress. Marathons are all about confidence, so I needed to be certain that my legs were ready for round six.

We walked a couple of kilometres to get to the start line and I definitely felt better, just for moving, but nothing could shake the feeling that I was doing this one cold.

On the walk to the start line, we met a lovely Canadian couple who had flown in for their first international race. I'd met quite a few running couples who'd travel to a place, run in the local festival, then wind down by hitting the beaches or sightseeing for a few weeks. I'd been thinking my ideal girl would be someone who'd run with me a couple of times a week, so I was a bit jealous of the Canadians.

The race was supposed to kick off at 8:30 a.m. but the gun didn't pop till around 8:45 a.m. Very Moroccan – everything gets done, but when they're good and ready. I'd been told there were 3000 participants in the event. I was surprised to see quite a few women wearing complete Arabic running suits, covered from head to toe, except for their faces . . . That's some impressive commitment to the race.

As I ran through the city streets, I got chatting to a guy called Tim, from Sheffield, who had been roped into this, his first marathon, on a dare. He'd agreed to do the run with a mate while they were drunk one night, saying they'd raise money for cancer research. He was ready to renege the following morning, but his mate's grandmother passed away from cancer that day, so there was no chance of pulling the pin then. In the end his buddy couldn't make it, but Tim had followed through on his promise, doing all the training and raising money for a children's hospice. I thought he was going pretty fast, but he said he felt good and my pace worked for him. At five-minute kms, we'd be set to go close to 3:40.

It couldn't have been more than 5 kms in, and I knew I was going to have a bad day. My left calf was locking up and I struggled to get it to loosen, even after a few stretches. I ran a few more kilometres, shortening my stride, so I wouldn't put too much pressure on my legs, hoping they'd warm up in a while. We passed through a gate and into a large olive grove. Immediately people were ducking behind trees and looking for somewhere to relieve themselves. There weren't any toilets at the start and I'd been told there weren't any on the track either. Everyone was making the most of the opportunity, though some people were already slowing to a walk here too. It looked as though quite a few runners had burnt themselves out in the early stages. I saw one young fella sitting with his head between his legs, throwing up his breakfast. His run was over.

Somewhere after this I lost Tim. I'd stopped to stretch and he continued on. As we passed the 10-km mark, we turned down another tree-lined street and came upon a very strange scene. Some guys in orange T-shirts were all crowding around some sort of trolley contraption. They were running, pushing and pulling. As I got closer, I saw that they were actually a pretty organised team. One guy was pulling, running with the poles supporting the trolley under his armpits, like with a rickshaw. Two others were on the sides, and two more pushed from the back and kept it stable. There was also a whole second team, rotating into the different positions to help. The contraption only had one wheel below, which I assume meant it created less drag. It looked like a difficult balancing act at the best of times, but on top of this, the team were pulling it along for 42 kms . . . What the?!

In the middle, nestled in a bucket, but sitting up to take in the scene, was a boy of around 13 years old. I discovered that these guys were a French fire brigade unit and the boy was a leukaemia patient. They were all chattering away, already 15 kms through their challenge and going strong. I was impressed by both their coordination and determination.

Further along, I got chatting to Clément, a Frenchman carrying a backpack who was in training for the Marathon des Sables, an intense 243-km six-day course across the Sahara Desert. The event is thought to be one of the toughest in the world. It turned out that Clément had been planning to do an Ironman competition in 2010, but when he heard about the difficulty of MDS, he got very excited and decided to take up the challenge. Clément had run quite a number of marathons and his stories of running in New York and Luxembourg were thrilling. His fastest marathon was 2:55, which immediately made me jealous, but also duly respectful of this Frenchman's running ability.

Clément had been divorced twice, and had a child by each ex. We chatted about this for a while and when I told him how I'd been made redundant at work, he laughed that the same thing had happened to him the year before. He'd lost his job for one weekend, but the following Monday he'd got it back on reduced pay. The Global Financial Crisis had forced the situation on him. He said at first he'd been devastated, but by that night he was happy again, thinking about all the cool adventures he could train for. Then when the job came up again, he knew he had to take it for his children. I agreed that his responsibilities as a father came first, almost apologising that I had done the exact opposite. He was excited for me, though, loving that I had taken my life into my own hands.

The kilometres passed, and conversation was put on hold as we began to labour. We didn't part; we both just acknowledged that there was work to do. I was tired, my calves were sore and my body was feeling pretty weak. I tried to maintain the pace, though, and Clément ran right along side me. I kept checking to see that he was okay, but he seemed as strong as ever, even with an extra 8 kgs attached to his torso. He was more machine than man.

We rounded the last turn and the finish line lay ahead. Clément and I crossed in 3:37.35. It was a big effort by me, but a mammoth display of power from the gritty Frenchman. We shook hands and vowed to stay in touch. Clément even said Daz and I should stay in his apartment when we hit Paris – he would be in the Sahara smashing his body at the Marathon des Sables, but he would leave the keys with his neighbour. What a generous guy. We arranged to meet for dinner later.

I was very happy to see Daz at the line, knowing that I could stop thinking and let him take over. Tim came through about 15 minutes later. He was pretty stuffed and said that the last 5 kms were way beyond anything he'd felt before. He'd done some crazy stuff in the army, so I reckon that was a pretty big statement.

Daz and I walked back to the riad. There, I got straight into the icy pool in the middle of the courtyard and tried to freeze my legs. It worked okay and Daz gave my calves a bit of a massage too.

Later on I caught up with Clément and a few of his mates. It was great to sit above the square and get to know these new French-speaking friends. They had such different lives to mine, but everyone had the same motivation: to make the most of every new adventure.

A few days later, Daz and I got the hell out of Dodge. Even though I'd been to more enticing places on holiday, we'd had a good time in Morocco. It was great training for dealing with whatever was thrown up in front of you – whether that's an arse-waggler or your sixth marathon in a row.

7

JOHANNESBAD THERMEN-MARATHON

7 February, Bad Füssing, Germany

3:17.30 PB

As we flew over the Mediterranean, I thought about how cool it was that I'd just run marathons on three continents – Asia, Europe and Africa – in as many weeks. People dream of running on all seven continents and I'd have five in the bag by July – assuming I could keep going.

We flew back over Europe and the further north we went, the more snow I could see. We descended into Frankfurt through a thick blanket of fog, the plane ferociously jolting and dipping with the turbulence. I hate that feeling, but Daz *really* hates it. The poor guy had his eyes closed and was gripping the armrests as the plane dipped suddenly and we slapped onto the ground.

When we walked off the aircraft, Daz and I looked at each other incredulously. So much snow! They'd had to scrape the snow off the footpath just so we could walk to the terminal. I had no idea how they'd kept the airport open.

The bus to Heidelberg took a couple of hours, then we got a train out to Zwingenberg to stay with Dave, one of Daz's New Zealand mates. As we cruised through the countryside, I couldn't compute how we'd just left the stinging Moroccan sun to enter a complete white-out. Daz and I just kept looking outside and laughing. I was very happy to see the friendly faces of Dave and Nina at the station after 12 hours of travel.

Dave drove us to their amazing three-storey cottage. It was very German in design, looking much like a ski lodge with a real retro-chic feel to it. Nina and her sister, Asa, had built an impressive snow bar outside. Apparently they had been inviting all the locals over for drinks, serving up icy cocktails in their driveway.

Dave and Daz had met the two sisters at Bora Bora beach bar in Ibiza a few years ago. The sisters were as crazy as the boys, so they got along famously and partied themselves silly. A week after they went their separate ways, Dave called Nina to tell her he'd bought a ticket to come see her. Anyway, long story short, they fell in love.

Daz hadn't seen Dave or the girls since Ibiza. Their reunion was impressive to witness, with everyone getting excited and reminiscing. We crashed out and I slept like the dead till 10 a.m. I was finding it difficult to sleep properly in hotels and hostels, but at a friend's house, you can let your guard down. I really needed that.

Over the next couple of days I was able to catch up on both sleep and work. There was so much snow that, unless we were going snow-boarding, there wasn't much point to being outside. A snowstorm a couple of days before had left thick layers of powder on the roofs, like thick icing on wedding cakes. As it began to thaw, you'd hear a loud rumbling noise, followed by a thud, as sections of the icing slid from the roof, clobbering unsuspecting passers-by.

Frozen landscape or not, I didn't want to enter this next marathon feeling nervous about whether my legs were working. On Thursday, the rain eased in the morning, and Daz and I decided to go for a run. It turned out to be quite difficult, with snow or slush covering most everything, so in the end we hit the roadway that follows the River Neckar out along the valley. We ran past old villages and castles that had stood for hundreds of years.

We spent some time sightseeing, and celebrated Daz's birthday early, on the Friday night. I bought him a present, a funny blue T-shirt with a picture of some guy called Bud Spencer as Banana Joe – a crazy '80s character from a slapstick action film. This guy has a huge following in Germany and Italy, so it seemed like an appropriate joke. We went to a nice little bar where we knocked back more than a few shots – I can't remember what they were called, but there were Tabasco, sugar and flames involved. I tricked Daz into having a couple extra than he meant to. The outcome was that Dave and Daz got drunk enough to take their shirts off and do a haka at the stroke of midnight in honour of Waitangi Day (New Zealand's national day). The other patrons were surprised by it all, but the boys got a round of applause for their efforts!

Next day, nursing a hangover, I went to pick up a rental car. It was half the cost of taking a train to get to our race in Bad Füssing, but better than that, it meant we weren't standing around bus stops and train stations in the freezing cold. It only took us an hour to get lost, though. I punched the co-ordinates into the Sat Nav and it told me I was a clown and shouldn't be driving on German roads. Well, that's how I interpreted the woman's tone when she implored me to 'Please make a U-turn if possible'. But we made pretty good time, covering 500 kms and the bottom half of Germany in just five hours.

The great thing about driving on the autobahn is that the speed limit on the roads is technically 120 kph, but you can drive as fast as 140 without getting booked. The scary thing is that everyone will do that speed even though there's snow everywhere and it's raining outside. The truly terrifying thing is that we were travelling at 140 kph yet cars/vans/trucks and donkeys were passing us as though we were standing still. Those Germans have fast cars and they're not afraid to use them. I do find it strange that most Germans are pretty regimented and stick to almost every regulation shoved their way, but when it comes to hitting the autobahn, they chuck the rule book out the window, mercilessly crush the pedal and rely on German precision technology to keep them from hurtling through a barrier and into a picturesque river.

We headed to Bad Füssing, powering along the roads in Freddy (as we named our car), following the commands of Veronica, the dominatrix in the dashboard. She delivered us right to the door of the Johannesbad Spa Complex. The marathon was an event organised and promoted by this huge thermal pool resort where Germans go to for holidays and rehabilitation. The foyer was bustling with a little running expo. We asked for Jürgen Knaus, the race director. When I gave my name, the guy said, 'Ah, the crazy Australians.'

Jürgen was pleased to see us, but also clearly very busy. 'I have your race entries downstairs,' he told us, 'and the directions to the complimentary hotel.' Fantastic! 'You should eat at the pasta party now, though, as it will end soon.' Okay, sounds good. Free food and accommodation, and a race entry – outstanding! 'Just one question.' He paused. 'Fifty-two marathons in one year? Are you guys crazy?' he asked, laughing.

Downstairs at the food hall people were packed at the tables in different team race jackets, eating bowls of pasta and drinking non-alcoholic beer. It had a good atmosphere and I felt tired but happy to be there.

The next day we drove back to the resort, where punters were all wearing bodysuits and SKINS gear. I was impressed at how many people were prepared to brave the cold, with around 1200 signed up to compete. Daz and I stood in the crowd, in the middle of snowy Bavaria, ready to start a race together for the first time. Daz was nervy, but pumped too. The race kicked off with a bang of the gun and we funnelled out over the line.

It was a lovely run. There were runners in costume and people were chattering away as Daz and I zigzagged through the crowd to get past some of the slower competitors. The Germans really get into this fitness stuff; everyone there was well prepared and had big smiles on their faces.

As we drew past the 5-km mark, we passed a drink station where they were handing out cups of isotonic sports drink. Daz grabbed one, gulped and made a face. 'Heated?' I asked. 'Yeah, man. That's weird,' he replied. It was weird, but it made sense in the conditions.

Daz was coasting and we were doing close to five-minute kms. It was really fun to run with my mate. Here we were, a couple of pals, blazing a trail through the snow in southern Germany.

People were mostly running in sets of two and three. I don't know why I noticed this, but it seemed kind of different to what I was used to. Maybe people huddle together against the cold by instinct, even in a marathon. Anyway, after about 8 kms, I began losing Daz. I'd be running with him next to me, then all of a sudden he'd be 20 metres behind. I slowed down for him a few times, then when I said I'd proba-bly go, Daz rallied and we stayed together for another 4 kms. The race is a double loop of 21 kms, so the longer we stayed together, the closer Daz was to home.

I looked at my watch and it was a little past the hour. I'd been plan-ning a new strategy and decided it was time to implement it. With all the travel and the recovery, I wasn't getting much chance to do speed work. I figured that I could run at least 10 kms of each race at my ideal pace and then expand on that as I progressed through the months. Now was a good time to start, as my legs were warmed up, so I said bye to Daz. My plan was to run faster now, and slow down again after 25 kms. I was passing people and feeling good, so it wasn't long before I was heading out for my second loop. I'd passed the half at 1:43, a fair way off posting a fast time, so I decided to look at this as a training exercise.

Daz's knee was seizing up when I left him. He told me later that he was really struggling around 17 kms and started to alternate walking and running. Then at 19 kms his legs were completely numb and he ran again, pushing with everything he had for the last couple of kilo-metres of the half marathon.

He finished in 1:58.58. He felt like a champion. He'd even taken breaks at every single stop, grabbing chocolate biscuits, drinks and fruit. That's what pulled him through apparently – 'It was free, bro!'

As 32 kms and a drink stop appeared ahead, I looked at my Garmin and saw 2:30 ticking by. Hmm, assuming I could hold under-five-minute kms, I'd be done by about 3:22. I was pretty sure I could do that. In fact, if I held my current speed, I might even go under.

That was a little silly . . . but possible. Crazy, crazy, crazy . . . but maybe, just maybe, I could pull it off.

I looked to my left. Frozen fields of wheat. I looked to my right. Fields and fields of nothing but snow, dotted with a few trees and houses, and mountains in the distance. Holy crap, what was I doing out here?

My watch beeped at me 33 kms in – I was doing 4.19 per km. *Hang on*, I thought, *I'm going quicker*. A kilometre later, though, I was struggling. I looked at my Garmin and the heart rate said I was going to be dead in the next couple of minutes, with my reading sitting at around 230 bpm. *Well, that can't be good* . . . But, of course, I didn't drop dead and I didn't slow down. As each kilometre came by, pace-wise I was still sitting under 4.30.

I thought about how great it would be to pull out another PB and decided it was possible if I could hold under 4.30 per km. I punched out a 4.19 in the next kilometre and knew I could do it. Everything was screaming and I had earlier passed a sign for a village called Hart. *All heart, buddy,* I thought, *all heart!* My brain was now saying no, my body was saying no, but my heart took over and drove me on for one last rush.

I turned the final corner and powered past the 42-km mark, stretching my legs for the final 200 metres. I was home, but not by much. The clock was ticking over 3:19 above the finish line, but I knew that I'd started a couple of minutes after the gun. I sprinted across the line and was stoked to see Dazzler waiting. I really didn't think he'd be there, because I was far too early. But here he was, with a 'Whoa, bro! That's an amazing time!'

I stopped to look at my watch: I had beaten my Las Palmas PB by 40 seconds. My body was screaming and my lungs were tight. My left calf was hurting and I felt a little dizzy. My face was frozen from the cold wind. And all of a sudden, I was annoyed at myself. That was a huge effort for 40 seconds. To make it, I'd taken seven minutes off the time for my first half, which was far too ambitious after such a huge month. It was dangerous and foolish, and I realised I'd made a mistake. But I looked over to Daz with a tired grin. 'That was for you, buddy,' I said. 'Happy birthday!'

We headed straight to the massage area. The real beauty of this marathon was the amazing recuperation resort – it was the perfect place to be after such a strenuous body beating. I peeled off my SKINS, which had kept me warm during the long run. They were caked in salt at the back, from absorbing the sweat as it seeped from my legs.

Then I made mistake number two. I didn't go outside to sit in the snow. Instead, we went straight into an outside thermal pool, 2°C above water, but over 35°C below. If you don't intend to run much in the following week, then submerging yourself in hot water isn't a big deal, but for a quick recovery, you really need to ice your legs. And I only had five days before the next marathon.

I knew where I should have been but stayed in the lovely hot water and let my body relax. I can't tell you how nice it felt sitting there while Daz kept laughing about how awesome his birthday had been.

We hopped in Freddy and powered to Munich. The next night we would fly to Egypt, but for now, it was still Daz's birthday. We drank tequila shots and a few beers, but it wasn't long before we crashed into a long and well-deserved sleep.

The next day we tried to walk around Munich, but at −4°C, we didn't last long. It was time to go to Cairo, and to 30°C weather.

8

INTERNATIONAL EGYPTIAN MARATHON

12 February, Luxor, Egypt

3:35.04

We left Munich on a late flight, about 10:30 p.m. on a Monday. It was another of my bright ideas to fly overnight to save some money on accommodation, even though we both slept badly on planes.

We exited the airport at 3:30 a.m. and became entangled in a battle with an official (well, he had a crappy badge) who was organising cabs. We were quoted one price, bargained it down, but then he tried to charge us the official price of 70 Egyptian pounds (LE). He kept saying he worked for the airport and that we should trust him. In the end we hopped into a random car (not an official cab) and were whisked away for the agreed price of 50 LE. The guy struggled to find our hostel, then demanded further payment, so in the end we were out of pocket by 70 LE anyway. An American guy we met later confirmed it should be a 30 LE taxi ride.

This was lesson one in Egypt. Everyone will screw you out of money if they can. Almost every transaction made, especially those involving tourists, is subject to a number of people colluding to squeeze every cent out of you. Avoiding this requires a certain level of street smarts and you don't wise up overnight.

We got to the Africa House Hotel at 4 a.m. We convinced the drowsy attendant to let us pay for half a night. Daz and I were given our own room and it's lucky there were three beds, because the first one I lay down in gave me some sort of skin irritation that freaked me out. I was gagging for sleep, but my skin was crawling and I tossed and turned till I couldn't take it any more, switching to another bed to try again. It was better, but not by much.

We were on a tight budget and needed what money I had left to last until a couple of sponsors saw us as a viable project. So we were stuck staying in crappy hostels, though Daz always selected the ones with a decent online customer-feedback rating. But these systems were flawed and, really, I wouldn't have stayed there if I'd had another option.

We'd arranged to be in Cairo for just two days. The plan was to see the National Museum the first day, head to the pyramids the next, and then in the evening push on to Luxor, where the race would be held. We'd been advised to see the museum first, to get an idea of the magnificence of the artefacts inside the Great Pyramids, as they'd pretty much all been emptied.

The museum holds a stunning haul. I remember Mum taking my bro and me as kids to see the Tutankhamen exhibition when it came to Melbourne. I thought that was pretty damn spectacular, but that was nothing compared to this museum's treasure trove. I'm telling you, there were mummies and sarcophagi of all shapes and sizes. There were paintings and drawings from all eras of Egyptian civilisation. Each vast space was crowded with tools, sculptures and vases, showing how people lived and what they wore, according to who occupied the throne at the time. It was absolutely extraordinary to see all of this up close. Kids were running about the stone tombs and rubbing them with their hands, trying to climb on top of some. I wasn't used to this type of indiscriminate groping of antiquities.

I am very interested in historical connections and understanding the way humanity has forged its place in the world. And what I was looking at was extraordinary, as well as overwhelming, mostly because it dated back so far – some pieces were 5000 years old. It's always my benchmark to consider the age of Australia and compare to these cultures. European settlement took place in Australia a little over

220 years ago. Christian culture is about 2000 years old. Roman culture 3000 years old.

The Egyptians win by about 2000 years. They kick everyone's arse in the historical stakes. And their culture was so advanced that it left these mementos to rub it in.

We went into the Tutankhamen display and I felt like a kid again, wanting to touch the cabinets but worried my mum would whack me on the head if I got too close. We walked around for a few hours, but after a while you simply can't take in any more information.

We grabbed some food on the way back from our first glimpse of the Nile (underwhelming), ducking into what looked like an Egyptian takeaway. And *bang!* we discovered koshari. It's a mix of three different types of pasta, lentil and tomato-based sauce, and comes with your choice of chilli or lemon dressing. It's *good*. We got a small tub each for about $1. One dollar! I knew right away what I'd be having the night before the marathon. It was a massive carbo injection and I couldn't wait to carve up another bowl.

The next day we had a driver take us to the pyramids. We'd paid the fellas at our hostel reception for the driver, costing us 200 LE. That's about $40, so it seemed like a fair deal for the day. Turned out you could do it for half that . . . Anyway, our driver jammed on the stereo in his cool little Hyundai, and 50 Cent rapping about his candy shop came blaring through. The driver asked if we liked the music and I told him it was my favourite song – I tend to say this about songs I hate.

When we got to the pyramids, our driver was kind enough to take us to his friend's tour company, where they offered us camel or horse rides for as little as 260 LE each. I told them as I was in training for a marathon, I'd prefer to walk. He seemed a little ticked off; I guessed this was because he would be going without his kickback that day.

We headed into the pyramid compound and SHAZAM! We were standing in front of the three Great Pyramids of Giza. They were so huge and magnificent! And HUGE . . . and MAGNIFICENT! The

Sphinx was crouched in front, like a lapdog waiting to do its master's bidding. The closer you got, the better you could see the immense size of the stones, therefore the more breathtaking the sight and greater your appreciation of the structure as an engineering feat.

We were accosted by a guy wanting to show us the 'right' way to get to the pyramids, then harangued by someone else who wanted to sell us a camel ride for only 100 LE between us. We were told it was a long tour and we couldn't walk it all ourselves. This sounded reasonable, so I agreed. Not long after Daz and I had mounted, our man hit us with the catch – it would cost more for the guide. How much more? 'Whatever you think it's worth,' said our old mate, Sammy. No, let's agree now. 'We can't, you just give whatever you think it's worth,' he said with a shrewd grin. He told us we should trust him, because he was older and had been here for many years. That word 'trust' again. I knew we were going to get screwed here.

Lesson two: set the price, tip inclusive, before you start and don't budge. Get off the camel if you have to. And don't pay more than $10 (50 LE) for two people to go for a 45-minute camel ride, no matter where you are. We paid four times that.

Sammy took us up to a point where we could see all nine pyramids at once. That's right – there are nine pyramids, not just the three big ones. The others are small though and, to be honest, going to the lookout to see them all together at once was pretty unimpressive.

I wanted to get up close to them. Get in them, on them, hug them.

The camel ride ended abruptly and we argued with Sammy about his tip. I stopped short of calling him a lying thief, but he persisted and I couldn't be bothered any more, so I conceded 200 LE in total. I laughed with irritation as he gave us his business card, telling us to be sure we referred him to our friends. We were finally next to the pyramids and I didn't want to talk to another crappy guide for the rest of our time in Egypt.

But this is where it finally got *really* good. We got the chance to go under one of the pyramids; the caverns inside were immense and terrifying. There was nothing left in each one, all artefacts having been long removed and taken to a safer place. But the size of the vaults gave an indication of the riches that must have once sat inside. In death, these pharaohs moved into palaces more extravagant than any that could have been enjoyed during their lives.

After a few hours walking around the park, we returned to our driver, who took us on to the Pyramid of Djoser at Saqqara. It has the oldest 'stepped' pyramid in the world, and at around 5000 years old, it is considered the oldest standing stone structure ever built. I looked at it for a while and then constructed my own version of their history.

What amazed me is that the king of the nearby city of Memphis, former ancient capital of Egypt, said to everyone: 'Hey, guys, we're all doing really well and we've got some spare cash, so I reckon we should build this enormous structure to celebrate how awesome I am. It should be completed in my lifetime, so when I die, I'll have eternal life through its existence. The only issue is that it will probably cost us all of our money for the next 40 years and all of the slaves will die in the process, so we'll be using most of our human resources. But the upside is, I'll be remembered forever as a deity and the greatest pharaoh who ever lived – which when you think about it is pretty rad!'

His officials must have all looked at him and pondered it for a while. 'You know, that might just work. You're the pharaoh and whatever you say sounds great. So, yeah, sure, let's give it a crack! Just don't throw any more tantrums or kill your eunuchs from now on, okay? And don't say we don't do anything for you.'

Whaddaya know? The crazy bugger was right. He did live forever!

Can you backdate Hero Time and apply it to the slaves? I'm not sure that works, because they didn't choose to step up to the plate, they were forced into it. I mean, do you commend the pharaoh for his foresight? Or the architect for the design? Or the project managers for making it possible at the expense of thousands of slaves and peasants?

Or do the slaves get respect for such sacrifice?

They were clearly all bonkers, but inspired at the same time.

Goddamn champions, all of them.

We headed down to Luxor, the town closest to the Valley of the Kings, on the other side of the Nile. The marathon was on Friday and I had picked up my race pack from an expensive hotel on Thursday.

It was becoming the norm for us to show up within 15 minutes of the start and this race was no exception. The start itself was in front of the Temple of Hatshepsut, the site of a bloody tourist massacre that had taken place 13 years before. Security was pretty extreme, but understandable given that the attraction is the city's bread and butter. Still, young lads standing around toting semiautomatics didn't help my race nerves.

We took off as the sun steadily rose above the Nile. I was glad Daz would be riding along out there on a hired pushbike. It gave me some-thing to look forward to later in the race. The race was a four-loop track that sat between the Valley of the Kings and the Nile. Apart from the start and finish line in front of this temple, we didn't see the tombs at all. But we did see some hot-air balloons ascending from a nearby field and they made the sunrise feel a little bit magical. Before I knew it, we were passing the 5-km mark. I was dismayed, though, as my watch only read 4 kms. That meant that the course was already short; I imagined the shoddy measurements were only likely to get worse.

We passed a couple of gigantic statues, including the seated Colos-sus, and the course took us through a few townships. Kids ran along next to us and whooped with excitement. I laughed and whooped with them. It tended to be the same for the second lap, though I noticed the temperature was rising sharply and I hadn't once seen a section of shade. I trucked along next to a couple of gents, chatting about our marathon experiences.

We pushed through the third lap, I noticed that the drink stations had significantly fewer drinks on them. Then I passed a couple of stations that were empty and completely unmanned. I also started to notice that the track was disappearing. As the front runner finished the final lap, the organisers had removed markers and traffic cones, making the track impossible to follow. Daz saw my distress in the fourth lap and rode next to me, coaxing me along. I was dramatically overheating, looking desperately for drink stops so I could toss more water over my head. Daz kept rotating drink bottles and pulling me forwards. I was running alone by now and any other runners in front or behind were looking similarly fatigued. The kids who'd been whooping in the early parts of the race were now running close to me and asking for money.

'*Baksheesh, baksheesh!*'

'Look, little mate, I'm running a bloody marathon. No money, no bloody *baksheesh*. Just give me a break.'

'Yes, yes, *baksheesh, baksheesh!*' came the insistent reply.

'I'll give you bloody *baksheesh* in a minute,' I spluttered, my patience disintegrating and my stress boiling over.

Daz tried to calm me down, but it wasn't working. I was done. I was walking for large tracts and my legs felt ready to be amputated; they had no interest in this kind of punishment. Daz took off on the bike to give me some time to myself.

I groaned and moaned as I covered those last 5 kms. I found the turn-off back up to the temple, and knew I was near the end, but whimpered anyway as I got closer. The problem was my GPS watch was telling me that the course was at least 1.5 kms short. I'd come all this way to run a marathon and I couldn't fairly record my time if the course was short.

I crested the last little rise and came to the finish line, with people cheering and the organisers ready to record my time. I told Daz to wait for a minute and I crossed the line, ran around a support post and straight back out again. It hurt – I was so dehydrated and mentally shot, I couldn't think of anything worse than running further in these conditions. But having to explain that I'd knowingly run a short race would have been far worse. Anyone who has trained for a marathon will agree that you don't want to be short-changed. If it's hard, then it's hard, but there is no excuse for anything less than 42.195.

I ran nearly 1 km out again with Darren gliding next to me on his bike, then when I knew I was plenty over the target I returned and ran towards the finish line again. I looked to the timekeeper as I crossed, pointed to my watch and said indignantly, '*That's* a marathon! Record *that* time.'

To me, this was the most glaring example of the Egyptian ethos that I'd seen throughout my short stay. Over-promise and under-deliver.

I was completely wasted by the run. Daz got me in a cab and we were taken to the ferries that constantly cross the Nile. I sat with my head between my legs, trying not to vomit and hoping I wouldn't cry. I had used every ounce of my physical, mental and emotional energy to get to the end of that race. Darren came into his own, taking control and thinking for both of us.

He got us back to our hotel and went on one of the most ridiculous adventures of the tour, tryING to get ice for an ice bath. The poor guy went from hotel to restaurant to look for enough cold rocks to cool my legs. It took nearly two hours, but he finally returned with a shopping bag full and we made the best of the ugliest, dirtiest bath I have ever sat in, just to cool down my legs.

I lay down for a while and then went to chat to some American backpackers we'd met. They were heading to the famous Red Sea resort town of Dahab that afternoon. It was a 17-hour bus ride, but the other end promised to be the perfect place to relax.

In a snap decision I decided that Darren and I needed a beach holiday too, a proposition to which Daz readily agreed. Within the hour we were packed, out of the hotel and standing with tickets in hand.

At the bus stop I was excited at the prospect of sitting on a beach, but anxious about my aching legs lying prone in a bus for longer than half a day. I'd bought a whole lot of snacks and beer from a nearby convenience store. Just as we were getting on the bus, the old man from the store ran up to me and handed me my Visa card, which I'd dropped. I looked at him in shock, then tried to hug him with relief. I'd spent a lot of time judging the Egyptians too harshly, and hadn't taken the time to recognise individual acts of kindness.

As the bus took us east and the sun slowly receded in the west, I took stock of my day. It had been a horrible race, but I couldn't expect life on this trip to be all roses. I thanked the old Egyptian gods that Darren was with me to carry a huge portion of the load that week. He didn't take offence when I was irritated. He stayed upbeat, even when I wanted to cry.

Dahab was a real gem. The whole town sits right on top of a huge bed of coral, so the snorkelling and scuba diving there is some of the best and most accessible in Europe and North Africa. We were only there a few days but it felt like two weeks. We sat in the lounges by the water and ate massive meals for a few dollars. Daz scuba dived for the first time and I did my fifth beginner's course. It was a little moment of heaven before we continued the grind. I will forever remember those few days as my happiest time in Egypt.

We bussed it back to Cairo and got on a plane to Milan. My experiences were so varied but the lessons were extraordinary, leaving me better prepared for whatever was coming next.

9

VERONA MARATHON

21 February, Verona, Italy

3:27.46

We flew to Milan and trained it to Verona. Fair Verona, what a beautiful place. An interesting CouchSurfing gent met us at the train station and gave us a roof for the night. We checked into a hotel the next day. I was finding the whole CouchSurfing thing a bit patchy, not liking that you needed to be polite all the time and fit in with a stranger's routine. I decided we'd stick with paying for cheap hostels, come what may.

This was my third visit to Verona. I went there for the first time with my mate Shaz in 1998, and returned with my then-fiancée in 1999. It's a truly magical little town, with its own architectural style quite distinct from other parts of the country. But they do have an old colosseum in the town centre; I'd read that the marathon would finish with us running right through the middle of it. I had remembered it as a romantic place, the home of Romeo and Juliet, so it was clearly the perfect place to hang out with the Dazzler . . .

The city has a large university and a huge number of international students too. One of Daz's challenges was to sneak into a university lecture in a foreign city, so while I was taking it easy one day, he took off on his own adventure. He found the university's city campus, showed up to a class and sat at a table in the back of the room. When rollcall came around, he answered '*Si*' to one of the names that was read out and then tried not to make eye contact with too many students. The whole class was in Italian, so Daz couldn't understand anything that was said. He took notes and secretly got out his camera and filmed some of the class, just to prove that he'd really been there. When the class ended, he headed back to the hotel to find me, his eyes wide and his heart palpitating as he relayed his story.

Verona is always abuzz, with the bars filling up late in the evening and some of the clubs and bars raging till well into the morning. Daz needed a night out, and this seemed to be as good a place as any. We went out on the Friday night and danced ourselves stupid, failing dismally to impress the local girls, but having a blast anyway.

The next evening we went out to dinner with some excellent French ladies who were staying in our hotel. Elisa was running the 10-km race and her friend Laurence was running the marathon, with her eye on a personal best. I suggested I could pace her if she was aiming for 3:30, as it would be about right for me.

Come race day, I couldn't find Laurence at the start line, so I ran hard for the first 5 kms, hoping I'd happen across her. Sure enough, just when I was ready to let it go, she popped up in front of me, well on track for her 3:30. We ran together steadily, constantly checking our pace so she wouldn't burn out. I talked to more runners, stepping around the ancient city, crossing the river a couple of times, trailing through the historic castle and finishing after a run through the Colosseum.

I cramped only 6 kms from the finish line and had to let Laurence go. She finished strongly in 3:25 and when I ambled home in 3:27, she gave me a huge hug and thanked me for my help.

It was a great finish, but my legs were in all sorts of trouble and afterwards I had to sit down for 20 minutes as blades of pain tore through my legs. I found that this was a basic routine for me now, especially in the races where I worked hard to get to the line. My legs would go into shock and it felt as if someone were sliding long cold knives into my hot, trembling leg muscles. It was worst in my quads, and I'd need to sit down until the waves of pain dissipated. My calf muscles were in all sorts of distress too, now feeling locked before, during and after the races. I could have sworn they were rocks taped to my legs.

Darren and I stopped off in Venice, before flying to Frankfurt and on to Beijing and then the Tokyo Marathon, where we'd planned to meet up with my Aussie running mates. I took in the romance of Venice and revelled in the fact that Daz hadn't yet seen this part of the world, so I was getting to glimpse it through fresh eyes.

But I developed a limp as we walked through those winding streets and historic piazzas. The last two races really had hurt me, and I was now finding it difficult to walk, especially with my big backpack on. The extra flights didn't help either but it was the cheapest way forwards.

It felt like my body was packing it in. Would I be able to continue?

10

TOKYO MARATHON
28 February, Tokyo, Japan
3:33.20

Tokyo is perhaps the greatest city on earth (yes, another one!). Everything looks like a novelty version of itself – cars, food, shops. The kids dress up like cartoon characters and the oldies are all so cute, you just want to hug them. Japanese people are some of the kindest in the world, though in Tokyo you can still see a staunch reluctance to relate to anything that comes from outside Japan. Once they were kings, a frightening enemy that tore through the Pacific; now they are mechanical geniuses taking over the world with technological proficiency and business acumen that nobody saw coming.

I was no stranger to Tokyo, or Japan. I'd had a Japanese girlfriend for a while. Mayumi epitomised all the fundamentally good things about Japan: kindness, simple beauty, generosity. I'd met her during my first time in Tokyo, while I was visiting a friend, Cris. I came back with Mayumi a couple of years later to attend the Fuji Rock Music Festival – another of those 'You just gotta do it!' events.

When I was working on my marathon list, Tokyo was right up the top. My old friends Brendan and Emma were living there, plus I was keen to catch up with a whole host of people I'd met on earlier visits. Cris's English mate, AJ, had offered me his room while he was holidaying back in the UK and, in typical Japanese style, we put as many people as possible in there. As the expense of hotel rooms in Tokyo was deeply prohibitive, this made the trip very cost-effective for all my

Aussie running mates, who'd lobbed over to partake in this episode of my international escapades.

My Tribal buddies arrived a couple of days after we did. Andrew 'Chippa' Wood brought his beautiful betrothed, Sian. Nicolas 'the Cougar' Marie is my closest running buddy – we'd done most of our training together and maintain a friendly rivalry, though he's a far better runner than I am. These were my Comrades buddies, so we were really racking up the air miles. Shane 'Yabby' Campbell, an absolute gun runner who can punch out a sub-three-hour marathon without much effort, was also over for the event.

The idea that we would run this race together was a huge spark for me. So far, I had only run with strangers, or new friends. When they got in, the first thing we did was catch up over a few beers – and a few tequila shots. They were all fantastically supportive and I really needed the boost. Having other friends there gave Daz and me some space too. I was pushing him a lot to do more – to take more photos and videos, to run more – but he was finding it stressful putting up with my demands. He simply didn't enjoy being pressured, but it was just how it had to be.

Daz and I stayed at Emma and Brendan's home, not far from Shibuya. It made a huge difference to be around people who lived in Tokyo and knew what to do, where to go, and so on. Emma was teaching at an international school and Brendan was working as a myotherapist, a practitioner who focuses on musculoskeletal pain, with most of his clientele coming from the expat community. I clearly needed Brendan's help, but he was not known for his soft hands. He worked through my legs and watched me writhing in pain. Have I told you I am a complete child when it comes to physical pain, such as that inflicted by deep-tissue massage? I freaked out and Brendo laughed at me.

'Jeez, mate, I've barely touched you. You might want to toughen up!'

He did his work and at the end said, 'Well, I reckon you'll get

another race out of them, but I can't promise too many past that.'
I sighed and looked at Daz, who shrugged. *Ah, bugger . . . Just keep
going until something snaps, I guess.*

Brendan showed me how to tape up my legs, the crossover binding
would stop my calves from going through their full range of motion,
which would in turn stave off fatigue. I tried it out the following day
and had to admit that it felt better.

A young fella named Toi had contacted me before I came to Japan. He
wanted to introduce me to his running coach, who didn't speak any
English but was interested in meeting me. It turned out that Akinori
Kusuda was a national treasure. He had become famous in 2009, by
running 52 marathons in 52 days, finishing with the Tokyo Marathon.
He'd set a new world record for the number of marathons run on consecutive days, and he'd done it at the ripe old age of 65.

We'd organised to meet at the Tokyo Marathon, where he had a
TV crew waiting to talk to us. I hadn't expected that, but Akinori's
world record was very important to the locals. When he invited me to
come and run with his club – the aptly named Smile Running Club –
I jumped at the chance.

Akinori-san had also connected with Alan Williams, an English
lad with cystic fibrosis. The average life expectancy of someone with
CF is 31, and Alan had just turned 32. In celebration of beating the
odds, Alan had decided to take on the challenge of running 31 races
in one year, and in the process raising £31 000 for cystic fibrosis –
his website was called Run31.org.uk. He was in Tokyo to run yet
another race and it was clear that this guy was on his own epic adventure. We had a great talk about our journeys to date.

We met with Akinori's club the next day and found out that they
were all *very* fast runners. The runners in his group were all ages and
had an impressive record of running 2:30 and 2:40 marathons, close

to elite. It seemed that Akinori-san was some sort of super-coach. I hoped to absorb some of his genius.

Race day was an absolute washout.

We got to the start line with 35 000 other runners there to attempt the 10 kms and the marathon. We were a big group at the start, with Yabby, Chip, Cougar, Brendan and I all running the marathon. Dazzler was running 10 kms and he'd come up with another brilliant outfit. Wearing a kimono and a headband, he looked like a character straight out of *The Karate Kid*. When we got to the race, however, we realised he'd been completely outdone: there were loads of runners in whacky outfits! Some wore full traditional dress, but we also saw a fella in a gridiron outfit and a guy dressed as Japanese Jesus, carrying a big cross and wearing a crown of thorns.

The race itself crisscrosses the city, running in and out of a central road three times finishing up at the harbourside. The rain was coming down in buckets but, once we were underway, we didn't feel it too much. All the lads wanted to stick together, but we lost Yabby before we'd even properly started.

We passed through the centre of town and I was once again blown away by the massive logistical effort it took to shut down a major city for a running race. I have been impressed before, but this was something else. It's a megacity that hosts 13 million people within the inner-city area alone. For all of that, it is a meticulously well-maintained place, with very little rubbish on the streets and not too many obvious signs of poverty. To have your run celebrated by locals waving fans, banging drums and shouting '*GANBATTE!*' (Do your best!), was wonderful.

Daz peeled off at 10 kms, just after we passed the imperial palace. It's a good place to go for a run, by the way, if you ever make it to Japan. It's a 5-km circuit and a popular place for inner-city inhabitants to meet for a trot. And, of course, it's as absolutely beautiful as you'd imagine a Japanese imperial palace to be.

At that point Yabby popped up out of nowhere.

'What took *you* boys so bloody long?' laughed Yabby.

The team was complete again.

Brendan was getting tired and began to lag. I kept stopping to take photos and videos of as many whacky things as I came across, but then I'd need to sprint to catch up with the lads. Everyone was still wearing rain gear of one sort or another, making it difficult to spot your friends.

We came around another corner and saw Emma cheering with the Boxing Kangaroo flag fluttering. The supporters were doing a hell of a job just trying to stay in touch with us!

We were all running according to Chip's plan. He'd done 18 marathons all over the world, describing himself as 'the consummate fun runner'. But he still hadn't cracked the 3:30 mark. We were sitting on track to beat that time, but I was trying to get the guys to run faster, just to give us a few minutes in the bag.

As we got closer to the end, you could sense the excitement build. But, to be fair, it may have just been me getting excited, because I distinctly remember rattling off what I thought was wise, motivational counsel.

'You guys are steam trains, you're heroes, you're completely unstoppable. I'm concerned about the explosion of raw power around here.'

'SHUT UP, BONE!' was all I got in response.

We came around the last couple of bends and saw the finish. Chip and I were sitting pretty, but we had lost Cougar and Yab, as both of them had hit the wall and dropped away. We slowed down and looked for them, but Chip was distracted by Sian, screaming from the side of the road. He ran over for one more kiss, then as one, we crossed the line for marathon number 10 in 2010!

We hadn't quite got under 3:30, though I thought the course was long. Nonetheless, I was very proud to have run with my buddies and, as we all hugged, the rain stopped and the clouds parted. Finally the sun emerged to bathe us in warmth to go with our glory.

If you're going to celebrate anywhere in the world, do what you can to make Tokyo your venue. For the next couple of nights, we drank and danced, checked out a few sights and even had the best karaoke sing-off of all time – in the same room as was used in the filming of the Bill Murray classic *Lost in Translation*. We were intoxicated on good beer and the Super Happy Fun Vibe of Tokyo.

I bid my friends farewell and a safe trip home. I would miss them, but they'd brought home to me, for just a little while.

On Monday night we watched the National NHK News. There was a 10-minute story on Akinori Kusuda, the Tokyo Marathon, and Alan, Daz and myself.

Would you believe that as we exited the plane the next day in San Francisco, a Japanese gent came up to me and asked, 'Did you run the marathon on the weekend?'

'Yes,' I replied. 'It was a lot of fun. Did you run too?'

'No, but I saw you on the news last night. I can't believe you've left Japan already. You'd be so famous there right now.'

'Thanks,' I said. 'But the show must roll on!'

But for a little while, just for a minute, I was Big In Japan.

11

NAPA VALLEY MARATHON

7 March, Napa Valley, California, USA
3:32.39 (started late – 3:20.43 watch time)

I'd added San Francisco to my list so I could catch up with Jackie Rogowski. She was a Denver girl who'd spent a few months in Melbourne helping our team at Google. Jackie was living with two other girls in SF, and Daz and I felt immediately at home in their place.

I love San Francisco. They say it's very much like Melbourne and I suppose it's to do with the shared relaxed attitude. SF is bright and pretty when the sun is out. The people are engaging and intelligent, with an ease that isn't as obvious in the other big American cities I've visited. The city is divided into distinct neighbourhoods and we were staying in one of the most overtly gay and thoroughly entertaining districts on the planet, the Castro. The rainbow flag adorns many businesses and residences alike and a number of the shops on the main street sell all types of pride products and quite a few sexy-good-time novelties too. Even better, the people sitting in the diners and bars are a classic mix of men and women of all ages who are refreshingly comfortable and open about their sexuality. It was a fun place to people-watch.

We went out for a couple of nights, saw some sights and I managed a run down to the Golden Gate.

I had some unexpected news from home. I was mid-conversation with my dad, chatting about other things, when he said, 'And Gay's going into hospital again, and hopefully that will be the last time.'

I'd been nodding on the phone, the way you do when you're only half-listening to your parents. Suddenly I stopped nodding.

'Sorry, Pa, but what do you mean, "She's going into hospital again?"'

'Ah . . . um, yeah, sorry, but we weren't going to tell you until you got home. Gay has cancer.'

My heart skipped a beat. My poor stepmother. 'Gay's sick?'

'Yes, it's breast cancer. But we think we got it in time.'

'Oh,' was about all I could offer. Dad told me a bit more and I asked if there was anything I could do. He said the best thing I could do was to stay the course. I asked Dad to keep me in the loop. Here I was, just cruising around the world trouble-free while the regular bad shit of life caught the people I loved unawares. Life's an evil bitch sometimes.

We headed up to Napa on the Saturday. I wanted to get to the marathon expo for the guest appearance of Dean Karnazes. I had been inspired by his efforts to run 50 marathons in 50 US states in 50 days – yes, you read that right – and motivated by his book, *Ultramarathon Man*. In fun running circles, he's an icon. His story is about experiencing a defining moment and using it as motivation to improve your life. He became an avid runner and his life has become more and more focused on this wonderful hobby. He has run 400 miles without stopping, over four or so days – and hot damn, that's a long way to run! Dean is by no means the fastest or strongest runner out there, but his story is accessible to many, and his is the kind of book you pass on to your mates, giving them hope that they too can achieve great things.

It was terrific to hear Dean's stories in person and he came across as a really nice guy. He told everyone about his 'next big adventure': in 2012 he was planning to run a marathon distance in every country around the world in just one year. I listened as a ripple of disbelief rolled through the crowd. It suddenly made my challenge seem piddling. When he opened the floor up to questions, I raised my hand.

'Hi, Dean, I'm really impressed with your challenge, and I can't believe you want to run nearly every day. I'm running 52 marathons in 52 weeks around the world and I'm a mess from the travel already. How do you think you'll get on?'

'Wow,' said Dean. 'That's really impressive! Well, I have been looking at my options and believe that I can get to 245 recognised countries in the world. I think it is possible to run the distance in all of these countries.'

'Hat's off to you, Dean; I've always been inspired by you. That'd be a phenomenal adventure!' I was amazed at his feat but, if I'm honest, I also felt a tiny bit outshone.

When I saw him at his signing soon after that, he shook my hand warmly and told me he'd be following me from now on.

I walked away with a thousand questions. Had I just been exposed as a pretender in front of this mighty running hero? Daz and Jackie assured me that I could still hold my head high. I tried to hash out the differences between our feats. I was spending time in each country, not just a day and a race. I was running races, participating in events, not just punching out lone kilometres in each new city.

I had to make peace with the fact that this was my path and anyone else's journey would be different. I had chosen to participate in running celebrations all around the world, not just for the love of the races, but because I thought these running 'street parties' were the best way to see a city come alive. When else do people swarm the streets, stopping traffic and creating that wonderful atmosphere? Tokyo, Rome, New York, Berlin . . . All of these places brightened up for such events and the enthusiasm was infectious. I wanted to feel that in as many places as I could.

But there was another side to running: the uncompromising effort it takes to run the long, lonely roads that snake across countries and continents. Some people loved this solitude and endeavoured to conquer each continent by crossing it. Dean was a true running enthusiast. I had enormous respect for them, but I wouldn't ever be that kind of runner. I am going to steal my friend Chip's turn of phrase, and say that I am 'the consummate fun runner'. I couldn't ever see myself traversing continents alone, but if you put a hundred races in front of me, with thousands of potential new friends and faces, I'd be there, for sure. I was in it for the good times, although there was no doubt that the tough times came wrapped in the same glory as that of the lone achievements.

We were staying in a small hotel at one end of the valley. I thought 40 minutes would be plenty of time to get to the start line. It was a perfect sunny spring morning as we drove up the highway, passing lovely little tourist towns. As the miles went past, though, I began to realise that I had completely misjudged the distance. Even if we sped, we would miss the start and probably get a fine to boot. I looked at Jackie nervously as I drove and she just laughed and said, 'Well, I told you we needed more time.' I wished I could have argued but she was right.

We got to Calistoga about eight minutes late. I gave the guys a hug and darted down the access road, passing crowds of supporters as they left the start area. I got a few laughs and shouts – 'You can do it, buddy, *RUN!*' – I was clearly the last to start. As I got to the line, the organisers were dismantling the beginners' arch. I looked at my watch: 12 minutes past kick-off. I paused to ask if it was okay if I started and got a bewildered look. 'Damn, they're long gone, so you'd better run fast to catch up!'

That was about all the incentive I needed. The road was clear in front of me and I belted along, passing the classic yellow schoolbuses. I got a couple of friendly honks from the drivers and incredulous looks from the road marshals.

'How far ahead is the last runner?' I shouted, running full steam.

'They passed through at least five minutes ago,' replied the guard as he stopped the buses to make way for me.

'Cheers!' I waved and kept legging it down the road.

I knew I'd catch them; I just didn't want to break myself in the process. It was only 3 kms in, while I was slamming out four-minute kms, when I saw the first walkers struggling up an incline. Soon, I found myself running smack-bang into the back of traffic, runners and walkers filling the road ahead of me. I began to dodge and weave to get ahead of the pack.

The course runs along a secondary highway, an old tourist road that sits a couple of miles east of the main thoroughfare. It makes sense to use this road, not just because it's easy to shut down, but also because it's a little elevated, winding high along the side of the valley. It treats you to extraordinary views of sprawling vineyards and dense forests below. As the sun rose higher, so did a number of hot-air balloons, floating lazily across the lines of grapes.

I saw Dazzler and Jackie 10 kms in; Daz's costume today was a bunch of grapes. With purple balloons pinned all over his T-shirt and a sprig of green protruding from his head, he looked so ridiculous that I burst out laughing at the sight of him.

Having supporters on these races gave me something to look forward to and kept me accountable for my time as well. I didn't want to have my friends waiting too long for me to show up. Jackie's flatmates had driven all the way up from SF to join the celebrations, so we'd have enough people for our own party by the end of the race.

I had started dead last, then run past what I estimated to be around 800 people. It was like emerging from a swollen river to find a thin stream of faster runners as I moved further along the valley. It was nice to be back around runners sitting at the same pace.

I finished in blazing fashion, almost knocking out another PB. My official time was 3:32, but my watch said 3:20. Fair enough, I would take any official time after the morning's fiasco! I'd ruined both nipples with the chafing, so my T-shirt was a bloody mess. I was extremely shaky at the end, legs wobbling, and felt almost ready to collapse. The team managed to get me to a massage table, then back to the hotel, where we filled a bath and I tried to cool the fire in my legs.

If you're going to come all the way to Napa, you have to at least sample the wines, so the girls drove us to a favourite winery. Artesa sat atop a rise and looked across the valley as it was washed in afternoon colour. I was all but broken, with my calves locked up, but hanging out with this little team made me happy and relaxed again. Everything was okay. Life was good. I said, mostly to myself, 'Another beautiful day in paradise and, hey, look where I ran today …'

We flew to Los Angeles for a stopover. Two days in a city like LA would normally be enough for me, but hanging out with my buddy Stuart made the whole place so much more accessible and I started to see its appeal. Stu had moved there the previous year, to pitch a screen-play he'd written and see where the adventure took him. We'd worked together in bars back in Melbourne, and I always remember him being such a joker, but now, 10 years later, he was a driven man, throwing caution to the wind in pursuit of his dreams. He had saved enough money to set himself up for at least 12 months, and in a place where connections meant everything, he was busy networking and under-standing the business.

Stu was making progress, but it was risky and draining. Still, as we both agreed, you gotta be in it to win it. Without putting his life under pressure, he would be left with only a dream and no real story to go with it.

I found myself in awe of Stu. He was on a long, stressful road. He said much the same of me, but I saw the fruits of my effort every week and my adventure had an obvious conclusion. His was more of a loose plan and no one could say how it might end up.

We went out on the town, checking out a Tuesday night at the Roosevelt. It was clear that most of the people were there to show off their money, something I didn't have a lot of. We were drunk too quickly and didn't stay all night. On the way out, Daz started rapping with a doorman. He was a *massive* black dude and Daz, the thinnest white man alive, was dwarfed by him. It was a perfect finish to our adventures and a day later we jumped on an Air New Zealand flight heading east.

12

CYPRUS MARATHON

14 March, Paphos, Cyprus

3:45.02

We bounced through London and landed in Cyprus. Alexis had arrived earlier that same day – she had a great package deal to fly to Paphos, which included a room in a nice resort. It was only for one, but we snuck in the side and all shared the space. To be honest, it was getting close to crunch time with the budget. Paying for both Daz and I to travel was wearing through the bucks and I was beginning to suspect we wouldn't last much longer.

I love the Mediterranean but I'd never been to Cyprus. It's a pretty place, easy to get around and so well frequented by the Brits that everyone spoke English almost without a local accent. The place was heaving with tourists, even though this was the low season. The sunsets were absolutely stunning and Alexis and I hired a car to drive around the island, learning about its history and taking in its immense beauty. We visited the Tombs of the Kings, a necropolis dating back to the Hellenistic period of 400 BC. It was very easy to feel like a speck of dust in the sands of time compared to the region.

We were only there a few days, but it was just the pick-up I needed. Alexis was running her first 10-km race and she'd been training in icy England. It was a resort race, something to stimulate tourism while the enormous hotels waited patiently for summer to roll around again.

I was concerned that it would be a little boring, but, conveniently, the race was a week before the Maratona di Roma, so we were in the right neighbourhood.

The start line was next to the Petra Tou Romiou, or Aphrodite's Rock. We were on a highway, east of Paphos, and the plan was to run all the way back.

We had some time to kill before the start, so I spoke to a couple of English lads. One of them, Steve, had done a few Ironman races. He was in Cyprus on holiday with some mates and had challenged them all to participate. Something told me that Ironman Steve enjoyed a challenge and loved to take his mates on the adventure with him.

Although Cyprus is very beautiful, it doesn't have much in the way of trees, so without a cloud in the sky, it was a very hot run. I'm going to blame the jet lag, but I think it was more the heat than anything – by 15 kms I was reduced to walking. By halfway, I'd lost momentum. Daz rolled up on a hired bicycle and encouraged me.

'You'll be okay, mate. Just keep moving like you always do,' he said.

'I'm struggling, man . . . too hot,' I gasped. 'My legs are on fire.'

Daz rode along beside me for a bit and told a few amusing stories by way of distracting me. Daz has the ability to find most things funny, so his morning had already supplied a few cracking tales. Even these, though, weren't enough to lift my mood.

At 30 kms, I was all alone. Darren got a classic picture of me running down the road. I love that photo, as it shows how lonely a marathon can be. It's just me, battling along, with the road stretched out ahead of me, a green meadow to my left with a few homes astride a rocky hillside. It captured a beautiful moment, one that I'd taken a snapshot of in my mind, running across a little island in the Mediterranean.

'So, this is where I'm running today,' I had said to myself. 'A field of grass instead of grapes. An island instead of a valley.'

As I pushed towards the end, I saw Ironman Steve again. I was losing a lot of time, but he was just kicking into gear. 'C'mon, Tristan,' he hollered at me on the way past in a thick Northern accent. 'Not far now, son!'

There wasn't much left in my legs, but I tracked Ironman Steve, trying to keep him in sight and use him as motivation to keep moving. Tourists, sitting in cafés, munching on their breakfasts and sipping their coffees, gave us cheers as we passed by. We came to the boardwalk and rolled around to the seaside fort, crossing the line in 3:45.02. Alexis was waving the Boxing Kangaroo and Daz was cheering alongside. I was crushed but happy. I went straight over to Steve and thanked him for leading me to the end.

Alexis had run well until about halfway through her 10 kms, then she'd struggled like hell to get to the end. She told me it had given her renewed respect for what I was trying to achieve.

Another unexpected delight, Cyprus is an island I'd definitely return to, though maybe just for a beach holiday.

Twelve marathons. Eleven weeks. Ridiculous.

13

MARATONA DI ROMA

21 March, Rome, Italy

3:11.27 PB

A drive across Cyprus brought us to Larnaca, then we took a cheap flights to Athens and on to Rome. We stayed near the central station, in a little hostel that we had waited too long to book a room in. At €35 a night each, this was going one of the most expensive beds of the year so far. On the plus side, I got to train in the gorgeous city gardens, Villa Borghese, which was really special.

Our invitation to meet with the marathon organisers coincided with a press conference; we were surrounded by Kenyans and Ethiopians, some of the fastest runners in the world. For the first time, I became aware of the brand power behind these big city marathons. The Five Majors – London, Boston, New York, Chicago and Berlin – had a near monopoly on marathon racing. They are seen as the most desirable international races to complete, even though three of them are in the USA. We found out that the Rome and Tokyo marathons had formed a partnership to leverage off each other to gain a stronger foothold in the market. If people were competing in only one international marathon a year, then these guys wanted it to be either Tokyo or Rome. I respected their efforts in trying to get higher profiles.

Marathoners are all about ticking boxes. First they want to run one marathon, then 10, then trundle on until they get to the 100 Club. They want to run in every state in the USA, every country in Europe, then all seven continents, and maybe chuck in the North Pole for good measure. Marathon junkies certainly want to tick off the Five Majors and when that's done, if this new Rome–Tokyo partnership played their cards right, they might be the next to get a tick.

At the press conference we met Dietmar, a mad German barefoot runner. He wore a crazy yellow outfit, with a bright-red afro wig that made him look like a rag doll, or a scarecrow, but never have I met a man less scary. He was, in fact, remarkably engaging and friendly.

Dietmar had been running barefoot in marathons for more than a decade, well ahead of recent running trends. He participated in a huge number of marathons and ultra-marathons each year and knocked them out at breakneck speeds. I remembered filming him at the snowy Thermen-Marathon in Bad Füssing, Germany. That day he wore a wild 17th century gentleman's costume, with a feathered hat atop a wig of long blonde curls. Today's get-up was tame in comparison.

I have to say, the Maratona di Roma is one of the most interesting races to which you could treat yourself. It's basically a sightseeing tour of one of the most majestic cities on earth. Rome is a town that just keeps on giving: it has the best value for money any tourist could hope for. At every turn, you are presented with a cathedral or a museum, a piazza or a fountain. From Trevi to Piazza Navona, the Pantheon to the Vatican, you are exposed to architectural wonders that light up a square or dominate the skyline.

The race itself was beautiful and painful all at once. It was a perfect day to race and we kicked off from the Colosseum. We trundled through the streets, passing icon upon icon. When we got to the centre of the city, however, we were pounding on cobblestones and the jarring footfalls shook my muscles from the bone. In and out of suburbs we ran, the whole first half of the race in sight of the three-hour pacer.

I had an interesting gamble riding on this race, which meant being close to the pacer was actually bad news. I had set up a competition at the beginning of the year, the prize being a free trip to meet Daz and me in Europe. For every $10 that was donated to UNICEF, the giver would receive one entry. To choose the winner I came up with a nifty idea: each entry would equate to a one-second time period in which I might finish. The person whose entry corresponded to my fastest time would win. I had anticipated finishing anywhere between 3:10 and 3:45, so the times began from 3:10 onwards. But here I found myself running through the halfway at 92 minutes, so I was way under the expected time. Whoops. At least I was on track for my third personal best of the year!

I couldn't let the chance to run this well slip away. I kept flying along, but in reality I was losing my grip on the race. I had the taste of a PB in my mouth, while trying to take in my historic surrounds. I was gasping to my camera, 'And here's the Pyramid of Cestius . . . And the Vatican . . . Wow, check out the Spanish Steps.' I powered through those last few kilometres on cobblestones and honestly thought my calves would give out, such was their shuddering with each impact. The last kilometre took us around the Colosseum one more time, ending where we started. My pace was broken, but I was still on track for a PB.

'Keep moving, Tris. For all the mighty gladiators who fell in this arena, lift one more time and share their glory! *Liiiiift!*'

3:11.27. A solid personal best – and just in the time frame to pick a winner for our competition! Melanie Bushby had won; she was a friend of the Dazzler's and a great supporter of our adventure. She would decide later when and where to meet us.

Daz found me at the end, shaking like a leaf from my exertions. He wore a gladiator's costume, about three sizes too small. It was a phenomenal race and Rome will remain a special memory.

Two extraordinary things happened that same day. My Nonna Netta (my stepfather's grandmother) passed away in northern Italy. She was in her nineties, and had a good life, but it was still sad news. I guess I felt it more because I was geographically so close to the family.

And then I found out that my cousin Miriam had her first child, Elsie, the first baby in our family. I was extremely happy for her. We'd had a loss and a gain, and I was reminded again how the real world continued to truck along while I was a long way from it.

I'd absented myself from being around my family during these highs and lows, but the detachment was only for one year, so I needed to suck it up.

You're okay, I told myself. *Just keep going.*

14

BRATISLAVA CITY MARATHON

28 March, Bratislava, Slovakia
3:30.15

Going to Slovakia was Daz's idea. He wanted to visit Mikhal, or 'Sharky' as Daz knows her, a friend who was nannying in Bratislava. She had been living there for about a year, working for a Slovakian banker and his family. If you're ever going to be a nanny, you could do a lot worse than working for a Slovakian banker – Sharky had a sweet pad, a car, reasonable flexibility in her work hours, and kids who were pretty cool by all accounts.

We flew into Vienna and got the bus to Bratislava. We felt lost – we knew nothing of this town, the local language or attitudes. But once we met up with Sharky, who introduced us to some of her friends, we started to feel much more relaxed. In fact, the days that followed turned out to be a real treat.

Bratislava has a phenomenal history, having been first settled on the banks of the Danube in 200 AD. It has been the domain of lords and seat of kings, with a striking castle perched above the town. It was always a 'window to the west' for the Soviets, with its proximity to Vienna making it a natural conduit city for east–west relations.

Sharky was a wonderful host, showing us that for a small town Bratislava has a pumping nightlife and a whole lot of beautiful women to go with it. Unfortunately, I'm far from at my best with gorgeous European women, let alone when they speak a language like Slovakian!

I met with the race organiser, Jozef Pukalovic – or Jozo for short –

a bright-eyed young guy who'd been working with his brother on building up the profile of this race. They were competing with the Košice Marathon, in eastern Slovakia, the oldest consecutively run marathon in Europe, which had its first event in 1924, so Jozo had some work to do. But he believed the capital city deserved to have the highest-profile event, so he'd made it his mission to deliver this crown. When he invited me to the gala dinner to celebrate the opening of their running festival, I was honoured to be included.

The Bratislava Marathon was only five years old, but each year it had grown by 30 or 40 per cent so that there were now more than 3000 runners in the different categories. I met at least a dozen runners who all had a story to tell. Like Steve from Gloucestershire, who was running his 498th marathon, aiming to have number 500 come up in two weeks' time. He'd broken the world record back in 1992 when he'd run more registered marathons in a year than had previously been achieved, with 87 races across the UK and Europe.

The race started in the city and ran through town for a while, then passed under the castle and headed out over the main bridge with a cool UFO restaurant on top. They'd shut down half the bridge and the highway for the runners, so it felt safe and spacious.

I sidled up next to a fella with a backpack on, intrigued to see what he was training for. Brian, a Canadian, was doing his final preparation run for the difficult 250-km Marathon des Sables, which was due to start at the end of the week. He looked determined and strong, but he'd been really sick and was coughing up a little blood on the run. It didn't seem to faze him. What an animal!

I moved from one runner to another as we passed water stops. I sometimes forgot that just saying hi to someone on these races, or giving a few words of encouragement, could turn into fascinating conversations that both taught me a fantastic lesson and introduced me to a new friend. There's just something about that camaraderie which makes the marathon such a special event.

Every time you run 42 kms you learn that the mind is the most amazing tool humans possess. It allows you to keep going when everything else is telling you to stop. Your willpower and ability to embrace pain and push through it to achieve your goals is a fundamental lesson in taking control of your life.

Put simply: go for a run, unlock your dreams.

Ha! Okay, maybe that's too simple.

Once we were through the new part of town, Petrzalka (which is dominated by communist-era buildings), we turned off into some lovely parkland near the River Danube and back towards the city and lap two. I saw Daz a few times, waving the Boxing Kangaroo flag. He'd tried to find a costume here, but it proved difficult and potentially very expensive. I loved seeing him dress up like a tool, but really I was just stoked that someone was out here cheering for me. So many times he was exactly what I needed on these runs. And Daz was loving being in a place where there were just so many hot women – he had plenty to look at while I was running about like a crazy bastard.

I was running with Brian the Canadian again at about the 35-km mark. He reckoned I looked in good shape and should step it up a bit. I had to admit I was feeling great, and I was in danger of missing my 3:30 target for the day by about two minutes. I wished Brian all the best and decided it was business time. I found myself cruising pretty easily at around 4.25 per km, which would give me back the two minutes I needed. It also meant that I wasn't taking this marathon too easy and I was getting a little speed training in. This was all very nice, until I hit an area that was basically a damn wind tunnel. Then suddenly I was working twice as hard just to keep my pace close to 4.30 per km.

'C'mon, champ, just a little more.

'The chips are down again, mate, but now's the time to punch through the pain!

'You can do this, you can do this. You're not a pussy, you're a god-damn *machine*!'

It never ceased to amaze me the crap I'd say out loud to myself when I was in the last 5 kms. But it worked.

I came over the last bridge and ran into town, dance tunes blaring from big speakers, supporters waving and shouting for everyone.

I finished the run solidly in 3:28.56 by my watch – though the official time on the site was 3:30.15. But I was happy with that result and very glad to have taken part in an up-and-coming race.

We had to leave the following day, so we weren't able to celebrate much. Just a few beers nearly put me in a coma, so I knew it was time to rest.

The plane left Bratislava as the sun began its descent late on Monday afternoon. Ahead of us was a flight to London, a night with friends, then a 20-hour flight to South Africa, via Dubai. It was a long haul and I was running out of steam, but Cape Town was near the top of my places to visit, so I was looking forward to it. But, holy crap, how could I hold it together for another nine months?

15

TWO OCEANS MARATHON
4 April, Cape Town, South Africa
5:29.00 (56 kms)

Leading up to the Two Oceans, we stayed with Vickie Francis, my running buddy Chip's aunty, who I'd met briefly at Comrades the previous year. She was also preparing for the race, looking to complete her 10th Two Oceans, an extraordinary effort.

Arriving in Cape Town was as close to going home as I'd get on this trip. CT is remarkable, not simply for its looks, but also for its character and the personality of its wonderfully diverse people. The weather was 23°C when we arrived, and it was the first time I'd seen Table Mountain without its cloth – the wispy cloud that often envelopes the top. It still felt like summer, even though Autumn was well overdue. I'd been travelling for 30 hours and the first thing I did was run through the streets to shake myself back into life. It was lovely.

That night, we met Vickie's partner, Joe, a cardiologist and a hell of a runner. He was aiming for his 15th Two Oceans. He'd also run some 16 Comrades, and was planning to do number 17 that same year. Listening to them both chat about the extraordinary feats they had achieved in the past months and years, you'd be forgiven for mistaking them for career ultra-runners. But it just seems to be part of the culture in South Africa. Everyone runs ultra-marathons. It made me want to move there, to see if some of that courage and discipline might rub off on me.

Everyone seemed to be on happy pills all the time, being friendly to each other and strangers, excited about the upcoming soccer World Cup. If people caught your accent, they would say, 'Welcome to Cape Town; enjoy your stay!' and they'd mean it. Maybe it was because of the terrible reputation the country had with its apartheid laws of many years ago, but you could sense that as the transition to a culture of equality continued, people wanted you to know that this was a safe and happy place. You needed to remain on your guard out when you're driving at night or walking about, but that was no different to somewhere like London.

CT was where Daz and I discussed some issues too. I admitted I couldn't afford to keep paying him for much longer. He said it was okay, that he'd been thinking about staying in London anyway. He was feeling pressured by me, said that I'd been treating him like an employee. I had been rude to him a few times, but I also couldn't get the results I needed from him either. I needed more photos and videos from him to justify the cost of travel. It was supposed to help drive the story online and perhaps get sponsors. The conversation ended amicably, but the cracks in the situation were clear.

The next day, Easter Friday, we went to pick up our numbers. The expo was a hive of activity and I enjoyed being amongst it. Later on, I swam at a local pool. I was worried as there had been ducks swimming in the pool, but the attendant assured me I'd be fine. I walked home after to find a lot of excitement as spaghetti bolognaise was being served as a pre-race feast. Joining us were Vickie and Joe's friends, who seemed to share my passion for a good balance of partying and staying fit. There was a bit of chatter about strategy, but mostly you could just feel that familiar shared buzz – part fear and anxiety, part mouth-watering anticipation. It was a world away from being holed up in a hostel waiting for the inevitable.

We had a 5 a.m. wake-up call to get to the marathon, which was due to kick off at 6:25 a.m. I was sure it was going to get hot, so I wanted to be able to run cool for as long as possible. My stomach felt funny, but I tipped this as nerves. In the car, I started to feel worse. We got near the start and I found a toilet. Yeah, I was in trouble. Okay. Never mind.

The buzz of the crowd took me straight back to my Comrades marathon. People were chattering in Swahili, Afrikaans, English and a variety of other languages, with quite a bit of back slapping going on too. So many runners came every year to participate in this wonderfully organised event and they readied themselves for another fierce battle with their old foes – the long road and the mountains.

I tried to be excited too, but I was already worried. Fifty-six kms is a long way to run, so you need to have your mental game right before you tackle such an event. Mine was already wavering. I smiled at the people encouraging each other, but it felt hollow. I worried this was not going to be a fun race.

The South African national anthem rang out and many people started to sing around me. A fine misty rain was falling as we stood under street lamps, waiting for the sun to rise and the race to begin. The anthem finished and the first strains of 'Chariots of Fire' began.

The gun went off and we ran through the streets into the dawn. Heading towards the beaches of Muizenberg, the road was lined with supporters. Our names were printed in large type on our bibs too, and every so often I'd get, 'Hey, Tristan, how's it?' Or 'You're looking good, Tristan.'

I needed to focus on something other than my stomach cramps so I tried to pay close attention to my surroundings. The mountains near Muizenberg were right in front of us. The town is squeezed in between the mountain range and the beach, and the view was absolutely beautiful in either direction. It had been a brisk morning with the rain, but now the heat was evaporating the early shower, making it humid.

I passed through Fish Hoek, the halfway mark, and was buoyed by the crowds. We'd just turned off to Cape Point (the base of the Cape of Good Hope) and were progressing over to the western side of the cape – essentially passing from the Indian Ocean side to the Atlantic Ocean. It's not entirely true that we were running alongside the Indian Ocean at any stage, as the magic line is further south-east at Cape Agulhas, but the idea is as inspiring as the scenery, so the name seemed perfect for this marathon.

From there I chatted to a local guy who said he was due for a walking break, which I must say was very welcome at that point. We'd only walked a few metres when we saw Deana, one of Vickie's friends, and the Dazzler on the side of the road! They were at about 27 kms, just before the hills began. Daz was decked out in a South African garb, including a flag, mask and a Nelson Mandela T-shirt. Deana asked how I was travelling and I replied that I wasn't feeling too good.

'Nonsense!' she said sternly. 'You're looking great and going well. You can run all the way and you're going to get a brilliant time!'

It wasn't the warm hug I was expecting, but it was what I needed. I stepped back into the flow of runners and faced the facts. This run was going to end one of two ways: with me on the right side of the finish line or unconscious. Time to switch on and get through this.

We hit the first hills. And boy, were they doozies! Slow, steep inclines that led up along some cliffs. I just kept alternating running and walking. Then, as I slowly crept higher, the view of Noordhoek beach came into sight. It was simply breathtaking. Even better, it was pain-taking! That was what I was here for, the most gorgeous views I'd ever taken in on a run. There were surfers on the waves and horses trotting along the sand. I forgot about my churning stomach, and spoke to my camera, 'Can you see what I see? This is where I'm running today . . . unbelievable!'

The road curved around and headed down again, but it wasn't long before you could see the stream of runners ahead climbing again. It was tough stuff, but every time I felt tired, I just looked out to the ocean.

I chatted to a couple more runners. The music was blaring and the kids were dancing at all of the drink stops. As we crested Chapman's Peak, the crowd lining the road were going crazy. I welcomed it, needing to snap out of my lagging motivation. Not much further along, they were handing out ice-creams! I wish I could have stomached one.

But as I started to head down towards Hout Bay, I felt better. The first big challenge had been thrown at me and I'd succeeded in getting over the top. Clouds had whipped up over the mountains and a light rain was coming down the side of the cliffs. I smiled as I looked up. I was cooling down. I hit another toilet and though I didn't necessarily feel any less sick, I knew I'd be able to hold out.

I made it to the marathon mark. At 42 kms I was wishing it was just a regular distance race; I could have handled that nicely. I'd swung back a bit, trying to take in too many Powerades to keep my salts up. I'd never stopped at so many drink stations in all my life. I started to gag and throw up a little. It was mostly just liquid, so probably the result of excessive hydration. It made me dizzy for a few minutes though and I slowed to a trot.

We passed a large township and the people out the front were giving great support. The kids couldn't have known what was going on, but they jumped about cheering anyway. Not long after, the hills began again. This was the road up to Constantia.

Signs began to appear on the trees by the road. They were placards with messages like 'Run, Forrest, Run!' and 'Pain is temporary, glory is forever!'

They made me laugh, but weren't particularly helpful.

The last hill was the hardest slog. With only about 10 kms to go, most people had slowed to a walk. I, on the other hand, began to pick up speed. I still had to walk here and there, but I wasn't completely knocked out. I knew somewhere, not too far ahead of me, Joe would be running with his son, James. I wanted to run with someone I knew for a while, so I booted along to see if I could catch up.

I passed more and more runners. People were spent, some even drifting off to the side of the road to stretch their weary limbs. I ploughed on and finally saw the top of the hill. I promised myself I wouldn't stop till I was over the top.

I was waiting for three smaller hills that had been named F1, F2 and F3. The locals had dubbed them 'the F*ck Its'. I knew I hadn't hit them yet. We were descending rapidly and I was worried I'd burn out before I reached them.

Then they popped up. One by one, I hit the base of a new rise and leant into them, thrusting my legs down to push my body up the hills. I thought about my friends back home. Cameron Blair is one of my oldest and dearest buddies, and I'd missed his wedding to the beautiful Katie. I hated missing such special events in my friends' lives. This race was for them, then, and for their little boy, Seth.

I ran harder. I got up the ramp and started to descend for the last time, entering the oval area in front of the university. Crowds of supporters pushed up against the fences, cheering their hearts out. I was so stoked to have finished. I pumped my arms as I crossed the line. The official time was 5:29.00.

Joe and James had finished just ahead of me. I must have been close to catching them half-a-dozen times. They'd run the whole way together. Daz was there too. He dragged me off to the massage tent and I got a little work done. It helped a bit, but I'd need that ice bath again before I left.

We went outside and watched some of the other finishers ending their torment. Vickie floated past, looking absolutely radiant. I left on a high. My body was a wreck, but I'd experienced one of the greatest races of my life.

16

PARIS INTERNATIONAL MARATHON

11 April, Paris, France

3:32.46

It took us 28 long and tiring hours to go Cape Town–Dubai–London–Paris. I wished I could have afforded direct flights. In Paris, Daz took up the offer of the friend I'd made at the Marrakech Marathon, and stayed at Clément's while he was in Morocco doing the Marathon des Sables. The night before the marathon I stayed in a hotel just a few hundred metres from the Arc de Triomphe. It was the first time that Daz and I had been separated before a race, but we needed some time apart. Being together all the time was intense. We agreed to meet at my hotel at seven o'clock the next morning.

That night I had a great time looking around the Paris Marathon expo with Eric Heine, a friend of my running pal Kevlar from home. Eric is a classic world marathon traveller who engineers his family holidays around his passion. I joined his family for a meal that evening.

In the morning, I got up early to prepare. Then 7 a.m. came and went – with no Daz. At 7:30 a.m., I sent him a text . . . Nup, no response. At 8 a.m., I was off to the race. On my way out the door, I tried calling: *nada*. I figured I'd see him on the track some place.

Outside my hotel I met up with John and some Aussies who'd recognised me from my website, and I was pumped to be able to head down to the start line with a group. This was going to be fun. We got to the Champs-Elysées and the crowd was HUGE! I got to my corral and found Elisa and Laurence (from the Verona Marathon) near the entry. We got in and the vibe got better and better. The idea of running through the streets of Paris had never seemed that exciting to me. I'd had my good and bad experiences in Paris over the years, but that day, there was something in the air: I was with great people, I was being supported by locals, and the Champs-Elysées was jammed with people who all had the same goal.

We finally got moving, parading down one of the world's most famous streets. We cruised further out along the River Seine, passing the Louvre and eventually the zoo. I was loving how revved up everyone was, with plenty of runners in costume. I slowed down to converse with a lot of people, then sped up to catch Eric and John. After about 10 kms we lost sight of Eric. Then I heard 'Tristan!' I turned to see a very sporty-looking girl bounce up next to us. She was wearing an Aussie touring top.

This was Judy, an Australian who'd read about me when I answered a Travelling Fit email, which puts travellers in touch with each other. I'd asked her to come say hello if she spotted me. We made the turn and started heading back into town. The closer to the city centre we got, the more supporters were out. It was getting hectic, both on and off the track. It took all my concentration to keep running at speed at not cause a bingle.

Further along, we ran under a bridge. As we entered a tunnel something very strange happened. It was dark and you could see the heat rising from all the bodies. Everyone was chewing up oxygen, exhaling more carbon dioxide. It's not nice sucking in that thick, sticky air. But just when I was beginning to sweat it and I could see the light at the other end, a rumbling sound came from behind us. I wondered if a train might have entered the 2-km tunnel – but there were no tracks. The sound got louder and I started looking over my shoulder for the lights of a truck. There was nothing but a sea of runners. Yet, louder and louder the noise came, until the rumble became a roar. I realised that it was the sound of thousands of runners creating an aural Mexican wave! I chimed in as the sound washed past us.

rrrrrrrrrrRRRRRRRRRAAAAAAAAAAAAAAAAAaaaaaaaaa . . .

It was FANTASTIC! The wave came back again; it was exhilarating and kind of frightening too. As we exited the tunnel, I was still giggling with the thrill of it.

It wasn't long before we passed the Eiffel Tower. I'd lost my team, so tried to jet forwards one more time. I caught Eric and Judy within a kilometre, panting, 'You guys need to slow down, you're getting difficult to catch!' Judy was coasting along. 'We'll need to grab another 15 seconds per km for the last 10,' I said.

'I will if I can hold it,' Judy replied.

I pressed on, checking the pace on my Garmin. They followed for a bit, but it wasn't long before I was alone. I slowed again and then tried to lead them forwards. *Nup. Not today.* It's wrong to push people in an event like this. I've tried it before and made the experience bad for my partner. I slowed again and ran with them. Judy was getting close to wall territory, but she was still gliding for the moment. I noticed the French crowd increasing both in numbers and volume. We were getting closer to the end and their support was growing to compensate.

We began to lose Judy. She'd pumped out a very brave 34 kms. I looked at my own time and saw that if I was to break 3:30, I'd have to really start powering now. I thought about it and ditched the idea. With so many people in front of me, running fast was going to be frustrating and tiring. I was so enjoying running in step with other people that I decided to just let it go. I dropped back to Judy for a second, who was still on pace for a PB. I gave her my last GU.

'Have it in about a kilometre from now, and good luck!'

'Thanks,' she said with a grin. 'See you at the end!'

Eric and I ran on till we reached a leafy boulevard that was tracing back towards the Arc de Triomphe. The crowds were cheering and the runners were responding, pushing home. I felt like I was seeing Paris in a new light – fresh spring air, supportive locals, a sense of kinship between the racers. I liked it.

I'd hit my wall too, though. I was beginning to flag and was glad that I hadn't tried to run too hard in the last 10 kms. Maybe all that travel from Cape Town had been more draining than I'd thought.

We rounded a couple of bends and the crowd was going absolutely bananas as we ran onto the wide Avenue Foch, which leads up to the Arc de Triomphe. The finish was still a few hundred metres away, but runners had started to sprint for the line. One girl powered past me on my right, her face contorted in pain, tears streaming down her face. She must have been trying to break 3:30. I wish I could have caught that moment. I didn't know her, but I could see she had conquered her fears and was living her dream. She was beautiful.

In the final metres I was almost bowled over as a big man came up behind me saying, 'Hey! Man, I read about you in the *Sydney Morning Herald*!' He was Aussie Jay, a tall, strong-looking dude who was working in New York, but running here with his mates. We crossed the line together. People were collapsing all over the place. Jay told me where they were meeting later and I agreed to try to find him. Judy crossed the line shortly after. She'd nailed her PB by seven minutes and gave me a hug. It was nice to know someone at the finish.

I retrieved my phone. There was a message from Daz: 'I just left hospital. I'm okay. Don't know what happened. Will sleep and see you later.'

I wondered what had gone on but felt relieved he was safe and left it at that. I thought I might as well let him sleep while I sorted myself out. I had another night in the hotel, so I texted him back to say I'd see him the following day. I was tired and concerned about Daz, but I wanted to celebrate my big day on the track.

I had an ice bath over at Eric's hotel room, then it was off to a bar in the city to catch up with my new friends.

I loved catching up with the Aussie guys; they were easy with their wit, fun with their jibes and encouraging of my efforts. They were all there supporting their mates and taking on another challenge. I loved that this was why they were in Paris – a casual weekend away from New York to smash out a marathon and have fun. Judy made it there after a while and we all hung out and chatted about the race. I was distracted, though, thinking about Daz and hoping he was okay.

The next day I went to Clément's to see Daz. He didn't look so good.

One of Daz's great qualities is that he'll talk to pretty much anyone. Sometimes when I'm tired, I find it hard to do that. So, apart from having someone to share the organisational load with, that's what made him such a great travelling companion.

Unfortunately this quality has its drawbacks. Sometimes the people Daz befriends don't have his best interests at heart. Daz had apparently met one of these sorry sorts. He'd gone out drinking with his mates and ended up in a bar by himself in the wee hours. Everything had been fine, then, all of a sudden, not. Next thing he knew, he was in the accident and emergency section of a hospital near Clément's apartment. The hospital staff told him that he'd been brought in by an ambulance, heavily intoxicated and perhaps even drugged. He must have had something slipped into his drink by the people he was talking to. Pretty scary, but as Clément said to me later, 'Paris is a big city . . . bad stuff happens.'

I was angry with Daz. To me, his only real workday was marathon day. It was when I needed him to show up, take photos and catch me at the other end when I was ready to fall down. He argued that it wasn't his fault he'd been drugged. I responded that he shouldn't have been at a bar at 3 a.m. anyway. He was scheduled to meet me at 7 a.m., so there was just no excuse. I was annoyed that he wasn't taking responsibility for his actions, especially as they had taken him into a potentially dangerous situation.

In retrospect, even though Darren was in no way responsible for being drugged, I can see that he was looking for an out. It makes sense now, but at that moment I was disappointed with my friend.

Clément came home from Morocco, the returning hero. He'd been through some of the most dangerous terrain in the world and had some hairy stories. There was one point during the Marathon des Sables where he thought he'd just passed through a checkpoint and stopped for a minute, but later found out that he'd blacked out for an hour and a half. He had also been so burnt out that he started bleeding from his nose. Even so, he cranked up his pace on the last day to overtake some of the other less mentally tough competitors to claim 97th position in a field of over 1000 entrants.

We were on the move at six o'clock the next morning to get on a plane to London, before transferring to Boston. Clément was heading to the airport too; he was on his way to Luxembourg to go to work . . . Yes, that's right, only seven hours after arriving back from a death-defying running adventure. He's crazier than me.

Daz was quiet all the way to London. I was tired and short tempered, having lost some gear on the Metro in Paris. When we got to Alexis's Happiness Centre, we had only half an hour to get our things together before heading to Boston.

That's when Daz dropped the bombshell. He wasn't coming with me. The incident in Paris had scared him and he wanted to go to a hospital in London to get checked out properly. He was stressed and tired and understandably wanted to make sure he was okay. He was at the end of his journey.

I was incredulous but I had no time to think about this; I had to go. I told him I hoped it all worked out and left.

It was a weird way to end the partnership. I'd known it was coming. Daz had done his best to support me throughout what was essentially *my* big adventure. He'd had some cool adventures of his own, but he'd also copped a fair bit of stress from me when I'd tried to do too much. I'm a pretty hard taskmaster sometimes, I'll admit. The last thing I wanted was for him to feel my stress, but when you live in each other's pockets, it's nearly impossible to avoid it.

I got on the plane to Boston. I sat there by myself, wondering how on earth it was all going to turn out. I knew I was going to see a lot of people along the way, but I also felt an incredible sense of loss: I wasn't going to be able to share it any more. It made me reflect on how the experience of travelling is far greater than the sum of the big adventures you have. It's all the stupid things that happen along the way, like getting a street sign wrong and ending up somewhere completely unexpected, or eating some strange foreign item from a vending machine.

Then there are those moments when there's no need for words: when you laugh at something you've seen and your friend next to you laughs too. Or you raise an eyebrow at each other to signal that a beautiful girl is walking past. Or you give a tiny nod of your head towards some local with a crazy haircut and your mate cracks up.

Things would be different from here on in.

17

BOSTON MARATHON

19 April, Boston, USA

3:19.22

In Boston, I was to stay with Teyah, the sister of my good friend Koya. Koya is part of Tribal and from this start of my year had been sending messages of support and encouragement. She's a straight shooter with a heart of gold. Teyah and her husband, Troy, had moved to the USA for Troy's work a few years beforehand. They had two little girls, Amelia and Georgie, aged seven and five.

After the last 48 hours, Troy's easy smile was exactly the welcome I needed at the airport. I was a little stressed and unsure about how the coming weeks would unfold, but as soon as I heard his broad Aussie accent, I instantly relaxed, as if with a brother. We drove across town to the suburb of Newton as evening darkened the sky. I was welcomed by a huge hand-painted banner in the bay window: 'Welcome T-Bone. RunLikeCrazy.'

The girls were excited, but also a bit apprehensive about having a stranger in the house. I resorted to bribery – lollies and Vegemite – to win their affection. It wasn't long before the girls were dragging me around the house, showing me their toys. Teyah was much like Koya, with a huge heart and a ready wit.

Teyah made the time to take me shopping and to check out the marathon course. All these things relaxed my mind and gave my body the time it needed to recover. Within two days it didn't even feel like I was on tour any more.

Still, I had work to do, and I couldn't ignore it forever. I was running the famous Boston Marathon on Labor Day Monday and wanted to fit in a visit to New York. It hadn't been in my plans, but I was beginning to doubt whether I'd make it all the way to November, when the NYC Marathon was taking place. I figured I'd better get my butt down there for my first view of New York, or I might never see it.

I jumped on the cheapo Fung Wah bus service from Boston to NYC. I'd emailed my old Google mate Andrew Olah, telling him I could make it for one night, and he insisted I stay with him and his girlfriend, Caroline. As the bus approached the city, I realised I'd made a grave error – one night was clearly not going to be enough. I don't know what I really expected, but the imposing buildings of Manhattan were a sight to behold. Everything was so much bigger than I had anticipated!

I took the train to Google's office. I could see that my friend Olah had certainly landed on his feet when he transferred to New York from Sydney. Sales and account management is largely about relationships and the ability to grow your network and Olah is fantastic at both. He's charismatic, smart and a natural athlete. On top of this he towers over me at around 6 foot 2. It was great to see his new digs; the Google office was a massive hive of activity and as cool as you read about in all the blogs.

We went out for dinner that night with some of Andrew and Caroline's friends, and I put in a call to Aussie Jay, who I'd met at the Paris Marathon. We met him in SoHo at a one of the funkiest clubs I've ever seen. We danced, met loads more people and as we walked home later, I admitted to Olah that I was having far too much fun to bother getting the bus on Saturday. As long as I was back in Boston by Sunday, everything would be fine for Monday's race.

Next day, Olah and I went for a training trot up at Central Park, taking in the massive public space that dominates the centre of

Manhattan. It's hallowed turf to anyone who loves marathons, as not only is it the home of the famous New York Road Runners club, but also hosts the finish line of one of the highest profile marathons in the world . . . I had to make it back to run the New York Marathon in November.

We hired bikes and rode right through the middle of Times Square, with the skyscrapers on either side of us and everything lit up by myriad flashing lights. 'New York City, baby!' Olah sang out. 'Livin' the *dream*!'

I was sold. I had to make it back to run the New York Marathon in November.

I bussed it back to Boston on Sunday morning. Olah said he wanted to meet up in Montreal in a few months' time, but that felt a long way off and I wasn't expecting anyone to go too far out of their way to see me.

Seeing Teyah, the girls and Troy gave me a settled feeling when I got back to Boston. I was booked into a hotel for race eve, so we hung out for a bit before I headed to a nearby auditorium to investigate the famous Boston Marathon expo. It was an enormous space, with every conceivable running gadget on show. It's amazing how many companies develop new shoes and clothes for running, promising increased performance and less fatigue. I enjoyed looking at what's new, but I didn't believe the hype. I think most of the gimmicks – barefoot running, vitamin drinks, compression wear – are just confidence boosters. I'm certainly not against this and I've tried my fair share of new 'technology', and sometimes it's enough to push me through the barriers. But when you get down to it, 42 kms hurt like hell, and all the technology in the world won't make you run faster or more efficiently if you haven't trained properly or prepared yourself for the mental battle.

The Boston Marathon is the oldest marathon institution in the world. It's been around for 114 years and has had many heroes, scandals and stories. It's a course that runs from Hopkinton towards the city along one major arterial road. It passes through many areas of suburbia, as well as some famous old colleges too. It is one of the Holy Grail races, with most people having to seek qualification in order to run. These qualifying times are difficult for most runners to achieve: I hadn't qualified to get in myself, so I felt like a bit of an impostor. I'd needed a time quicker than 3:10 to qualify, and when I entered in 2009, my fastest time was 3:23. So I bought a touring package from Travelling Fit, the sports tour company that Judy from the Paris Marathon was part of. This was a shortcut to securing an entry. The costs were pretty high but Boston had to be done, as did London, New York, Chicago and Berlin. No matter the price, these were the Five Majors and I wanted a piece of them.

I won't deny that I had been caught in their marketing net. Boston was to be my first Major for the year and I was to immediately follow up with the London Marathon, six days later. My friend Chippa Wood had all five of his Major medals framed in the hallway of his home, so that each time his runner friends came by, we'd all gawk at them in awe.

Behind all the race preparation, there was a potential spanner in the works. Many people flying to Boston from Europe had been stranded due to a volcanic eruption in Iceland. I hadn't thought too much about it, as my trip to Iceland was still months away. But the ash cloud had been menacingly floating down into transatlantic flight paths. Most airlines had grounded their planes for fear that the silt and magma particles might get caught in the engines and cause temporary or permanent loss of power to their aircrafts. Otherwise they'd be in danger of having a fleet of 400-tonne gliders!

Heathrow, one of the world's busiest air hubs, had all but been shut down. I'd made it from Paris to London to Boston, but the following weeks included races in London, Belfast and Prague. If this got worse, I could be stuck in one place without racing for nearly a month! The backlog of travellers alone would mean that I'd have to wait a week if

I missed a flight to London. I knew I couldn't do anything about it, so I just kept checking the news, six times a day, hoping things would get better.

On race day, we competitors all piled into old yellow school buses, which took us from the centre of town out to Hopkinton. The atmosphere on the buses alone was enough to excite even the most sombre of early-morning risers. Everyone was comparing race plans and talking about their previous marathon experiences. It was a good place to be, but a long ride out.

The rain clouds were clearing, but it was still blustery pre-spring weather. I sipped coffee to keep warm and had an extra pit stop before wandering towards the start line. As I came over a rise, I could see a huge throng of people cramming onto the road, cutting across my path. As far as I could see, in both directions, the road was packed. I looked for a sign of where I might start and just had to accept that it didn't really matter – it was going to be an obstacle course from start to finish. I just walked straight into the belly of the snake of people and got comfortable.

I chatted idly to those around me until we all heard the gun go. The eager rush was checked 100 metres later, as everyone crammed across the start line. It was a common issue with such busy races, though the problem was exacerbated by the fact that the road to Boston from Hopkinton is only two lanes. I'd heard it was a fast track, though, descending to the city. This was most notable in the first 5 kms, and I needed to control myself and coast a little, instead of hitting top speed too early.

Within 10 kms we were passing outlying suburbs and being cheered by the locals. Even at 9 a.m., some of the supporters had beer cans in hand, enjoying the street parade of mad runners. I laughed at the juxtaposition of healthy runner and boozy supporter.

I kept an eye out for Teyah and the girls. They were heading down with some of the other families to cheer us on, but I was off my predicted time due to the delayed start. I gauged that I was passing through their suburb, but I couldn't see them anywhere. I was ready to give up when I spied the green of one of Australia's best-travelled flags, the Boxing Kangaroo. It meant so much that they'd come out to see me run, so I stopped for a quick chat.

I continued along the course and found the famous Wellesley College. It's a female-only campus and traditionally all its young women come out to cheer runners along. From the fence lines they hold up signs that encourage the bucking heart of any man who goes past: 'Kiss me, I'm a Senior', 'Kiss me, I'm Asian'. These signs encourage runners to hit the sidelines and jump up to the fence, planting a kiss on the nearest bearer. The girls are young and just having fun, but some of these lads were so eager, they were all but hurdling each other for the opportunity of a kiss. It was a crazy sight and mixed with the sound of the women screaming encouragement created a powerful scene. I was swept up in the excitement and ran up to a girl for a quick kiss on the cheek.

It was a moment's respite before the long slog continued. I was buoyed by the fact I was running faster than most around me, but when I reached the notorious Heartbreak Hill, I thought I would bust. By the time I crested it and started the descent towards the city, my legs were dragging and my chest was heaving.

Around the 35-km mark, many more college students were out by the course, cheering their hearts out. I'd written 'T-Bone' across my front and some of the lads started hollering my nickname while I ran. They offered us ice-creams and beers as we passed: the supporters had pretty much turned the race into a drunken street party. Their enthusiasm was infectious and I started to laugh, even though all I really wanted to do was walk. I was burnt out, but still moving, and this final lift to my spirits urged me on to the end. I powered home to finish in a respectable 3:19. My legs started to give out almost immediately, but I was so proud to have knocked off the oldest marathon event in the world.

The next day, I went back to my foster family. I had one more experience to tick off – a baseball game. Troy took me to a match between the Red Sox and the Texas Rangers. I loved sitting in the stands of Fenway Park, listening to the Boston accents and watching the regular 'swing and a miss' that seems to slow the game to a snail's pace.

I didn't really get it, but I got a buzz from the enthusiasm of the fans and hanging out with Troy; it reminded me how lucky I was to have such excellent friends.

I tried to tell Troy how much it meant to have been made to feel so welcome in a foreign land. I tried to explain that I'd felt like I was on the brink of disaster a week ago when I lost Daz, but time with his girls had settled my nerves and inspired me again. I tried, but the words were mostly jumbled into a pathetic series of thank-yous. Anyway, I was going to miss them dearly.

The following day I'd head back to London for more adventure . . . as long as the Ash Cloud of Doom didn't foil my plans!

18

LONDON MARATHON

25 April, London, England
3:28.33

Luck was on my side and the flight paths were open.

I checked into a hotel, using another package provided by Travelling Fit. It was up near Holborn Tube Station, a stone's throw from where I'd lived during my time in London, some 12 years before. Another buddy from my bartending days, Matt Opray, was heading to London around the same time and we made plans to catch up. He'd been travelling around and by the time he got to me, he was talking about getting a job . . . or just taking off to Europe . . . or maybe just getting drunk for the duration of the summer.

We exchanged tales of our adventures and I had to stop myself from enjoying too many beers with him. It had all the hallmarks of a night that could get out of hand and I really needed to keep myself in check before I took on another Major. He'd caught up with Daz and I asked how my beleaguered friend was doing. Matt told me Darren felt guilty but that his actions were justified. I disagreed, but found myself trying to see things from Darren's view. He'd been put through a lot and needed to forge his own path. I was frustrated, but as Matt said, 'You can't hate him for helpin' you out, bro! You just put too much on his plate.' He was right and the message was clear: let it go.

The expo for the London Marathon didn't have the same energy as the

Boston show. I think the Americans are intrinsically more excitable than the English, in all things except for football and cricket. I bought a tonne of gear, trying to make sure I'd be amply covered in the logos of the really big marathons when I got back to Australia and started running with my mates again.

Race day rolled around and in the pre-dawn darkness a bus took all the Travelling Fit people to the start line. There were a lot of empty seats. The Dastardly Ash Cloud of Doom had destroyed the hopes of many travellers, leaving them at foreign airports, only to be told that they may be waiting weeks – well after the London Marathon had packed up for another year.

We arrived at the beginning of the race to find it completely bereft of competitors. Apparently the English are late starters! Dawn illuminated only the huge blow-up monsters that had been positioned near the start line. They stood there like crazed hot-air balloons, the first witnesses of the race. I chatted to some Aussies and caught up on news from home. I struggled with the idea that Aussie news doesn't matter much while you're travelling. Even though the bad news, good news and general gossip was all forgettable on the world stage, it was still nice to hear about when you're homesick.

A bitter wind whipped up, bringing with it drenching rain, but it didn't douse people's spirits too much. The London Marathon is known for its costumes, so plenty of people were dressed up in wild outfits, with the Guinness Book of Records announcing a huge number of record-breaking attempts: fastest marathon dressed as a golfer; fastest marathon dressed as a clown; fastest marathon dressed as a donut, and all that type of thing.

By the time we finally got underway, I was freezing. We'd been in the cold for far too long, but the sun was emerging again and the rain eventually petered out. The race began in two waves, kicking off at the same time and merging around the 5-km mark. I heard a yell and turned just in time to see Ironman Steve from Cyprus. We chatted for a bit and took in the atmosphere before I said goodbye and hoped we'd meet again.

I trundled along, more entertained by the mad outfits around me than the run ahead. I was sitting on a good pace, but it wasn't going to be my best run; I could feel that already. We wove through the streets of London, on the south side of the Thames. The miles (as they were set) slowly clicked by and as we got to 12, I could hear cheers rising up. I knew what was coming.

We rounded a corner to see the majesty of the Tower Bridge in front of us. The pain in my legs melted away. I was running across the world's most famous bridge. The footpaths on either side were densely packed with supporters and I heard a shout on my right: 'T-BOOONE!'

'Dazzler! Opray! And who's this? Hey, Adrian!'

Wow, my buddies had come all trussed up. Daz was wearing the battle garb of St George, looking as noble as could be in these perfect surroundings. And I hadn't seen Adrian for years! I stopped for a few hugs and a photo, getting over my shock at their unexpected appearance. We agreed to meet at the end.

Not 200 metres further on, I saw the Boxing Kangaroo flying on the other side of the road, right in front of the ramparts protecting the Tower of London. Alexis was screaming out and Michael, my sister Rebecca's fiancé, was taking PicturesLikeCrazy. It was awesome to see them too and I slowed for another couple of hugs. I was losing time, but I loved all this support.

The next 10 miles were a real grind, taking us east to Canary Wharf. We toured Millwall and the City, crossing the docklands and then pulling west again, back to the Thames, and past the Tower of London. A lot of the costumed runners coming the other way were looking a lot less festive by now and they still had a long way to go.

Now, it just so happened it was Anzac Day. I had 4 miles left and not much go in my legs. I had a lot rolling around my head at this point, but it boiled down to one thing – those lads died so that we could live free. Australia wouldn't be what it is today it weren't for the sacrifices of these soldiers. It turned over in my mind as my legs kept moving under me.

'For the Anzacs,' I repeated softly, breathing heavily, running on.

I entered Hyde Park and ran up to Buckingham Palace. The final stretch was awash with fluttering flags and cheering masses. Spring sun drenched the park, shimmering through the green leaves above. This was all very nice but my legs were straining and I really needed this race to be over. We turned east one last time, towards the finishing chute.

There were stands lining the boulevard. I remember noticing this, but it was just a swirl of faces. I wondered if the Queen or any of the royal family would stick their noses out for an event like this. The finish line loomed ahead – a great archway across the road, with photographers perched on top. I yelled a few words to my camera, over the din of the crowd, thanking my friends, my sister, the Anzacs. I was elated to finish my second Major in as many weeks.

I celebrated with a lot of friends after that race, including Daz. April had been exciting . . . surprising . . . exhausting . . . massive!

19

BELFAST CITY MARATHON

3 May, Belfast, Northern Ireland
3:28.35

On the plane to Belfast I felt sick, with a sore throat and a stuffed nose. I was tired, having slept an average of only four hours over the last few nights. I seemed to be spending even more time travelling to airports than I did in the air.

I didn't know anyone in Belfast. I figured I'd get there, hang about, get up to date with some work stuff and then punch out another marathon. Yes, I thought I would come to Ireland and take it easy. I even considered not drinking.

What an idiot, eh?

Matt Opray joined me at Belfast's Lagan Backpackers the day after I arrived – his birthday eve. We hit some pubs and clubs over the ensuing days, dragging out anyone from the hostel we could browbeat into joining us. We smashed it up at a cheesy club called Stiff Kitten. You had to be drunk to enjoy it, so we cranked through some quick rounds until everyone was DancingLikeCrazy.

The next day we headed to Dublin, hangovers and all. Opray and I wanted just to take a quick look at another city and, well, as it turns out, Dublin is a hell of a place to party too . . . We got in at 8 p.m., just in time to dump our bags and join a pub crawl. We told them it was Opray's birthday and were given the star treatment, which seemed to justify our being out drinking.

You might wonder then how we justified drinking the next night as well. Well, Dublin is a nice-looking city, but if the weather's crap, which it often is, there ain't so much to do. Except, of course, head to one of their 4000 pubs! We did manage to get to Kilmainham Goal, though. The gaol bears extraordinary significance to the birth and shaping of the modern Republic of Ireland. It housed the leaders of the 1916 Easter Rising and was the site of most of their executions. The uprising did not have a lot of popular support in the beginning. But when the public found out that the men had been summarily executed for treason, the republican cause gained a huge amount of favour, eventually giving way to the formation of a free state in 1921.

We got back to Belfast on Sunday. After the expo I crashed for a bit and finally caught up with Alexis who'd decided to come over and support another race.

The next morning I wanted to be anywhere other than that start line. I didn't miss the starter's pistol but I did miss my opportunity to hit the loo. I was tired, a little stressed and struggling with a head cold. None of this would help me run a fast marathon. There were some 18 000 participants in the race, but most of them were part of the relay teams that spanned the length of the course. It made the race seem pretty bulky but full of spirit.

It wasn't long before I struck forwards; the runners around me were pretty slow and I didn't want to get caught up in their plodding pace. I bumped into a few people I'd seen in previous runs but didn't get into lengthy conversations. I was pumped to see Alexis – Opray was trying to keep her from falling off the fence she'd perched on.

I ran through an area called the Falls Road, which is a staunchly Catholic strip. Opray and I had taken a black-cab tour of the area a few days before and had been shown both the Protestant and Catholic sides of Belfast's security wall. As the runners passed the office for Sinn Fein on Falls Road, we were suddenly surrounded by people holding up placards, demanding things like 'End Prison Brutality.'

I actually found it pretty confronting to be presented with this kind of rhetoric during a city fun run. I knew it was an election week, but it weirded me out to see a marathon being used as a forum to spruik political messages.

After a few short crests, we finally got onto the 'big' hill. It was a long slow 3-km rise and by the end of it, I was losing my willpower. I never reached the point where I seriously considered stopping, but it felt like this race had got the better of me: my right hip was stiff, making movement quite uncomfortable.

Running along the edge of the bay before heading back into the city, I was in a world of pain. But I just tried to remain calm and keep up a reasonable pace. I passed a couple of musicians belting out tunes. They'd changed the words of the Black Eyed Peas song to 'Tonight's gonna be a sore night.' I nodded along to that sentiment.

With about 5 kms to go, I was beat. We hit a canal and ran right back along the side of the city. The path took us down to a bridge, where Alexis and Matt were going nuts. I found one last spark of energy and with just 4 kms to go, began to lift my head and my game.

As I moved closer and closer to home, I focused on a strong rhythm and kept pounding the pavement. Just as I came up on the last kilometre, a guy I'd met at the London Marathon, Keith, jumped out of the crowd and started running with me. He'd taken me for an excellent training run on the Friday before, down south along the canal. He caught me at a perfect time, pumping along next to me and taking my mind off things just a little longer. I was having a bit of an out of body experience, with my brain feeling completely separate from my legs.

Keith peeled off when I only had about 500 metres to go.

I kept barrelling home. I was tired and just wanted it over with. I finally crossed the line in 3:28.35.

Maith thú, well done, read one of the posters someone was holding up. *No kidding*, I thought.

Me and Daz, 12 September 2009, the day I sold my flat to fund my big adventure.

JANUARY 2010

My first marathon completed, we got stuck in Berlin. Time to celebrate my 33rd birthday in style.

Marathon 4, Dubai. The star of the show was world champion, Haile Gebrselassie. All I could say was, 'You're my hero, Haile!'

Marathon 5, Las Palmas. I had just beaten my own best time by five whole minutes.

Marathon 6, Marrakech. From left, Albert, me and Tim. We shared stories along the way. I also met Clément, on the right, who would play a major role in my journey.

Marathon 7 in Bad Füssing. Daz's first half-marathon. In one week we'd gone from the heat of Morocco to a white-out of snow in Germany.

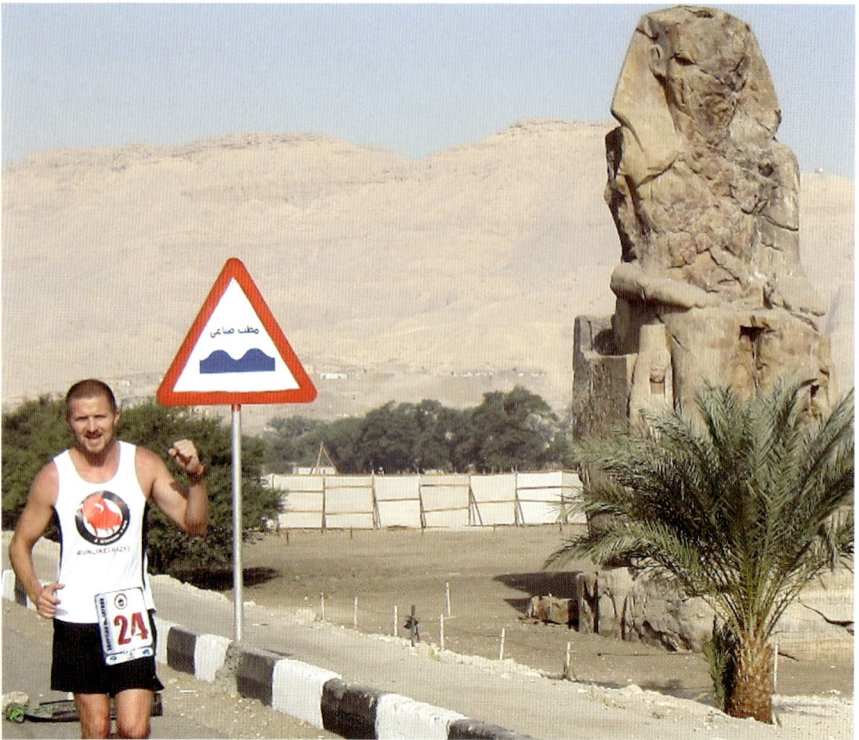

Marathon 8, Egypt. This is one of my 'Look where I'm running today' moments with the seated Colossus in the background.

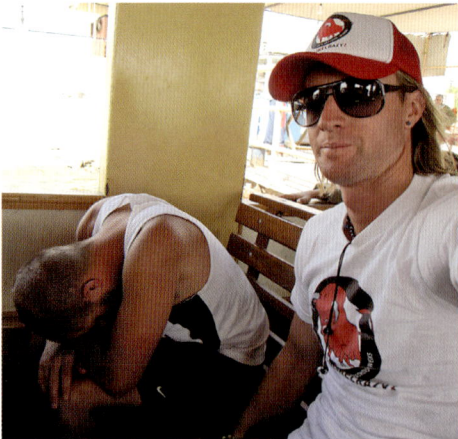

I was completely wasted by the Luxor run, but came good a couple of days later in time to go scuba diving in the Red Sea.

Marathon 10, Tokyo. Locals supported us along the way, celebrating our run.

I've always been inspired by Ultramarathon Man Dean Karnazes so it was great to meet him at the expo for my eleventh marathon in the Napa Valley. Daz's crazy costume for this marathon was in keeping with the vineyards we ran through.

Marathon 12, Cyprus. I love this photo. It captures a beautiful moment, showing how lonely a marathon can be. It's just me, struggling along, with the road stretched out ahead.

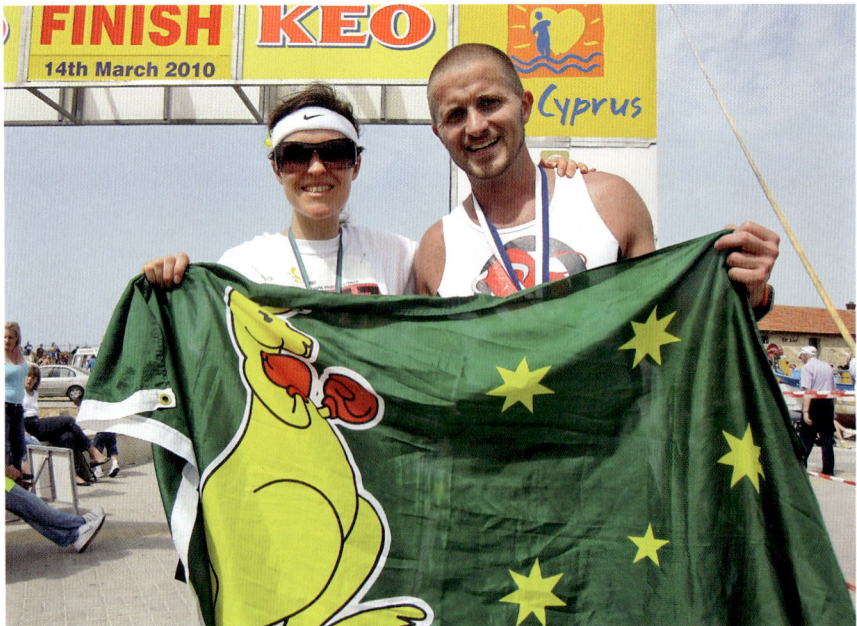

My sister Alexis with the Boxing Kangaroo flag that accompanied me around the world.

Marathon 15, Cape Town. Two Oceans Marathon is 56 kms, the views are magnificent and the challenge is enormous.

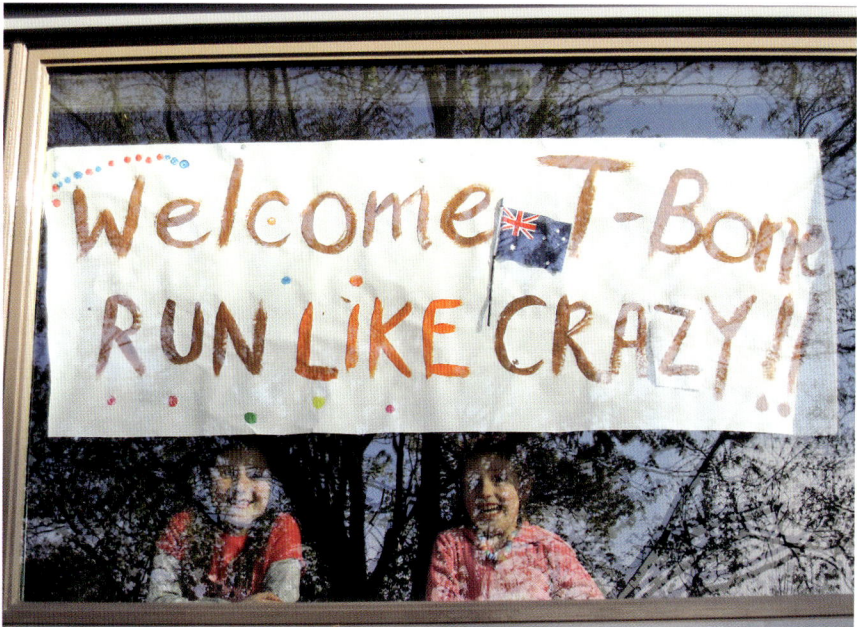

When I turned up for marathon 17 in Boston, I was made to feel very welcome by Millie and Georgie, part of my 'foster family'.

Marathon 21. Of all the runs, this was the most difficult, and the most emotionally charged too, especially at the end with Sharon and Lisa. We dedicated our Wall-smashing Bonanza to their late stepdad, John.

A $20 tour to a village on the other side of the Wall gave me a glimpse of local life.

I went to Rwanda to see the mountain gorillas and to run my 22nd marathon.

So far from anywhere that it was kind of scary, Easter Island was an amazing location for marathon 24.

St Petersburg. Halfway.
Only 26 marathons to go.

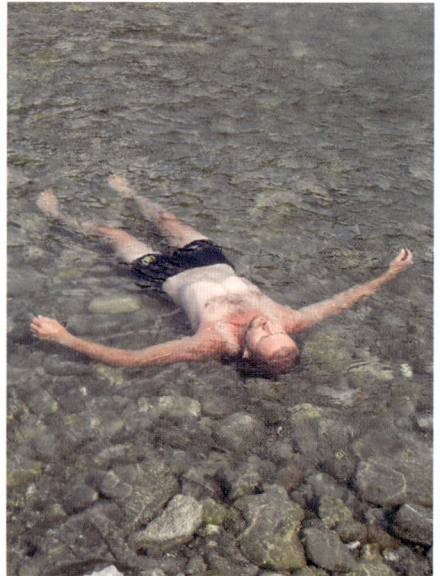

Post marathon 29, Busana – my shoes
after ten races. I'd completed two
mountain marathons in two days,
so cool mountain water was the best
substitute for an ice bath.

The hills of Lake Hovsgol where the 100-km Mongolia Sunrise to Sunset Marathon is run. This was my thirtieth marathon for the year.

AUGUST

At the 99-km mark of marathon 35 in Bornholm, Denmark.

Me and Clément in our Super Mario Bros. outfits for number 37, the Marathon du Médoc which runs through one of the world's finest wine regions. You drink wine instead of water along the way.

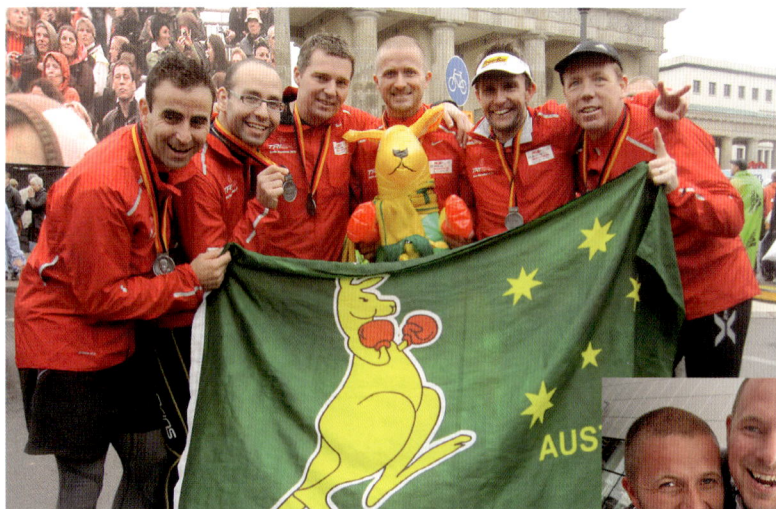

The Tribal lads joined me for marathon 39 in Berlin. From left, Nanfra, Kevlar, Mossy, T-Bone, Yabby, McGrath. And K-Bone in the middle! My brother, Chris, also cheered me on.

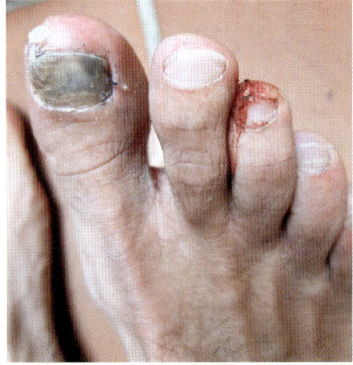

Marathon 40 at Loch Ness
came at a price: smashed toes.

Marathon 43, Ljubljana: my fitness regime was lugging these bags around the world.

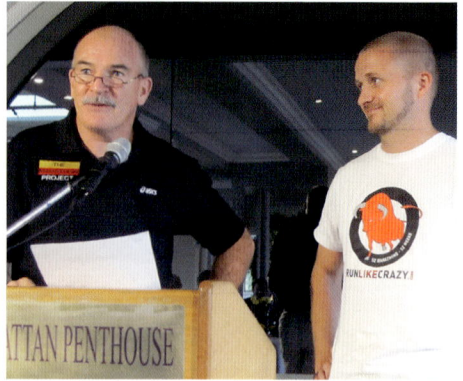

Marathon 45 in New York City. I met two Australian national icons in a day; Kurt Fearnley, winner of numerous Paralympic and World Championship gold medals, and Rob de Castella, former marathon world-record holder. My sister Bek and Mum came to cheer me on.

Transport to marathon 50, Cayman Islands, with Jane the pilot.

DECEMBER

Running marathon 51 in Antarctica.

Behind the scenes of the last leg: Nick McCormack and Bec Sherwill.
Daz ran his first full marathon covered in red body paint.

The finish line, marathon 52. I felt like I was going to cry with happiness
as I ran into history.

20

PRAGUE INTERNATIONAL MARATHON

9 May, Prague, Czech Republic

3:19.08

I'd dodged so many bullets in the past few weeks, I was beginning to feel like Neo from *The Matrix*.

Getting out of Belfast was another lucky break. Both the Irish and Scottish airspaces were closed on the morning of my flight, but were re-opened for a small window later that same day, allowing me to get to London. Poor old Opray got stuck the very next morning – more ash, fewer flights. I was on my own in Prague.

Prague is a great city, with a rich mixture of Eastern and Western European architecture and culture, plus it's decently affordable by Euro standards. You can do a lot of cool stuff there without blowing your entire budget in one night. I have fond memories of the place: I proposed to my ex-wife on the banks of the Vltava River, a long time ago.

I arrived there on Wednesday. It was nearly the end of spring, but the weather was struggling to reach 15°C in most places. It was wet too. I didn't mind that it was raining; I was terribly tired and had plenty of work to catch up on indoors.

Far from being a concrete plan, my calendar was a best laid one and I knew I'd need to start making compromises.

My plan had been developing a few gaping holes. Many races had changed their scheduled 2010 dates due to the soccer World Cup, and I'd been waiting to find replacements that wouldn't mean my having to rebook too many flights. Another problem, the most intractable one, was my dwindling finances. Paying for Daz for the last few months had been pretty tough. It was a good investment in many ways, but I always knew it was a risky manoeuvre. I really had believed, though, that I would land sponsors during the first quarter. That hadn't happened, and I was running low on dough. I didn't see this as the death blow for my adventure, but I had to consider reducing my itinerary considerably, perhaps sticking to Europe for most of the year.

I sat for two days solid in the Czech Inn. While it rained outside, I emailed and phoned, strategised and reorganised. It was a slow process, because every change in destination ultimately impacted on every movement in the weeks before and after. Mongolia was back in; Rio was out. Marathon du Médoc in; Moscow out. Phuket was just impossible to get to from South America, without spending insane amounts of money and time ($3000 and two days' flying each way). Easter Island looked as if it'd go on the chopping block, but the organisers did me a deal, so it was on. Rwanda was expensive to get to, but when would I get another chance to go. And I'd see the gorillas there too . . . *on like Donkey Kong.*

By Friday, my brain was pretty fried. That's when the sun came out and Opray showed up, looking relaxed and scruffy. He'd finally got to Prague from Dublin. I had someone to hang with and my wallet was looking in a much healthier state. I was immediately happier. I'd booked us tickets to the Electronic Beats Festival with Booka Shade and Hot Chip for that night. We had a couple of drinks at a bar on the way. Who'd have thought that 'a double vodka on ice' meant 'fill up the entire glass'? Those Czechs know how to drink. By the time Hot Chip came on, Matt and I were both pretty drunk and neither of us recalls a lot of that show.

Somehow I lost Opray on the way out from the gig. I headed down to the metro station and jumped on the first train. That was at 4 a.m. A journey that should have taken 15 minutes, including one train change, took me two hours. I kept falling asleep and missing my stop.

Having incessant jet lag and crap sleeping patterns had cursed me with a strange form of narcolepsy. I fell asleep at the drop of a hat, during conversation, on planes and evidently sitting on trains. Add alcohol and a night of dancing and I couldn't even keep my eyes open for three stations. So I kept missing my stop, waking up, swearing, getting off and switching trains to head back – only to fall asleep and miss my stop again. At 6:30 a.m. on Saturday, I finally walked into the hostel and fell fast asleep in my bed.

I didn't sleep for too long. I headed out to the expo to pick up my bib, and it was pretty festive out there. They had all sorts of games for kids and things to try, like spring-loaded stilts. They even had a dog race! The owners ran with their dogs – dressed in their own race bibs – on a 5-km track.

After heading back to the hostel, I met some newcomers to our room. Greg was from the States, Barjan would be my first-ever friend from Kazakhstan, and there were two Aussie girls, Jen and Danielle. The girls were awesome; Opray and I could relate to them straight-away and the Aussie jokes started flying.

Preparing for a marathon in a hostel room with seven other people asleep is a bit awkward. I woke Opray and he came with me to the race, a big effort considering how little sleep he'd had.

The race was to kick off in the Old Town Square. Walking the deserted narrow streets towards the start line was strange; it didn't feel like there was an event on. The lanes twisted a couple of times and then the square came into view. It was packed! Runners and support-ers were jammed into the old plaza. I wove around to the entry point, said my goodbyes and jumped the fence to enter the throng.

The atmosphere was good, although I didn't understand a lot of what was being said. Flags from all the neighbouring countries were represented: Slovenia and Slovakia, Latvia and Germany.

We got started with a cheer and the streets filled with runners, heading to the river. The track is in a bit of a star shape. The last 8 kms is basically a repeat of the first eight, and the rest of the track covers different parts of the city.

I started off at a decent pace, but it was a sunny day, and I warmed up very quickly. I tried not to slow down too much, but a messy night on Friday hadn't helped my energy levels. Thankfully there were plenty of drink stations and lots of running alongside the Vltava. There weren't loads of people on the sidelines. Czechs tend to be a little stoic, with that post-Communist chip on their shoulders, but there was a feeling that those who were out were genuinely happy to support the race, and they cheered for all the runners, not just their mates.

As the course came back into the city, I saw Opray up ahead – I was pretty happy to see a buddy. I stopped running and had a quick chat. He asked me how I was doing and I laughed, saying I was struggling with the heat and had just let the 3:20 goal go. When I kicked off again with a nod and a chuckle, I tried to put my head down and get fired up.

I had one more section out and back to go, crossing the river a couple more times. If I picked up the pace, I might be able to retrieve a decent result from this outing. I was tired, but not out. As I was thinking this through and doing some quick calculations, clouds began to roll in above me. Fat, juicy rain clouds. I don't mind a little rain and if it means less sun, then I'm all for it during a race.

'Right, guzzle another carb gel, put your foot down and let's get this show back on the road,' I told myself.

And that's what I did, cruising at a solid speed again now, punching out 4.30 kms. If I saved five minutes over the next 10 kms, then I'd have a sub-3:20 time. I was cooler, more motivated and passing runners galore. *Bring this shit on!*

I kept moving, focusing on the beautiful scenery. I'd been emotionally attached to this place for a long time, having got engaged here. But far from feeling sad at the way things had turned out with my marriage, I was finding this visit thoroughly therapeutic. Who'd have thought that the next time I'd be back would be to smash out a marathon, five years after the divorce? I really had become a different person to that dude. Every hurdle changes you, doesn't it?

I didn't want to keep up the pace any more, but I knew I was dragging the minutes back and looking to get a fair time. I hit the cobblestones and my legs felt like they were jackhammers being pounded into granite. I couldn't find a flat footfall, so I was stepping uncomfortably on the solid stones.

I made the final turn back in towards the Old Town Square. Only 500 metres left. I was heading home, another run done – 20 down, 32 to come. It was Mother's Day back home so I gave my two mums a big shout out on the video. This one was for them.

My time: 3:19.08! Wow, I couldn't help but wonder what I might have done with some real rest.

Getting back to the hostel, I realised I wasn't going to have much luck getting an ice bath. Then, to my surprise, the receptionists at the Czech Inn offered to help me out. Lauren, an American girl working on the desk, volunteered to let this stranger into her home to use the bath. We walked the back streets of Prague together and it was great to see more than the main roads of the city. I had my bath, using ice from the hostel.

Later we went to a very cool outdoor bar area. Apparently there were a few of these gems hidden away around the city and it's common for locals to spend many long summer nights chatting over a few beers in these park-side beer gardens. Opray and I had feasted on massive sausages with our beers and I wondered how the Czechs went on a diet of so much meat, bread and potatoes. Not fantastically well, it seemed. Lauren told us that the Czechs have one of the highest colon-cancer rates in Europe. We went out dancing again that night. I knew I should stop celebrating every week, but it really was far too much fun.

My time in this city had been unexpectedly excellent but now it was time to say goodbye to Prague and to Matt as well. I'd miss Opray and I looked forward to catching him in Hungary later in the month. At the airport, the flight was delayed – of course.

When we finally boarded the plane, they told us that the engineers had to check the engine for ash in the UK. Everyone stopped complaining immediately. When you hear that engineers have to check the engine on your flight, you're suddenly less concerned about the time issue. I still had a flight to Dubai to come and then on to Beijing the following day.

I was still running, still dancing, still dodging bullets. And the world just kept on delivering extraordinary moments, week after week.

21

GREAT WALL MARATHON

15 May, Tianjin Province, China

4:26.23

The last time I was at the Great Wall of China was in 2001 with my brother Chris 'Smokey' Miller, my sister Rebecca and friend Kerry. I remember all of us being on top of the Wall, blown away by its magnificence, when Bek suggested we try calling Dad. We were pretty confident that a call to Australia couldn't possibly work in rural China – it was 2001 after all. Sure, if you dug a deep enough hole you might get there, but to just dial it in? Imagine our surprise then when we called and the connection was as clear as day.

'Hey, Pa, you'll never guess where we are right now!'

That was one of those world-so-small moments. Standing on a wall that had its beginnings 2000 years before, when Mongol warlords had raided the civilised empire of Qin, was pretty extraordinary. That had withstood the hordes was pretty incredible; the Wall's statement was probably much stronger than its function, I mused.

Back in 2001, I never imagined I'd be back to see it, let alone trying to run across it.

After around 52 hours of travel, I was too tired to be excited. I'd got to bed at 2 a.m. that morning, but was up again at five to catch the bus out to the Great Wall, around two-and-a-half hours away.

The 'technical day' allowed people to familiarise themselves with the course and get a feel for how tricky running on an uneven surface atop of a narrow wall really is. The course crisscrosses over the Wall and parts of a fort down below; it's actually pretty confusing, so it was well worth going through it.

I didn't realise how many people were involved – there were some 2000 participants overall. The technical day was the first time everyone had been in the same place and the square was full of excited people. I kept my eyes peeled for my friends and tried not to look like too much of a loner.

Sharon Eyre is another mate from my barkeeping days; we toured Europe together when we were 21. After 15 years of friendship, she is more like a sister to me than a friend. Things hadn't been easy for Sharon: tragedy had struck her family the year before. Shaz's stepdad, John Pelling, had passed away quite suddenly, leaving her mum, Susan, devastated by the blow. John had served in both the British and Australian armies and was an adventurer at heart; he was also funny, in that dry, jibing English way. No one escaped the sharp end of his wit. We had always got along well and Shaz thought he would have been very proud of my journey. She had asked if I would dedicate one of my races to John.

'Of course!' I'd said. 'Any race you like, just pick one and I'll run it for him.' Susan decided on the Great Wall Marathon, which at the time looked as if it would be financially difficult to include in my itinerary. But it was for John, and I was resolved.

Then Sharon, her sister Lisa and their mum started talking about coming to China to support me. It wasn't long before Shaz was talking about running the half marathon. . . . Then Susan and Lisa decided it was time to get active. All of a sudden, we had a RunLikeCrazy brigade heading to the Great Wall of China for a John-inspired Wall-smashing bonanza!

I was so happy to see Shaz and her family. I'd had bugger-all sleep in transit, but I was thrilled to be able to enjoy the company of people I knew.

'You look tired,' was one of the first things the girls said to me.

'Yeah, but I feel great!' I lied in response.

The girls had some mementos for me, including a letter from another of our back-in-the-day nightclub friends, Dee. Damon, Dee's husband, had been diagnosed with bowel cancer over a year before. A large section of his intestine had been removed and he'd been fighting hard and doing well. Then in October the doctors told them Damon was back in the thick of the fight. My absence meant I hadn't really understood how bad things were. Sharon gave me Dee's letter and told me that Damon had passed away two nights before. I was in complete shock. I hadn't even considered that Damon would lose his battle.

We were to go up the Wall in our respective tour groups. The drive was 5 kms, so I had time to open Dee's letter. It had been written about 10 days before and, in typical Dee style, opened with her saying how proud she was of me. Then she wrote of Damon, explaining that his battle was drawing to a conclusion. They'd been told to say goodbye to him two weeks before, but he was hanging on, true to his 'stick it up them' attitude.

She wrote about her rock – their little girl Jacqueline, two years old, trying to be grown up to help Mum. That was about where I had to drop my shades and look out the window as tears welled in my eyes. Dee was one of life's absolute givers, one who nurtured and protected, who showed understanding and patience to all around her, even when others turned their backs. And Damon, whose passion for life, pragmatic nature and love for his family should have earnt him so many more years of happiness with his wife and child. At age 35, it was too early for him to leave.

The team caught up on the Wall, to walk the section we would run a couple of days later. I saw Sharon and hugged her. She knew why and we both started to tear up. There wasn't much to be said. We pulled ourselves together and then headed up onto the Wall.

The thing that gets you is how high it is. Not so much the structure itself, but the natural wall of the mountain ridges that it snakes across. The Wall stretches for 970 kms across the Beijing area alone, cresting mountains, splitting into multiple threads, creating a spectacular pattern that you can see for miles in every direction on a clear day. In sections, the wall is quite deteriorated, not even offering steps, just well-placed rocks. In others, they must have got tired of putting in so many stairs, because the blocks are two or three times as big as the others, and you begin to wonder how many giants were roaming the ramparts in those ancient days.

It took an hour and a half to cross the 3 kms and get back down to the fort. We had something to eat in the square, then our groups split again. Mine was staying near the Wall, while Sharon's tour group would head back to Beijing to take in as many sights as possible before the sun.

The next day, I figured I'd do something vaguely touristy in China. I'd done all the Beijing stuff the first time around, so I thought I should do something different and stay in the regional area near the Wall. I decided on a $20 tour to a village on the other side of the Wall – and, boy, was it different!

We were put on these funny old three-wheel tractors with trays on the back and driven a few kilometres up to the village. We were easy targets for crappy tourist gifts, the type of tat the locals buy in bulk from some factory, but we were also welcomed into a few of the locals' houses. We went to a small school, where the kids were playing basketball and running around in circles. It was really quite cool to see them having fun, unbothered by us, safe in their village and just doing the same things I did in my school playground many years back. Some of the boys were even doing pretty impressive karate or judo moves on each other.

We ate at the local headman's house. Well, he *was* the headman, back when the Communists operated each village like a functional cell, providing food for themselves and the People's Army. Many old men in the village still wore the basic blue workers' garments from the

1950s, and many older women donned the old-school green tunics. Life hadn't changed much, because it simply didn't need to. Communist ideals, as flawed as they are, essentially developed to help working communities like this find equality, so that lifestyle still made sense to these people. Who was I to judge their way of life anyway?

The next day, race day, and the atmosphere at the start was good. People were pretty revved up and I had a whole team of runners around me. Susan was smiling. She was doing the 5-km run with Lisa. We all had pictures of John on the backs of our singlets, a hilarious snap of him with a reggae wig on. It felt great to honour a really good man and to be helping Susan deal with his loss. 'This one's for you, John,' read the singlets.

The sun was breaking over the edges of the mountain range around us. You could feel its heat immediately – it was going to be hot and uncomfortable, no doubt about it. There was a little bit of confusion as to who was starting in which wave; really, it was just a jumble of people in the first group, but I entered the back of that bunch after giving Shaz a big hug and wishing her luck in her half marathon.

I tried to find a good speed that I could maintain through the first 5 kms up the hill to the start of the Wall. People of all abilities were around me, with most runners taking it slowly, as we entered into a completely unknown type of race. I was passing a lot of runners, figuring I'd slow down when I got to the top of the winding road. But I didn't slow down at the top the hill and continued to pass huge numbers of runners who had started ahead of me. By the time I was up to the entrance of the Great Wall, I was right at the front of the first wave, possibly even in the top 50.

I bounded up the first flight of stairs and then I was able to let the awe of it all wash over me. I was running on the Great Wall of China! You could see where I was from space!

Some runners would fly down the stairs, then walk up the next group, only to rush downwards again at the next opportunity. I was the opposite, as I've never felt too comfortable going downhill or downstairs at speed, so I just took it slowly, stepping deliberately. I took note of another runner's technique and began to track back and forth across the stairs diagonally, elongating the possible foot space and allowing me to confidently step faster.

As I got over the first sections, and finally onto the downhill run, I came upon some familiar faces – Susan and Lisa, most of the way through their 5-km challenge. They were cruising along very well, loving the experience.

We got down to the fort again. As I got going on the flat, I became aware of two things. It was hot already, really bloody hot. And second, my quads were on fire. They weren't used to that kind of climbing. Even so, I maintained a pretty good speed, keeping the pace around 4.45 per km and chewing through more of the competitors, seeing them struggle to find form after coming off the hill.

At the 21-km mark, I thought I was okay. Pretty baked, for sure, but still going. As long as there were no big surprises, I thought I'd be able to get through without falling apart, so, at 25 kms when a random turn in the road became a long, slow, leg-shattering climb that lasted 3–4 kms, I knew I was sunk. I grappled with it for a while, but eventually succumbed to the heat and slowed to a walk. A guy was chasing me up the hill, making very good time and we encouraged each other forwards. As he drew ahead of me, I yelled out, 'Hey! I've been looking for you, Number 52! You've got my number!'

'You can have my whole bloody singlet when we get to the end!' the guy called back over his shoulder. I had just met Deano from Reading Roadrunners.

We finally descended, but I didn't get far before I was met with another hill. I passed through a little village, then entered a plantation of some sort. I was no longer running on a road, but on a dirt track.

There were barely any markers and certainly no easy footing. I tried to stay focused, making sure I hit sturdy ground, but a few times my feet turned dramatically on the soft dirt and I was lucky not to have fallen on my face.

I kept moving towards the fort and the last leg of my run. As I entered the square, a commentator called out my name and told the crowd about my year on the road. Lisa and Susan were there, shouting there heads off. I appreciated it, but could barely react as I walked a few metres, took a few swigs of water and got ready to take on the final 8 kms, which were on the Wall itself. With a little fist pump, I climbed the stairs to get back on the Great Wall of China one more time.

I ran along the ramparts, over a bridge and started to climb up a goat track that takes you to the Wall. Not more than 30 steps up, I came to a sad, painful halt. I bent over double and coughed. I wheezed a few times, looked down to the crowd in the square and looked back up the hill. 'Bugger me!' I sighed, knowing that this was going to be more challenging a task than I'd steeled myself for. 'How the hell am I going to . . . ?' I trailed off, knowing that there was no answer, there was just the doing ahead of me.

I began to climb again, pushing past some tourists, trying to keep my footfalls solid and drive through my quads. I charged up a few more sections and hit another intersection with my eyes rolling in my head. 'Just keep moving, champ. One step at a time.'

I saw the Wall looming as I steadily climbed the track. As I got to the final steps, I felt my hamstrings tighten, and then came the pain. I tried to stretch, but couldn't find anything to hold onto for balance. A few of the volunteers were looking at me quizzically, seeming to consider whether I was worth helping. I finally found a rock to lean on and stretched out my leg. It relaxed and I downed the rest of my electrolyte drink, hoping a little more salt would help. I then finally surmounted the Wall.

I'd told myself that getting on the Wall was the hard part, and everything else after that would be easy. But, of course, I then had to tackle the different sections of the Wall, and that meant finding the momentum to climb each set of stairs. I was tired and my focus was shot, so running down each series of stairs was becoming more dangerous. This was not going well . . .

I hit another section and the guy ahead of me, having climbed halfway up, had taken a seat. I bounded up and plonked down next to him, sweating, wheezing, but laughing at the insanity of it all. He looked out at the valleys below, at the sections of wall that snaked away into oblivion.

'Beautiful day, eh, mate?' I mused, thinking it might be a good time to make light of the situation.

'It'll be a better day when this damn run is done,' he replied, getting up and turning to face the rest of his challenge.

I sat for a moment longer. I looked at the tired runners following along the Wall below. I gazed across the valley at the ancient-looking landscape. I took a deep breath, got to my feet, and started to climb again.

When I finally got to the very top, a young Chinese guy was waving the national flag and his two companions cheered. I wasn't in much of a state to respond, but I nodded my appreciation.

Then it was down, down, down again. A couple of sections later and I was off the Great Wall, with only 5 kms of winding road to go. You would think that my legs would have been happy about this but they were a mess and for about a kilometre I had to stop every 200 metres just to stretch out the cramps that were gripping my hamstrings. I knew I was okay, that I would get to the end, but I was finding it hard to stay focused and in control of my body.

I thought about John. He'd have been making jokes at my expense right now, probably completely inappropriate ones too. I laughed a little at the thought of him giving me a kick up the arse. I thought about my stepmum, Gay, too, who was now facing the fight of her life.

Then I started to think about Dee and Damon. It just made me so sad. I felt like such a fraud, running around the world, having the greatest year of my life. I didn't have the responsibility that Damon had. I didn't really have anything any more. All Damon had wanted was more time with his lovely wife and his daughter. I couldn't quite reconcile why I was allowed to live to the fullest yet Damon couldn't have just a little more time.

I began to weep. I was running, tears streaming down my face, wishing I could do something to help. Damon was being buried while I was running in China. It just didn't make sense and I couldn't get a handle on it.

As I slowed to a walk, another runner was coming down the road behind me, the third guy to pass me in that section. I hated being so defeated this late in the run. I rubbed my eyes and tried to pull myself together.

'Fifty-two in 52 weeks!' the runner shouted as he ran by me. 'Come on, my friend, come with me!'

'I'm sorry, mate, but I've got nothing,' I responded weakly. He gave me a wave and kept charging down the hill. I saw his number – 21 – and it gave me one more spark. It was my twenty-first race and here was my totem, leading me forwards.

It wasn't long till I was off the hill. I turned back towards the fort, knowing that I only had one more kilometre to go. 'No more walking,' I said to myself. I kept running, finding just a little more juice in my tired old legs.

And there it was: the entry to the fort. I ran into the busy square and there was Sharon, Susan and Lisa, shouting and cheering. I'd made it. I couldn't believe it. I was broken as I crossed the line.

They gave me my medal and I made my way to Sharon, giving her a half smile. I started to tell her what I'd been thinking on the hill but instead just wept. She knew why and we hugged and cried. It was all a little public for me, as people were coming over to congratulate me.

Of all the runs, this was the most difficult, and the most emotionally charged too. I was deafened by my feelings, unable to process everything that had happened. I was done. I had to sit.

It took a while to pull myself together. I think having a beer helped. Sharon had pulled an amazing time for her first half-marathon, finishing in 3:25. Susan and Lisa had finished together and they were elated to have completed the run.

In the end, I finished 19th of 580 marathoners, in 4:26.23. It was a much better result than I'd anticipated. I couldn't have performed any better: I had been punishing myself for weeks already and had no race-specific training and very little rest.

The following days were full of sightseeing in Beijing, dinners with Sharon, Susan and Lisa, plus the gala dinner hosted by the race organisers in town. There was even a bit of Chinese nightclubbing.

I was tired as hell and didn't want to leave my Great Wall family but the gorillas of Kigali were calling me.

22

INTERNATIONAL PEACE
MARATHON OF KIGALI

23 May, Kigali, Rwanda

4:06.39

There were a few reasons I wanted to go to Rwanda but the most important one was to see the mountain gorillas. Native populations live predominantly in one volcanic area that straddles the borders of Rwanda, Uganda and the Congo. The gorillas are a source of huge revenue for all of these countries tourism-wise, so they're reasonably well protected, but this wasn't always the case, as we know from films like *Gorillas in the Mist*, a homage to Dian Fossey. Back in the 1960s and '70s, it was more profitable to poach and steal the gorillas' young to sell on to zoos and private collections. And the only way to get a baby gorilla was to shoot its entire family first. There are now only around 800 mountain gorillas left in the wild.

After my plane landed, I went straight to the tourist office in Kigali to book a gorilla-scouting trip. It turned out, however, that you need to buy a licence, and the office had already exhausted their daily supply. I ended up doing it the 'backpacker way' along with a couple of girls: catching a local bus to Musanze, then hiring a truck to take us up to their park habitat.

It was night by the time we got to town. My new friends and I booked into a cheap hotel together and went to find a bite to eat. I glanced at the horizon and caught sight of the bright, sparkling Southern Cross suspended above the hills. 'Wow!' I exclaimed to my travelling companions. 'The gorillas live under a Southern Cross too!

They're as good as Australian!' All of a sudden, deep, dark Africa didn't seem so far away.

The next morning we hopped in our truck. After quite a journey, we reached a point where the guides stopped the vehicle; from here on in we'd go on foot. Then we walked 50 metres through the jungle before I was faced with the most beautiful family I have ever seen. Two female gorillas were wound around each other in a strange knot, while a baby gorilla rolled about on top of them, harassing them for attention. I was nervous and elated at the same time. I'd heard many bedtime stories of the mighty apes tearing people limb from limb (anyone remember *Greystoke?*), and where there is a mother and baby, a papa is sure to be nearby.

To get their attention, the guides mimicked the grunting sounds that the gorillas themselves make. Apparently they have visitors every day, so seeing us wasn't an unusual experience for them. The guides pointed this way and that, so that we would see where the rest of the clan was. A blackback gorilla was behind us. He was massive, sitting by himself a little higher up, and we all moved around to get a better look. I swear, he wasn't more than 15 metres away. I wondered what he was thinking, and he answered me by rolling sideways and scratching his butt.

Charlie, the big silverback patriarch of the family, took stock of where the rest of his family was and began to move further into the jungle. He looked around at us with an assured glare. He knew we were no threat. One of the mothers walked into a section of seemingly impenetrable wilderness, mowing down bushes and trees as she progressed. These guys owned the jungle.

We left after about an hour. I thought about a lot of things after that experience. I had no doubt these animals would be extinct in my lifetime, that my own children would never see them. I'd seen some amazing things this year, including structures and carvings as old as civilisation. Yet these animals predated us by a long stretch. How could we not protect them with the same effort as our oldest works of art or constructions?

Humans are nuts.

I ran the marathon the next day. The International Peace Marathon was a well-organised event, put on by a Belgium running group. I was impressed to hear that 25 nations were represented. The young African guys were extremely fidgety at the beginning, so you could tell the race meant a lot to them.

The race began in the Amahoro Stadium, atop a crest. The track took us out along a downhill road, and at around 4 kms we turned around and ran back up the hill. After that, we would skirt through a couple of neighbourhoods, swing back anti-clockwise around the stadium, run through the centre, which would make up the first of four 10.5-km laps.

I won't lie, it's not the most dramatically interesting marathon in the world, but you do get good views of the city from Amahoro. The joy came from running with such lovely people. The locals looked like they were having a wild old time, whether they were running or supporting. The expat community came out in force too and I got a lot of cheers from random people who'd read about me on a local website. I had little African kids running along next to me, and I was kept company by an old man who huffed and puffed as he went. I saw all sorts of people pushing through in magical displays of courage – one fella was missing a leg but managed to cover 21 kms on crutches!

I was still wrecked from my race across the Great Wall, and I hadn't rested. My legs were lead from the beginning and the day got hotter and hotter. I looked good around the halfway mark, but by the third lap I was ready to walk home. I ran down the hills, but could only walk up them. I staggered through the stadium for the final time. It wasn't my finest run, but I had completed marathon 22 in 4:06.39.

The Africans in that race were incredibly fast and able to post times as quick as 2:17 even running up and down hills. Unbelievable. I have so much respect for those guys and their abilities, especially considering how hard it must be to make time to train while you're trying to feed your family on shockingly low wages.

I'd spent a lot of time looking at the bright side of Rwanda, but I also wanted to know more about how things had played out in 1994. At that time the country was in the middle of a civil war with a basis in ethnic conflict – the Hutus against the Tutsis.

I headed to the Genocide Museum, where I learnt a great deal about the horrors that had taken place in the streets of Kigali. For 100 days, Hutus roamed the towns, massacring the minority Tutsis in an attempt to ethnically cleanse Rwanda. Some 800 000 men, women and children died – hacked to death with machetes or shot. Many women of all ages were brutally raped by gangs of armed men. It must have seemed that Armageddon had descended on the country.

I looked at the wall of remembrance and the names of entire families etched into the black granite. I wandered slowly around the photo galleries and sucked back emotion as I looked at the hundreds of pictures of maimed children and women. Then there were the bones piled up in glass cabinets with skulls of all sizes. It was sickening.

I read the stories that surrounded the massacre because I wanted to understand. Essentially, it was a case of mass hysteria, ignited by Hutus in the upper echelons of society, but the fire was fanned from the state-run radio stations that filled the air with messages of hate. Obviously the history of aggression went back a lot further than the event itself, but I wondered how many of the smiling people I had seen in the streets must have witnessed – or maybe even committed – mass murder. I had seen the scars on any number of guys my age and younger – results of machete attacks. Some were missing limbs, which could be attributed to many things, but there were far too many instances to ignore. How could their neighbours have perpetrated such acts? And how could they then live next to these neighbours when peace was returned? It freaked me out a bit.

I went to Nyamata Church, a massacre site in Bugesera, on one of the crammed local buses. I walked in to see the pews covered in blood-stained clothing. The museum curators – I guess that's what you'd call them – had piled all the clothing from the dead onto the seats. The blood had blackened, but you knew what it was. Around 10 000 people had been killed in Nyamata on 10 April 1994. The local Tutsis had gathered in the Catholic church when the killings started, for protection. The frightened villagers barred the doors, but the militia smashed their way in and did their bloody work.

The curator then led me out of the church and down behind it into a crypt. The walls were lined with wooden storage shelves and on each level were bones that had been separated and stacked together, with skulls laid out in many neat rows. I made myself stay and look. The skulls had gashes across their surfaces, where they'd been carved with knives. They had holes, from bullets. Some of them were as small as my hand and I wanted to imagine they were anything but those of children.

I left shell-shocked. I didn't smile much for the rest of that day. I remembered again how lucky I was to be Australian. We're just so far removed from this kind of violence, or even the potential of it. I hoped desperately that Rwanda would maintain its peace.

It had been a huge week, from the emotional upheaval of the Great Wall run to the intense cultural experience of Kigali. I was definitely ready to leave but I was glad I came to Rwanda. I went to my Heart of Darkness and saw magnificence, madness and atrocity.

23

KESZTHELY MARATHON
31 May, Keszthely, Hungary
3:25.32

The trip to Budapest was a late inclusion. I had intended to do the Budapest Marathon in September, but a new date was set at the beginning of 2010, and it turned out to be the same day as the Berlin Marathon. Berlin was the easy winner. I'd never been to Hungary, though, so when another gap appeared in my schedule, I decided to do a race in the small town of Keszthely.

Matt 'the Global Gift of' Opray had been drifting around the Czech Republic since I left him in Prague. He made his way down through Hungary, arriving in Budapest a few days ahead of me. Lauren from the Czech Inn decided to come down too.

Good times are what you get when you hang out with good people, and it was here I had one of the most brilliant nights out of the whole year. We went to a strange warehouse club/bar with multiple rooms inhabited by a circus of crazy and interesting people falling about wasted. I kept myself reasonably nice, but even so I was pretty drunk by the time we headed home to the Loft Hostel.

Lo, Opray and I pulled ourselves together early enough the next morning to get our train to Keszthely, the oldest town in the Balaton region. Apart from my hangover, it was a lovely trip, a couple of hours, cruising along by a breathtakingly scenic expanse of water, Lake Balaton. And when we got to Keszthely itself, I gave myself a little high five for being clever enough to come. It's a stunning rustic holiday town, boasting a fantastic range of old establishments. The most impressive is the Festetics Palace, built in the mid 1700s, and therefore older than white Australian history.

Opray decided he couldn't let me run this one alone, so he donned the most ridiculous body-glove bike outfit I'd ever seen, sourced from a local op shop. He's a good-looking lad, but, seriously, there was purple spandex wedged where purple spandex had seldom been. The following morning, when we lined up at the race start, he generated more interest than I had in five months.

It was great to be able to share the excitement with someone as the gun cracked. I was going to try to knock out a fast one for my 23rd marathon of the year, while Opray was going to run his first half-marathon. We stepped out together but I lost him after a few kilometres. I pushed along Lake Balaton's shoreline, realising quickly that there were some fast runners in this race and I'd better not get too caught up in the excitement.

In the first half I was running really strongly and liked my chances of scoring another personal best, but after an hour of slogging it out, the heat of the Hungarian early summer kicked in and my wheels began to fall off. I felt terrible and, even worse, I snapped at Lo because she wasn't at the place we'd agreed on for a GU drop.

I dragged my butt to the end, where I quickly apologised to Lauren. Opray had nailed his maiden run in a very respectable 1:45. My time was 3:25. The pain of the race was forgotten reasonably faster than that. It wasn't long before the three of us were sitting by the lake with beers and smiles all round, watching the swans, taking in the serenity.

We had a couple more days in Buda, wandering about and making the most of the famous Széchenyi Baths. It was quite a short stay in the end, but definitely a worthwhile one.

I had a long journey south ahead of me, heading to Argentina and then on to Chile and Easter Island. So I hugged my friends goodbye and rushed off for yet another lengthy solo flight.

24

EASTER ISLAND MARATHON
7 June, Easter Island, Chile
3:31.28

On the way to Argentina I got stuck in Madrid for a night, because the national Iberia airline decided to sell more tickets than seats. I was annoyed at the time, but they paid me €600 as anti-flip-out money. I needed that dough, so I copped it on the chin.

Finally, I was hanging in another lump of metal, looking down at the dawn creeping across South America. Clouds hugged the mountains below, flowing through the valleys, between the peaks. This was new land to me. Somewhere down there, society got its start. The Incas had gone about cultivating the land and chopping off heads for the same sun that was now rising behind me.

This was the fifth continent I'd run in this year, and the sixth continent I'd set foot in, at the beginning of the sixth month. I only had one night in Buenos Aires, not nearly enough time to appreciate that immense city. I stayed at the Tango Inn, which was not as exciting as the name suggested. I decided to go to their tango night to see some local culture. But I was jet-lagged, so as much as the meal was good, and the Chileans I hooked up with were nice and the dance spectacular was fun, I nodded off at the table.

In Santiago I stayed at La Casa Roja, a beautiful old building run by Aussies and Chileans. The owner asked me what I was doing there and I tried to be enthusiastic when I told him, but I was so exhausted it just came out all wrong. I was a babbling mess. But he was still impressed (or felt sorry for me) enough to give me two nights' free accommodation.

A riding tour around town the next day made me like the city immediately. The residents' great national pride was evident in the numerous flags that were flying everywhere to celebrate 200 years of Chilean independence and to support their squad for the upcoming World Cup. I enjoyed the ride so much that it inspired me to run 11 kms along the river, looking up at the snowy peaks of the Andes.

My next marathon was on Sunday, two days away, and my flight to Easter Island was the next morning. But when some of the people from the hostel asked if I wanted to see how much fun Santiago was on a Friday night, I could hardly say no. We hit a club, and I started to see how much South Americans like to party. We danced most of the night away.

One glance out the window showed just how much of a void the endless sea created around Rapa Nui. I wondered why anyone had populated this little rock called Easter Island in the first place – we were so far from anywhere that it was kind of scary.

I rested and ran the marathon the next morning, still hurting from China and Rwanda's marathons. Easter Island was surprisingly bare. With green hills rolling in from the sea, I thought I would see more palm trees and foliage, but there weren't too many trees on any of those hills.

I ran fairly quickly for the first 10 kms, enjoying putting quite a bit of distance between myself and a number of the other runners. For quite some time, I was sitting on the tailpipe of the police motorcycle that was guiding the lead runner. But the further across the island I got, the more the unexpected hills and heat got to me. I slowed down a little, then I slowed down a lot. As I crested the largest hill, at about 17 kms, I realised that I was in for a whole lotta hurt. Running down that hill made me want to cry – I was going to have to turn around and run back up every one of those steps to get back to the top.

But I did run back. For as long as I could, I tailed a nice Chilean guy, using his consistent pace to measure my bursts and walks, but I struggled to keep going. I want to say I had a great race, because I came fifth overall, but I felt crap and no sooner had I crossed the finish line than I ripped off my singlet and collapsed into the bay.

The other runners were a very interesting crew indeed. Pancho had won the full triathlon that had been held on the island a few days earlier, which included a huge swim and a mountain-bike race. Irwin had run this marathon to complete his seven-continents marathon journey. He'd headed down to Antarctica a couple of years before as part of his quest, and when the weather was deemed too foul to proceed with the official race, he'd opted to run 480 laps of the ship's deck instead. That is commitment!

The next couple of nights, I hung out with a lass who was so in love with Australia that she'd taken up citizenship. We had a good laugh and I enjoyed doing the whole island thing with someone, rather than walking around by myself. A tour of the quarry was where the island really came alive for me. These were the different sites where the famous stone heads were either lying face down or standing proudly. Hearing the tales of the Moai (the heads) and why they were so prevalent on the island really gave the place an amazing sense of character.

Here's my version of their history.

Little Champions showed up by boat from Polynesia. The island had been trading with Hawaii and Samoa for a long time, but some large event in the ninth Century AD cut them off from the other islands. At some point the local fellas became a bit bored and started getting carried away with the idea that the town elders watched over the villages after they died. So they made a large stone head for each important old mate who'd passed on. They faced inwards over the village to protect their descendants.

As time moved on and these kids got more and more lonely, the number of heads being produced in the central volcanic quarry got a little out of hand. To move these mammoth craniums, weighing as much as 80 tonnes each, they cut down trees to help slide the stone up to 21 kms across the hilly island. As their population grew and the resources provided by the forest disappeared, the locals started warring with each other. A fair few village heads were pushed over – Eventually most of the Moai were face first in the dirt, and sometime around the 19th century, production of the huge noggins stopped, possibly due to the discovery of the islands by European explorers.

Whatever the case, the remnants of a few monster scones that were in production can be seen today – specifically the Colossus Brain Bucket, which if completed, would have stood some 21 metres and weighed around 270 tonnes. He must have been a hell of a headman!

There were a couple of things, though, I didn't quite understand.

I was told each head took about a year to complete and they would do most of the work at the quarry, just completing the facial details when the stones were transplanted to their village. But if the head wasn't managed properly while they were moving it, the fragile neck would break and they would need to start again. What I didn't get was why they didn't just move the solid block, then carve it up on site? Apparently the quarry was a sacred site . . . well, that was their excuse anyway.

Secondly, how the hell could these islanders afford to take a year to carve a head for Grandad? Surely someone's kid was starving while old mate was dicking around in a quarry for months on end?

These conundrums added to the unique and wonderful experience of visiting this magical little place. The fact that these carvings have lasted so long is a tribute to the amazing ingenuity of the natives of Rapa Nui, but there's also no doubt in my mind they were all Head Cases. No wonder I felt at home running there.

25

MARATÓN INTERNACIONAL DÍA DE LA BANDERA

21 June, Rosario, Argentina

3:09.35 PB

Getting back to Buenos Aires, I narrowly avoided yet another disaster. A week before, it hit me that I'd underestimated the flight time to Santiago from Easter Island, and that I'd forgotten to account for the switch in time zones over such a long journey. So I would land at almost exactly the same time as my flight would be taking off for Argentina!

Not good. I looked at buying another ticket, as my Super Web Deal Fare was not changeable, but it would cost me $700 one-way to BA. That's a lot when you're budgeting $15 per night in hostels.

I looked at myriad other routes to get there – bus, train, rental car, even rental motorcycle – trying to stick to my schedule, but it was going to cost about the same and mean a lot more travel time. I had pencilled in the next week as a rest period, and didn't want to waste it on a lengthy, lonely bus trip.

I decided to take a punt on my negotiation skills. If the flight landed right on time, I could run across to international departures and beg my way onto the plane. But when we took off late from Easter Island, I knew I was in trouble. I arrived in Santiago 20 minutes after my scheduled departure and tried not to look too disheartened as I approached the LAN Airlines support desk. I explained my situation and just as I saw the pretty girl shaking her head, I blurted out that I was running around the world trying to raise money for charity.

'Please, if I miss this flight, I will miss the next and the next and

I won't get to my next marathon in time!'

It was a slight lie, but I had to turn that shake into a nod. I pleaded and showed her my T-shirt, translating the words into poor Spanish. '*Correr como loco!*' I repeated, hoping they would laugh.

The girl turned to her burly male counterpart and he looked me up and down. I tried again and he smiled, registering my panic. 'Sir, it's okay, we understand you,' he said. 'We just need to find out if we can fit you on a later flight. We shouldn't do it, but we'd like to help.'

Bless them, they got me on a flight two hours later. I could breathe again. Having booked such a huge number of flights and hostels in advance, I was destined to make mistakes like this, but my finances had taken such a beating, I couldn't afford to do it too often.

In BA, I found my way to the Mill House, a famous hostel in the centre of town. It was much nicer than the Tango Inn. I was bone tired, so passed out quickly and quietly, hoping to enjoy a little holiday even though it was a bit cold – much the same sort of weather as Melbourne's during winter. I'd given up on trying to get a race in that weekend. I had one race in hand anyway, from way back in January.

Some awesome lads from Sydney gave me a few tips on what to expect from the nightlife around town. Their tales of misadventure got me excited about spending a week in this wild Latin town. The hostel was full of really nice people, including Brazilians and Australians, Yanks and Irish, and we hit up the extraordinary Argentine steakhouse La Cabrera, consuming so much food and wine I thought I'd burst. My stomach had definitely shrunk, along with the rest of my body, but I needed a good protein boost and made the most of it. We took in a few nightclubs and I drank and drank, danced and danced. It was a real holiday and I celebrated my year to date with whatever energy I had left.

South America was grinding to a halt over the next few weeks, because it was a holiday period as well as the opening ceremony of the World Cup. A huge screen was set up in San Martin Square, but every time I planned to head down to watch a game, the rain set in. I got there for one Argentinian game, but the hill was so crammed with supporters that I couldn't even see the screen and left at halftime. It was a sea of sky blue and white, with even the tourists donning local jerseys.

BA seemed to disappear in the blink of an eye, flashes of dinners, wine, dancing and laughter, amid echoes of 'GOOOAAAALLLL!'

The South Australians guys from the hostel wanted to head to Iguazu Falls up north, before crossing into Brazil. I decided to go with them. The boys promised me an awesome experience on the South American bus system, and they were right. We booked tickets on a luxury vehicle. The buses certainly showed signs of wear, but the seats were enormous and fantastically comfortable, like business-class seats on airlines. And it was a treat to be served food and alcohol.

Sixteen hours and about six movies later, we arrived in Iguazu to soak up the warmth of the tropical environment 1000 kms north of chilly Buenos Aires.

We headed to the falls the next day, wandering around the jungle paths, seeking the source of the dull roar. When the falls finally came into view, the five of us had our jaws on the ground – the sight was awe-inspiring. A boat ride later and we were under a section of the falls; it was a unanimous 'yes' to getting up close to the surging water. With life vests on and cameras rolling, we floated close, but within about 50 metres of the base we were drenched and deafened by the crushing force of water. I loved it – the time and money to get there was truly well spent.

The lads were heading north in the days to come, but I needed to go south. I'd gatecrashed their travels for long enough. I was jealous of their easy schedule, but they were doing the backpacker thing and

I was on my own mission. I booked a trip to Rosario, the birthplace of Che Guevara. Another long ride on a very comfy bus . . .

I arrived in the university town of Rosario on Friday and I was picked up by one of the event organisers, Iván Bianchin, who was working as foreigner support. I really liked Iván right away. It turned out he'd won the half marathon in Rosario and was generally an absolute rocket as a runner. He worked in internet marketing and strategy, just as I had at Google, so we understood each other. When he took me down to the event expo, he introduced me to everyone from the race director to the regional sports director. I felt good about what was to come.

That day and the following one, we toured the city. It is said that Rosario girls are the most beautiful in Argentina and I reckon I saw a bit to support this claim. The Sunday was to be National Flag Day, which is akin to Australia Day, part of a holiday weekend that extended to Monday – race day. The main event, a festival with fireworks and free bands, played out along the Paraná River, where the city is located. There they unfurled the longest flag ever made, or so they said. I held a piece of it, along with thousands of others, as a plane floated overhead taking pictures. There were flags everywhere, flowing from monuments and towers, apartments and shops. It was a bloom of colour over a concrete city, blue all around and in the sky above. All that pride and happiness around me made me fall in love with the country.

The race felt as much of a celebration as had the day before, with so much energy and happiness in the streets. They're all heart the Argentinians, there's no doubt of it. Iván had got me into the elite area up the front, so I immediately started out fast. I hung on to those front runners for as long as I could as we headed off for a loop around the city, then charged back to the river for the second half of the race.

I ran with some really nice guys, who, even though they spoke very little English, encouraged me anyway. I felt welcome on this course and decided it was time to step it up. I downed a GU much earlier than normal, at 10 kms, deciding on a new strategy to increase my carb intake. I ran a little too hard through that first half: when I clocked my 21-km time, I was at 88 minutes and holding, faster than I had ever run a half marathon. I had expected to see Iván, as he was holding a couple of gels for me. But, alas, I was ahead of my expected time and he was nowhere to be seen. I charged on and hoped I'd hold out, but my strategy relied on more GUs.

The next 6 kms still went quite well, but when I hit 27 I felt like a car door had opened into me. I almost stopped on the spot, but I was still hanging on to the three-hour dream, so pushed myself forwards. Ahead of me, runners were becoming ragged, so I used that anti-energy as best as I could, admonishing myself for wanting to slow down, when so many around me were crumbling faster.

'C'mon, c'mon, c'mon,' I kept saying to myself. 'You got this. If there was ever gonna be a day to break three hours, you're having it right now.'

It didn't work. I had gone past the point of no return, dipping below that invisible line where to recover would take way more energy than you have in your body. It doesn't matter how many drinks or carb gels or anything else you have, they won't stimulate you enough to get back in charge. You're cooked . . . all you can do is manage the pain.

So that's what I did. I hoped I would make it under 3:05, but that slipped by. I aimed for 3:10 and kept battling my way along the river right next to the rows of wild supporters, heading to the finish line. Guys were patting me on the back as they passed, a couple even stopped and tried to call me on with them, even though I was stumbling and walking. And I knew that you can't carry anyone in a marathon.

It now came down to how bad I wanted a PB – and, man, after that much pain, I wanted it bad. I lifted one last time and ran the last 3 kms.

The crowds were going ballistic at the end and as I made my way into the chute, the clock had clicked over to 3:09. I gritted my teeth and sprinted, crossing the line for marathon 25 with a personal best of 3:09.35, my fourth in six months.

Everything after that was a blur. My legs were practically smoking and I tried to sit, but a TV camera was in my face and I had to smile and answer some questions. There were so many people around, still celebrating the holiday, it was hard to even find a place to sit.

Iván drove me to his home and put me in a bath of ice and made me some sandwiches. I got dressed, picked up my bags in one hand and my lunch in the other, and then Iván drove me to the station just in time for the bus to BA. I couldn't thank him enough; he gave me a hug and a laugh. '*De nada*,' he told me. 'I will see you again!'

A few hours later I was back in Buenos Aires. I dragged my body and my 20-kilo bags on shattered legs, from the bus station to the airport shuttle and got on another bus. Two hours after that I boarded the first of four planes to St Petersburg, Russia. I was busted up and tired, so as I lowered my aching legs into that tiny economy space, I was full of dread for the long haul ahead.

As the plane lurched into the red and purple evening sky, I knew that Argentina would forever have a special place in my heart. Then my brain switched off.

26

WHITE NIGHTS MARATHON

27 June, St Petersburg, Russia

3:38.35

I disembarked in Madrid, then flew to the island of Majorca to get another flight to Copenhagen, Denmark, where I had an über-cheap return ticket to Russia. This meant I could come back a week later for the Roskilde Music Festival without too much difficulty. It all seemed like a great idea – until I arrived at Copenhagen Airport just as the lounges shut for the night. I slept-sat on a bench in front of a 7-Eleven for nine hours till morning. Not great.

By the time I dropped off my bags at the Atmos Hostel in St Petersburg, I had been travelling for 44 hours. I was now on the other side of the world, in the midst of summer, rather than the depths of winter. I'd gone back in time around 10 hours and I was so far north that it was 'white nights', meaning the sun never fully set. I felt sick, tired and irritable, but I wanted to make a good impression, so I just smiled at the lovely Anna at reception and asked for a bed to die in.

I slept long and ate a little that evening, before watching some football and passing out again. It never got dark, so I had to keep looking at my watch to figure out what time it was. It also really screwed with my already heywire body clock. I was wide awake at 3 a.m., so I just got up and wandered the empty streets. It was a bit cold, but already bright. I didn't go too far, but got a little taste of the pretty city.

Later, I went for a longer walk. St Petersburg has only been around for about 300 years, initially built by Tsar Peter as a fortress against the Swedes at the beginning of the 18th century. It wasn't long before it was turned into the seat of local government and in 1712 the Tsar moved the capital to Petersburg – a little egotistical, but he was Peter the Great, after all. It flourished and remained the centre of politics until the Communist revolution of the 20th century. The city has always been considered the most Western city of Mother Russia.

It's a staggeringly beautiful place, with wide roads and gorgeous architecture. The statues on many of the bridges depict wild stallions and brave soldiers. St Petersburg is also a romantic city, albeit one with a tumultuous history. Under the Communists, it was renamed Leningrad for their fearless leader, in another pitch of egomania. The city took an absolute pounding during the Siege of Leningrad, which lasted for 872 days, from September 1941 to January '44, becoming all but depopulated as a million people fell victim to the German invaders. The city was rebuilt and renamed and now thrives as a centre of culture and entertainment. The museums were restored to their former glory, too, and none is more famous than The Hermitage, which houses much of Russia's art collection.

The beating sun had the locals wearing as little as possible. Russians definitely have their own style, which sits somewhere between eclectic and just plain weird. There was a lot of bright, flashy gear on display and some uncomfortable-looking spandex stuff that had probably been sent from East Germany in the '80s. And since this was the most Westernised city in Russia, I couldn't imagine what the rest of the country got around in. But, in fairness, the Russians don't seem to give a crap what anyone else is doing. I liked that attitude. Plus, they can back it up with the fact that every woman in St Petersburg is *ridiculously* good-looking. I'm telling you, I was fumbling with words in front of the ticket stand, the café, the bar, at traffic lights, in front of cop stations, in museums. I like to think that I'm a reasonably subtle guy, but every time I looked at a girl I gawked. Then I'd look at her mother and fall in love all over again. It's true, it's true: if you're a lonely bloke, sell your house and go live in St Petersburg . . . they're growing on the goddamn trees. And I've never seen so many giant guys in one place. Handsome too. I felt utterly outclassed. Sure, they dress like their mum suggested the outfit, but they make up for it with their giant awesomeness.

I went out with some Italians, Iranians, Americans and the owner of Atmos Hostel, a crazy Russian dude named Nikita. Niki took me to a bar late one night and told me to wait and watch. A couple of locals spoke English with accents so thick and so different to the Latin I had become used to that I found it hard to understand what they were saying. But once I'd offered them shots of vodka, everyone seemed happy and I got hugged often. After a bit, a stunning woman came out and did the most amazingly athletic and artistic strip tease I had ever seen! The women in the crowd were whooping a whole lot more than the men and I was transfixed with what I'll call cultural curiosity.

Now, it probably seems like I'd been celibate on this trip up to this point, but there had been a couple of flings and lusty nights. It's not easy meeting someone when you're prone to passing out during conversation, or you have to run a marathon the following day, or head to the airport at 5 a.m. You get the idea.

Anyway, on the Thursday night, Nikita took a group of his hostel guests and a couple of Russian girls on a pub crawl. We had a great night: Nikita pulled funky robot moves, while the Italians and Iranians danced like the world would explode if they stopped. The Iranian girls were certainly gyrating like they knew what they were doing, but I stayed well clear, worried I'd end up with a bounty on my head if I got too close.

That night I was enamoured by Alya, one of the absolutely gorgeous Russian girls, and, somehow, I kissed her. We danced and drank, but too soon she said, 'I have to go!'

'What?' I was surprised. We'd only just started having fun.

'I need to get bus to Helsinki. It leaves in few hours.'

'Really? Are you sure you have to go? Go tomorrow,' I told her, clutching at straws. 'We may not get another tonight!'

'No, I must.'

'Well . . . how far is Helsinki?' I asked.

'Four hours on bus.'

'Okay. I'll come with you!'

Alya looked at me with wild green eyes, 'Ha! Really? You want come with me?'

'Hell, yeah!' I said with drunken bravado. 'Let's do it!'

We were soon back at the hostel collecting Alya's gear. Then we were negotiating a fare in a small taxi bus that took the St Petersburg residents to Finland for shopping trips. I've said before that I'm prone to making mistakes and I consider them mighty lessons, but this bit of stupidity really took the cake.

I was drunk and still having a great time – until the bus got pulled over by cops and we were told that the driver didn't have a bus licence. We left at a nearby petrol station for three hours while they sent for a replacement driver. It was hot and sticky by then and I'd more than sobered up. Alya was still beautiful, but the whole idea didn't seem so crash-hot any more. By the time we crossed the border and made it to Helsinki seven hours after departure, I had a thunderous hangover and seriously regretted ever getting on the bus.

We went to stay with Alya's friend, but I soon found out it was a national holiday in Finland, so nothing was open and there was nothing to do. It was great hanging out with these girls and even better when Nastia cooked us a fantastic meal, but I was feeling a fool for leaving all my gear in another country. If I wasn't back the next day, Saturday, to get my bib, I'd miss the race.

Nastia put me in the spare room and the girls shared her bed. I felt silly for chasing Alya this far, but they were two of the sweetest, friendliest girls I had met on my travels. I passed out quickly and woke up early. Alya walked me to the local train station and said goodbye.

173

One last kiss from this green-eyed glamour girl and my heart melted again. The doors shut between us and the romance was over before it had even begun.

I paid a stupid amount of money to get the only available train back to St Petersburg. For a few hours I watched the countryside change as I crossed borders again. The scenery wasn't vastly different on either side of the border, but it seemed, from my window, that life was more organised and easier to deal with in Finland.

I got the third degree from both sides of the border police because I was travelling without luggage and only had my passport and wallet with me. I told them I was visiting friends and when they asked for an address I made one up. I didn't know how that would go, but I couldn't remember where I had been.

I arrived back at the Atmos Hostel as the revellers from the night before were emerging from their rooms. 'Man, where have you been?'

'Don't ask,' I said.

I got changed and made it to the expo just in time to register. I wandered the streets for a while and then tried to rest for my marathon the next day, but I was still jet-lagged, and couldn't settle down. I wrote for a while and ate some food, then finally went to sleep around 9 p.m., but the loud *bang!* of a suitcase dropping woke me up at 11 p.m. Sleeping in dorms on a Saturday night definitely has its drawbacks. I tried to go back to sleep, but the light outside the room and the loud talking of the backpackers kept me awake. Finally I got up and saw one of the Italians. 'Tristan! We go out. YOU COME!'

'You know what? You're right. No sense lying here doing nothing!'

So I went out again, in the dim half-light of midnight. We went to a bar in Dumskaya Ul, a small court off Nevskiy Prospekt, where there are a swag of cool haunts. I sipped on a couple of beers while the others danced, and hoped I'd get some sleep soon. I chatted to yet another stunning local girl and thankfully she spoke English well enough to hold a good conversation. When she asked me what I was doing that day, I said, 'I'm here to run your marathon.'

She looked at me, confused. 'What marathon?'

'It's the St Petersburg White Nights Marathon,' I explained. 'It runs around the city, even up Nevskiy Prospekt, just out here. It's a big event, haven't you seen the signs?'

She hadn't noticed, but then asked, 'When is it?'

I looked down at my watch, raised my eyebrows and then looked at my half-drunk beer. 'In about three hours,' I said. 'So I need to go.'

With that I was off. I walked back to the hostel, past drunken youths and girls in the most revealing outfits I'd ever seen in public. At 5 a.m., I walked past monuments and beautiful girls with horses, offering people a ride down the street. Madness. I got back to the hostel and put my head down for an hour or so, before heading back the way I had come to the huge square in front of The Hermitage.

It was an absolutely gorgeous day. The sun was well above us and everyone looked excited to be there. I was not so excited, even though it was marathon 26, the halfway point.

The race was a blur. I ran well for the first half, but there weren't many foreigners in my space, except from neighbouring post-Soviet countries. I tried to talk to a few people, but I was just met with mumblings of Russian or looks of agony. It was a very scenic run, with many river crossings, but by 21 kms I was flagging again.

'To be expected, you idiot,' I chided myself, watching the worn road pass under foot as we ran through the old town. 'You do the crime, you gotta expect some punishment.'

I pushed and pushed, then I walked and ran, then I walked and walked. I was getting cooked by the sun, high in the sky by that stage. I felt sick from lack of sleep and frustrated at myself for taking the marathon less than seriously. I had put myself in a bad position: by rights I should've been collapsing from exhaustion, not running 42 kms.

We crisscrossed the city for a while, and ended up on a road that follows the Neva River all the way back to The Hermitage. Gusts of wind blew against us on the last 7 or 8 kms and as hard as I tried, my legs gave out and I was reduced to walking a few hundred metres at a time, then leaning into the wind and trying to cover another kilometre or two. I had local runners pacing next to me, each in their own worlds of pain and torment. We would look sideways and grunt encouragement and keep moving together. We got there in the end.

I was shot to hell and couldn't make much post-race conversation. I picked up my gear and went back to the hostel, grabbing some food on the way. I sat down and ate in the common room, as a few of my dancing friends emerged from their rooms and said their good mornings. One Italian said, 'I knew it, man, I knew you weren't going to run the marathon today.'

'What do you mean?' I asked.

'You were at the bar with us at 5 a.m., so I knew you had changed your mind.'

I just grinned and pushed him my camera across the table.

The next few days were very strange. I couldn't sleep for more than two hours at a time and I couldn't stay awake for more than two hours straight. When I was sleeping, I was dreaming of running, or being late for a plane or a train. I would snap awake and then just get up and start moving again. After 48 hours of this, I thought I might have broken something in my brain.

I had to sleep, or I would be ruined, so I bedded down one night and didn't get up until I knew I had been there for eight hours.

But then, of course, it was time to go.

I couldn't believe I'd made it halfway, but that meant I had to do the whole thing over again to complete my journey. I wondered if my mind and body could take it.

27

COAST MARATHON

3 July, Kristianopel, Sweden

3:59.11

I'd always wanted to go to the Roskilde Festival, one of the biggest music extravaganzas in Europe. It's an eight-day festival, but the bands only play for the last four days, so plenty of punters show up early, set up their themed tent cities and enjoy late nights drinking and falling about before they even get into the music. It sounded well worth shelling out the cash to go.

But when the Sultan of Dubai (aka Adam) and I arrived at Roskilde, I was sans my ticket. It seemed it'd been lost in a paint storm back at the Happiness Centre. We met up with an old mate of the Sultan, Dr John Barnes, who was living in Sweden, and, lucky for us, had some sway with the locals. He'd been at the festival from the start and was wearing some rather interesting trousers that I was tempted to describe as pantaloons, but whatever he was wearing, the good doctor managed to conjure up a ticket for me. Yet another crisis averted.

Doc John and the Sultan knew each other from Melbourne's eastern suburbs and we discussed the fact that I was from out that way too. It wasn't long before we worked out that the Doc and his brother, Sam, were the two kids down the road who my brother and I played with when I was about eight.

'We played Frogger on your Atari, dude. That was 25 years ago! Hot damn!'

And so the shock of accidentally meeting a childhood friend in the middle of a massive music festival in Denmark continued to sink in. Suffice to say, Dr John is a magnificent lad who had met a beautiful Swedish girl in Adelaide and realised that to keep her he had to move anywhere she wanted, even if that meant taking up professional gambling. Ain't love grand?

We were all stalwarts of Meredith Music Festival (the greatest music festival on the planet, held annually in country Victoria), so we were ready to see what the Danes had to offer when it came to going crazy. And, boy, do those kids like to party. For four days, 120 000 people got loose, then they actually started the music! The next four days saw the rest of the punters show up and the whole area copped a good battering. They had a number of different stages going; there were beautiful Scandinavians everywhere, and plenty of drunk Aussies too, and, strangely, no police. Security people were around, but their presence wasn't obvious. A relaxed fun time was had by all, with no particularly aggressive behaviour that I could see.

There was a catch, however, to including this madcap music adventure in my packed marathon schedule. Somehow in the midst of the partying, I needed to complete a marathon. It was midsummer, so Scandinavian countries had a lot of races on. A couple of months back I'd stared at a map and my trusty race calendar for a while and found that there were two marathons planned in nearby southern Sweden. One was in its inaugural year and the other had been going for a few, so for safety's sake and thanks to some spectacular-looking pictures form the 2009 event, I chose the latter – the Coast Marathon. It did mean that my crazy schedule looked something like this:

Thursday
Arrive from St Petersburg, Russia, hire car and meet up with the Sultan. Head to the Roskilde Festival and meet up with the Doctor.

Friday

Chip (my Tribal mate, who'd last joined me for the Tokyo Marathon) arrives at the festival, coming from Australia via London.

Saturday

Get up at 4 a.m. with Chip, leave campsite, drive to Kristianopel, Sweden. Run marathon number 27 with the mighty Chippa, get back in car and drive to Roskilde. Rock the hell out in celebration!

Sunday

Enjoy day off at the festival – watch Prince dance the house down!

Monday

Fly to London and head to Pamplona, Spain, for the Running of the Bulls.

As far as Saturday went, that's exactly how it was planned and exactly how it was executed. Chip and I got to bed at about 10 p.m. on Friday night, did our best to sleep in a tent, with tunes still pumping across the hills around us when the alarm startled us at 4 a.m. We dutifully got up, with glorious Scandinavian sunlight welcoming us to our epic day. We didn't mess around; we got in the car and drove towards Sweden.

We made great time, stopping only once to get a couple of bread rolls. Our destination was a tiny little village at the Kalmar Strait, on the eastern coast of Sweden, and the number of yachts moored in the marina told us it was a popular holiday retreat area. And yet it was also obvious that the local community was responsible for creating the race's relaxed, friendly atmosphere. We walked into the town hall and registered, told them our story and they were thrilled to have us at their event. The organisers couldn't believe that we'd come all the way from Roskilde, let alone the music festival, just to participate.

To be honest, we couldn't believe it either, but we wore our festival armbands to prove it.

There were only about 60 runners in both the marathon and half marathon, but it was also the regional championships, so the field looked like it had some pretty quick runners. The race kicked off and everyone eased into their own paces pretty quickly. Chip was having knee trouble, so we aimed for 3:45 and decided to see what happened. During the first 10 kms, I was having difficulty shortening my stride, and was dragging Chip along faster than he liked.

It was a rare opportunity to share the experience with a good mate, so having Chip next to me, taking in the sights and sounds of this remote race, was special. And it really was beautiful. Every time I looked up from the road, I took in the lush country – green forests on one side, golden hay bales on the other. It was hard to imagine this paradise stuck under metres of snow in winter.

We pushed on and saw the strong runners powering back along the outback course. Chip needed to slow down from the halfway point, so we backed off some more and lost the feisty Iranian we'd been chatting to. His tales of persecution as a Kurd in Iran certainly passed the time.

Many of the support crews at each checkpoint knew what I was up to, and they got more and more boisterous as we moved towards the end. We were cutting it a little too fine for the four-hour mark, so I started getting on Chip's case every time he needed a walk break. It was hardly surprising he was running out of juice. After all, he was jetlagged from the flight from Australia and I'd made him sleep in a tent at a rock festival the night before. He had recently got engaged, and I managed to get some decent conversation out of that, trying to take his mind off how much the end of a marathon sucks.

We got through it just in time. In the final kilometres Chip found another gear and pushed on, scraping in at 3:59.11. We both had a massage and ended up next to the docks eating a feast and soaking up the beauty of Sweden in summer.

A lengthy drive back to Denmark got us to Roskilde in time to watch a few big acts on the main stage and I kicked on till 4 a.m. I even had a couple of girls up on my shoulders – probably a pretty stupid thing to do after the marathon, but beer and music makes you do strange and wonderful things. When I did pass out, I had a little smile on my face.

The next day we lazed about and did our best to catch a few more acts despite the heat. I thought I was done, but after a little kip in the grass, I fired up just in time to see one of my favourite Aussie bands, the Temper Trap. Then late that night, the one and only Prince hit the stage. I really didn't expect too much, but once he got the crowd moving and played 'Purple Rain', the show became one of the most impressive musical events I've ever witnessed. All he had to do was turn and shake his butt a little and the whole crowd lost their crap. It was wild! There were three encores and I loved it all.

On Monday, nice and early, Chip, the Sultan and I packed our tents and left the festival. We had plenty of time till our flight, so we wandered around Roskilde – a gem of a town.

We ended our journey together at the airport. The Sultan headed back to keep Dubai afloat and Chippa and I flew to London, where we hugged our goodbyes at the airport. In London, I bee-lined it to the Happiness Centre.

I must have looked terrible. My sis seemed really worried about me. But there was no time for worry – Pamplona and the Running of the Bulls awaited. I was meeting a friend from Australia at Luton Airport, so I had to get going. I was comforted by the fact that after running a marathon in the middle of a music festival, things couldn't possibly get more crazy.

28

ZERMATT MARATHON

10 July, Zermatt, Switzerland

5:30.40 (alpine marathon)

I spotted Bec Sherwill at the airport before she noticed I'd arrived. She had been at the World Cup for a few weeks, managing a tour group associated with the bank she worked for, making sure the clients enjoyed themselves and nothing strayed too far from the plan. She was looking forward to a three-week holiday, mainly in Croatia, with some much needed sun, sand and relaxation.

She finally saw me and gave me a huge hug. We caught up on news during the flight to Bilbao, in northern Spain. Bec was hung-over from a huge weekend with friends in London. And when I say 'friends', she had pictures of Prince William and a number of celebrities at a polo match that she'd been invited to. Yep, she'd been having a lot of fun.

We landed pretty late, hired a car and belted our way south along the freeways to Pamplona. It was a longer drive than I expected and we got in around 1 a.m. There would be no sleeping in, though: we needed to be in the town centre early to watch the opening celebrations for the seven-day festival of San Fermin – the main attraction of which was the famous Running of the Bulls.

The celebrations didn't officially kick off till midday, but things were already out of control when we arrived at about 10 a.m. Kids were wildly running about with different-coloured dyes, squirting each other in technicolour mayhem. Everyone was wearing white pants and shirts, with red sashes and scarves – the traditional dress of the festival. It wasn't just the teenagers getting up to no good either. Locals aged from five to 75 were packing into the plaza, their whites streaked with the dull maroon of spilt sangria.

I'd always thought that this festival was a tourist thing, but it soon became apparent that it is really a local show and the foreigners are a side act. We weren't made to feel unwelcome at all, but it takes a few days for the tourists to learn the ropes and I could see how that might be aggravating for the locals.

We found a local lolly shop that had fridges full of sangria on sale. Sangria is a pretty potent mix of red wine, Coke/soda and fruit punch. It's very easy to drink, so you can neck about a litre before you realise you're drunk. Each bottle contained 1.5 litres, so I bought three to get us in the right frame of mind as fast as possible.

In a small square, packed with locals and tourists, the mayor announced (with fireworks) the beginning of the fiesta. It was an extremely hot day, with temperatures soaring to 37°C. Observers on the balconies above the jammed streets threw buckets of water onto ecstatic drunken punters. I took Bec's hand so I wouldn't lose her – everyone was wearing exactly the same clothing, so it was near impossible to spot each other when we were separated by more than five people. The further into the town we got, the more intense the madness became.

She didn't know it, and I'd never told anyone, but I had a bit of a thing for Bec. I had got to know her a little at the Canberra Marathon more than a year ago and I'd seen her at a few Tribal events. All of a sudden, here we were on the other side of the world, holding hands, drinking sangria, dancing and laughing out loud at all the wild Spaniards. I plucked up the courage to lean in and kiss her. I wasn't sure what to expect, but when the kiss was returned, I felt a whole lot of sparks that came with it. This was different. This was special.

We headed back to our hotel for some rest and took it easy for the evening. I was intending to run with the bulls the next morning, and

I didn't want to be drunk. It seemed dangerous enough without adding alcohol to my stupidity.

We were in the city by 7 a.m. Every day for the week of San Fermin the bulls were to run at 8 a.m., so the plan was for me to get down onto the track and for Bec to head into the stadium. It's about a 1200-metre course and you need to be halfway along if you're to run with the bulls *and* make it into the stadium. I knew it was an issue to hold on to a camera, and I was going to give it to Bec – before making the snap decision to try getting a couple of pics from in among the action. Bec hugged me and told me to stay safe. I didn't even try to reassure her. Truth was, I was scared shitless and didn't know how to tell her that I thought I was going to die.

It turned out that the track was all closed off by 7 a.m., the runners having jammed in an hour earlier. I darted through the streets of the city, asking locals and other frantic tourists where to go. I was repeatedly told it was too late. Bullshit! I wasn't going to be defeated by something as stupid as time. By now I was down near the beginning of the run, where the bulls are released, on a platform a few metres above the actual course. I pushed through the crowd of observers and got to the rail. I told the Spanish guy on the rail in sign language that I was going over. He looked at me incredulously. Then he just shrugged and moved aside. I leapt the rail and fell to the cobblestones below.

And with that, I was in the thick of it. The parade was only 10 minutes away. I was nervous, but excited. Plenty of people around me were taking photos, so I pulled out my camera and did the same. Then I heard a shout and someone tapped my shoulder. I turned to see a cop reaching out towards me from the barricades that protect the street crossings. I couldn't understand what was happening at first, but when he pointed at my camera, my eyes went wide and I apologised, putting it back in my pocket. He was having none of that and reached towards me to pull me out. I turned to run into the crowd, backing away a bit, but the look of anger that flashed across his face made me realise that this decision would result in a lot more than a slap on the wrist if I was caught. I conceded defeat. He dragged me through the fence and with that, my assault on the World's Bravest Matador title went up in smoke.

Minutes later the first firework went off and runners started to bolt. Another minute, and the second firework *kaboomed* across the city and the bulls began their stampede. It was quite a sight and in some ways I was glad to have seen all the action from that angle before I attempted to run myself – I wouldn't be leaving before I gave it a shot.

After a day of being electrocuted by the madness in this place, I was ready to have a quiet meal that night, but most places were just cranking out tons of drinks and tapas to keep the festival-goers happy. Plus it was the World Cup semi-final, with Spain taking on Germany in a fight to the death. In the end, Spain came good and the whole place went bananas – the biggest party in Spain just had a reason to get bigger! We were leaving the next day and I had to admit, I was ready to get out. But not before I'd attended to some unfinished business.

We headed into town again early in the morning. I left my camera with Bec and headed straight down the mouth of the course from the stadium and looked for the point where the runners collected. I was leaving nothing to chance. It was 6.45 a.m., already warm, and I was ready for some bull action. As I walked down the course, I passed a guy covered in sangria and leaning against a wall, whispering gently to the bricks about all the amazing time they were going to spend together. He didn't know the bulls were on their way in an hour or so, and that he could be a speed hump in no time.

We collected in the straight before Dead Man's Corner. Many runners looked like they needed sleep, a shower, or at least a slap in the face to sober up. As it got closer to 7.15, the section where the runners had collected was shut off. 'It's full!' the crowd roared. We were all packed together like sardines and it was getting very uncomfortable, very quickly.

Success here is all about the stadium. If you're too slow, you get locked out. But if you run too fast and beat the bulls in by a country mile, you'll be the subject of scorn for all the onlookers in the stadium. The chant '*Puta Madre*' needs no translation and will ring in your head and your heart till your deathbed.

There were some shit-scared faces around me and when the first 'warning' firework was set off, I was amused to see many people bolt around Dead Man's Corner and up the road towards the stadium. *Stay calm*, I thought, *wait till the second warning*. A few seconds later, the next blast came. It gave me a shock, but I chose to wait for a few more seconds. I felt like I was in *Braveheart*.

I strained my ears listening for the bell of the lead bull. I eyed Dead Man's Corner and saw people skidding around the bend. Basically it's a sharp right-hand turn, so tight that the bulls slip to the left on the cobblestones as they try to round it. If you're caught on the left side at the same time as the raging brutes, then you can say goodbye to your ribs as they're crushed into your lungs by the huge masses of meat landing on you. I thought I heard a tinkle and looking behind me I saw more men running like blazes. I took stock of my situation. 'Who the hell are you trying to kid, idiot? RUN!'

Fifteen steps had me rounding that corner. On the other side was not what I expected. A mass of bodies were huddled right around the edge. All of a sudden, this right-hand safety zone was at gridlock: the runners created a wall that seemed impenetrable. But the fear in their faces was what terrified me the most. My heart rate tripled, my eyes dilated, adrenaline exploded through my body and I'm pretty sure I exhaled the F-word. Then I just threw myself headlong into the mayhem and hoped I'd live.

The crowd caved forwards in front of me, not so much from my impact, but because everyone was ready to get the hell out. People clawed at each other until the crowd finally spluttered onwards down the thin city street. All I knew was that it was time to run and I started to grab others who weren't moving, thrusting them forwards or to the right to get out of the way. I was now officially shitting myself. The panic around me was palpable and I could taste sweat in the air even though my mouth was now stone dry. Then *clang, clang, clang*. The sound of a surging bull. The death knell. Time to run. *Faster.*

I looked forwards and sprinted as fast as I could through the crowd. But the clangs got louder and all I could see while dodging arms and legs was the frightened faces of the guys who had looked backwards. And eventually I looked too. *Shit.*

There was a steam train of bovine malice heading straight up the centre of the narrow cobbled street. The biggest one had the bell and its eyes were wide as it charged. The four others with it were running wildly in line, but as I turned, one of them tumbled further back, slipping on the stones and collecting a runner. The bulls were now passing me and I shouldered my way further from the centre and into the right-hand wall of shouting people.

Clang, clang, clang . . .

Another group of bulls was coming. The screams around me were more from people just wanting to get the hell out, but I was determined to dodge this second onslaught and still make it into the stadium. I kept running and looked back in time to see the next herd pass just a metre away. I saw another fella get thrown to the side by a confused bull. The movement tripped the bull and he slid onto his face. Everyone scattered again and I took the opportunity to keep running forwards while there was a gap. Some of the officials made room for the young bull, gave him time to gain his composure and move into the stadium. As soon as he passed me I followed behind, thinking that this might be my last opportunity to get in. Sure enough, they started to pull the big gate closed.

I pushed with the crowd, the stragglers who wanted the glory of being inside. I was pushed back by an official, but the crowd behind me was bigger than his weak shove. In a second, I was through. I ran into the arena with a sense of euphoria. The crowd around the arena were up on their feet, cheering and clapping. The adrenaline in my body was going ballistic, but the run was over, so I didn't know what to do with the energy. My eyes were wild and I tried to shout, 'YEEAAHHH', but it came out as a quiet 'Yeerrr'.

It took a few minutes, but I found Bec in the crowd. The feeling was just coming back into my legs when she gave me a big hug and a kiss.

'Let's get out of here,' I said.

'Absolutely,' she replied. Job done, no injuries. It was time to go. But I was still shaking a bit as we were leaving.

The idea was to get to Switzerland the following night – Friday – for the infamous Zermatt Marathon, running from 1000 metres above sea level to nearly 2600 metres, below the glorious Matterhorn. Once that was completed, we'd jump back in the car on Saturday afternoon and drive for about 550 kms to Reggio Emilia, where we'd pack in some sleep and then drive another hour or so to Busana, for the mammoth task of racing another alpine marathon on Sunday. Two marathons in two days. I'd never run at altitude and I'd never attempted a trail race, and it seemed like a good idea to practise both before I went to Mongolia for a 100-km trail race at altitude, in just 10 days' time.

Stepping up from the marathon distance to 100 kms scared the bejesus out of me, without the added complications of altitude and trail. After Mongolia, I'd have a two-week gap to catch up on rest before my next run. Two weeks of hell, then two weeks of rest – there was some method to my madness.

A drive through the Pyrenees and across the French countryside seemed to be just what the doctor ordered. By the time we crossed the border into France, I was settled again, laughing and chatting to Bec about all sorts of nonsense. There was plenty to get to know about each other. I had never realised just how much I talked until that trip.

I mean, I knew that I was pretty chatty, and I've got a fair old tank on me, so whenever I started to run out of breath I knew my talking bordered on ridiculous. Bec was kind enough to point it out a few times but mostly she let me prattle on, probably because I was driving and it was keeping me awake.

Bec had changed her plans to come with me for the runs that weekend. She was finding it fun to be part of the adventure, and I think she'd decided to do her bit to keep me alive for a few more days. I figured that a stop somewhere on the Mediterranean would be a nice gesture. We'd been driving for hours, so the perfect break on a very hot day was a dip in the water, and that turned into us staying the night.

Problem was, I made the most of the hotel's reasonable internet connection, and we didn't hit the road again till nearly 3 p.m. on Friday. I was sure it was only another seven hours' drive, travelling at around 130 kph. I thought that would give us heaps of time so we stopped for dinner in Chamberey, a beautiful town where they came up with America's favourite shirt material.

By the time we hit the road again, with Bec driving, it was getting late. She let me sleep, in the vain hope that I'd be rested for the morning's race. But when I woke up around midnight, we were still a couple of hours from St Niklaus. We finally arrived at the small ski village at 2 a.m., only to cop an earful of German from the landlady about how late we were. A few hours' sleep and then we were up and getting organised to run.

I felt surprisingly awake, mostly because my anxiety at the task ahead was kicking in. Bec had been outside and was full of cheer about the beautiful scenery, but looking up at the mountains reminded me too much of what I was up against so I sat on the couch, taping my legs. I wasn't relishing what was ahead, but I was soothed by watching Bec as she filled my water bottles with Gatorade powder. I liked that Rebecca was with me. I liked Rebecca a lot. *Maybe she's the one*, I thought, following her with my eyes. *She makes everything okay.*

Everything is brighter around her. I smiled, as a wave of calm enveloped me.

The run through the town of St Nik was fun, because many family members were out to cheer everyone on. Swiss dudes in lederhosen were even blowing those enormous horns that look like water slides! Once we'd exited town, it was a long 6-km trek on a reasonably low-gradient rise. I noticed my shortness of breath almost immediately, but at only 1000 metres above sea level, I knew there was worse to come.

The course eases slowly up to 1500 metres, where it reaches Zermatt, which was the halfway point of the race. Then the incline becomes much steeper, getting up to 2900 metres by its end. I had no frame of reference for dealing with this.

Most of the first half of the race was on trail and dirt road, so it was interesting to see how much more slowly everyone was progressing on the unsteady ground. I found it pretty taxing, and with the combined problem of being quickly out of breath, it wasn't long before I was taking short walking breaks.

We closed in on halfway, and the powerful snout of the Matterhorn came into view. I exhaled. 'Biiiiiig!' was all I could muster. As we ran into Zermatt, large cowbells being rattled and monster horns being blown made the atmosphere of this picturesque town very festive. We looped around the top side of town, crossed the river and headed up to the eastern slopes. Looking at my watch, I was surprised to see it had already taken 2 hours and 15 minutes just to get through the first 22 kms. And the hard bit was yet to come. 'Long day, Bone,' I said to myself. 'Just keep moving, buddy.'

As we headed out of town, the locals were spraying as many people down with water as possible. The Aussie comes out in me when I see that kind of water wastage and I avoided being covered. The water was coming from the melting snow, but I was still uncomfortable seeing it being poured all over the ground.

We hit the edges of the forest and a road so steep that running was near impossible. With that, the real challenge began. I hadn't been running quite as fast as I should have in the first half of the race. I figured I should sandbag a little – hold a bit back for the race the following day. Suddenly I came to a grinding halt. All I could do was lean forwards and pump my legs to push up the side of the mountain. I tried to run again and again, aiming to run for at least 1 km and then a few hundred metres' walk. I managed a whole 400 metres before I was walking again. I tried again . . . 300 metres. 'What the hell?' I panted.

I walked as quickly as I could, looking to the efforts of an older fella who seemed like he was walking with a strategy in mind. I tried to keep up with him and got frustrated, starting to run again. But no sooner had I blown up at 300 metres than my old mate pumped past me. 'Bastard,' I breathed at him. I walked on, trying to get my breath back.

The amount of effort needed to keep going was extraordinary. After a while, I seemed to find a good rhythm and wasn't gasping quite so hard. I even ran again for a few hundred metres, but slowed to a walk so I could stride without sucking blades. I passed a stream cascading down the side of the mountain from the melting snow above. It was pristinely clear and a few runners filled their bottles. I did the same and took a swig. Holy water! It was the most delicious mouthful of water I'd ever had.

Finally I saw some runners getting excited ahead, as the path's gradient began to subside. People were beginning to trot again and even run. I took the opportunity to move my legs too and it wasn't long before we were running on a flat road, edging along the side of the mountain. I thought my legs would fail me, but they seemed to revel in the feeling of running again, so I let them flow. There were a few more points on this road where the path shot sharply up for a while, but I was certainly making real progress by now. I passed Old Mate Walker within 2 kms.

We climbed further and hit some trails that led us over ice-cold streams, funnelling water down the slopes. The sting in the sun was really getting to me, but I kept on running. It wasn't time to give in, not with less than 10 kms to go!

One section was the bottom of another ski slope, the junction of two lifts showing where the skiers would normally head. We crossed over and started to climb a goat track, cursing and slipping single file along a mountain pass. Then it was down into another shallow valley; we had to run quickly down the rocky trail, trying not to fall, and on up the other side.

This race had everything.

With only 5 kms to go, I thought I was safe. I'd heard there was one more hill to come, but I wasn't worried. My hamstring and my adductor on my right leg were pulling pretty heavily, but it didn't warrant me slowing down just yet, so I soldiered forth. I finally came to another checkpoint, where I grabbed copious amounts of isotonic drink.

I came out of the drink station, situated at a busy crossing and train stop. It seemed to be the last big stop before the top of the mountain. It couldn't be far now, surely. But then I saw the runners ahead of me take a sharp left turn. Straight up the side of the mountain. Three kilometres of the steepest mountain road yet. This was why they had a train and ski lifts that went to the top.

'Shiiiiiiit.' I stopped for a minute and looked at the distant trail of people winding up the hill in front of me. At the highest point, they were no more than ants, marching in line up the mountain.

I started to walk again, leaning forwards and trudging up the hill. There'd be no more running in this section except maybe at the very end. To give you some idea of how disheartening that is, I normally run under five-minutes per km. Even as fast as 4.20 per km if I feel good at the end of a race. So the last 3 kms should have been a mere 15 minutes of hell. But with that kind of gradient, you're looking at 14 or 15 minutes per km. So it was going to be another 45 minutes minimum of the toughest path yet. And I'd been going for 4:45 already.

Wonderful.

It was a slow burn. I was tired, my legs ached and I was now scorched from the sun. The beauty of the Matterhorn was on my right and to my left a train ferried people glued to the windows up to the end point of the race. I tried not to look up too often. A couple of 'walkers' passed me and I passed a couple myself. A few people shouted at themselves to 'keep going' or something similar in French or Italian. A few others encouraged those around them with 'Not far now!' One task, one focus – keep going till it ends.

I could see the bottom of another ski lift, in an area that doubled as the station for the train. Surely this would be close to the end. People were gathered at this point, cheering the stragglers as they got closer to the top. I expected to come over the rise to see a finish line. But I was in for another little shock, for the finish was off to my left, looping up the hill some more: it was probably only another 800 metres, but I was really at my wit's end. I shook my head and laughed.

I'd committed to the extra loop when someone came bounding down the side of the hill from the finish line. 'Hey!' shouted Bec. 'You've made it!' She had a big cheesy grin and looked like she'd been waiting for a while.

'Well, I haven't quite made it, but it's nearly over.' I slowed for a minute to let her join me, then continued on.

It was a joyous scene at the end with a backdrop of some of the most breathtaking mountain scenery you're ever likely to see. I was so happy to finish that I would have jumped for joy, if I'd been able to feel my legs. So I grinned, or at least I would have, if I'd been able to feel my face.

Bec did everything she could to make me feel better, but I was fading fast. My legs were cramping and I was eyeballing the beer tent as though I was going to rob the joint. There was no indication that I was ready to hop straight in the car and drive to Italy for another marathon the next morning. I had my doubts about this being a good idea after all. This was pure HurtsLikeCrazy.

I sat down. Bec got me a beer. I stared at the Matterhorn for a while, wondering what on earth I was doing here. I wondered this after every race; it took me a while to absorb what just happened. All around me, people were exhausted, lying in the sun, soaking up its rays, even though many of them were as sunburnt as me. At this altitude, it was pretty cold no matter how much the sun beat down. The slightest breeze felt like it carried a thin layer of ice from the highest peaks, tickling your skin and turning the red sunburn to blue. These guys and girls had been training for months and put all they had into conquering this mighty goal. They'd succeeded and would spend their afternoon and the night licking their wounds and celebrating with beer. I envied them. I wanted to celebrate with them and relax.

But no. Alas, I'd said I would try to do this and it would go against everything I stood for this year to not even try. Time to get off this mountain and hit the road again. We got the train down the hill and I watched as more people edged up the same path I'd struggled with an hour before. *Poor buggers. God speed to you all*, I willed them. In Zermatt, we stocked up on pre-cooked vegetables and snacks for the trip.

One more train took us to Täsch. I got changed in the car park, washing myself with anti-bacterial gel and wet-wipes. I had some serious chafing problems in my shorts, so a combination of a soothing cream that breastfeeding mothers use and Vaseline was applied to the inflammation. I rubbed what was left of my busted old tube of Voltaren into my pulsating leg muscles, in lieu of finding an ice bath on the long drive south.

We had 550 kms, half a tank of gas, an iPod full of disco tunes, heaps of great stories and a mission half complete. It was no *Blues Brothers* movie, but it was a pretty good road trip so far.

29
ECOMARATONA DEL VENTASSO
11 July, Busana, Italy
5:46.17 (alpine marathon)

We got to Reggio Emilia at around 8 p.m. There was just enough time to go for a walk to stretch out cramped legs and enjoy a simple, hearty meal. Bec was still looking fresh and very pretty, even after nearly seven hours in the car, while I was a wreck. We could see that this town had a vibrant nightlife so I felt bad that I was ruining Bec's holiday by hitting the hay so early, but she swore she was having fun.

In no time at all we were on the road again, driving another 100 kms along the back roads of Tuscany as the sun began to rise. Around 6 a.m. we arrived at the small village of Busana – very quaint, very Tuscan. The organisers of the marathon were welcoming when they realised we were the 'crazy Australians' – I got some slaps on the back and big grins.

The race took off without too much ceremony. We looped around the narrow streets of the town for a few minutes, cramming through a few stone alleys, before we were off down a hill, on a road that took us away from the village. We ran along leafy trails, and up steep roads, then off into the trees again. We passed through villages and I felt like we were going in circles until, after about 10 kms, we were running past Busana again, but now at the top of the town.

We started to ascend the mountain that dominates the northern side of the town. We wove along roads and tracks, getting higher and higher. My legs were burning. I was surrounded by strong runners, but it was clear that the really good ones were already miles ahead. I walked a bit, but did my best to keep moving at a constant pace. As we ran into the forest once more, I found myself on a very steep dirt track. My head was down, but I glanced up every so often to see if the ridge was near. I came around another bend and there ahead, on top of a stump, was Bec! She'd gone for a run and followed the markers till she found a spot to wait.

'Hey!' I said, trying not to sound too defeated.

'Hi,' she said with a grin. 'I wasn't sure if you'd stopped.'

'Well, I sure want to, but I've got a ways to go yet. We haven't even made 15 kms.

She jumped down and gave me a hug. 'C'mon, I'll run with you.'

Up and up we went, chatting to some of the runners who understood English. Bec lasted a few kilometres before she realised she had a long way to go back. I continued wearily up the hill. I'd thought that this course would be easier than Zermatt because the highest point was halfway through the race and only about 1700 metres above sea level, a rise of around 1000 metres from the start. But the course was so extraordinarily steep that I couldn't get up any momentum or speed. I just wasn't getting to the top fast enough, and my energy stores were waning while time was ticking away.

We emerged from the forest near a lake, where families picnicked and kids played with toy boats. The bald top of the mountain was visible above the next tree line, complete with swirls of mist. I could just make out a trail – ants marching to the top. There were only around 500 runners in the race, but it felt like they were all in front of me. As I pushed up the hill, emerging from the last lot of trees, I was practically frothing at the mouth, shaky with exhaustion. I was pushing my hands down on my knees, trying to dig each strike into the side of the hill. About 300 metres from the top, I stalled. I stood up straight, rock-still on the path. I could not go on.

My watch said I had only come 24 kms in 3:30. I would normally be finished by now. And there was still so far to go.

Tuscany, in all its glory, was in front of me. Forests, fields, lakes. It struck me that I was on top of the world, for the second time in two days. 'Look where I'm running today!' I said into my camera. I thanked my lucky stars that I had taken on this adventure. If I could force my body up another 300 metres, I'd be at the top of this bloody hill, then there'd only be the steep decline to go.

After a couple of minutes, with the encouragement of passing stompers, I shook myself loose and continued up the hill. Ten minutes more and I was high-fiving some random marshal at the peak. I started to run again, as did others around me. It was a steep drop on either side, but with stunning views both ways. A blanket of clouds hugged the mountain below the crest on the western side, while to the east, the countryside extended out to the horizon. It was surreal to look down to the left and feel like I could step out onto that thick cotton wool, or dive into fields of gold on the right. The fantasy had my heart pattering as quickly as my feet were hitting the narrow path.

I descended quickly, trying not to slip. I was passing more runners now, though we were fairly well spaced out. I didn't even try to put the brakes on. One misstep and I could have twisted my ankle, yet I was going faster and faster. I skipped over rocks and jumped a couple of fallen trees. At one point there was a hairpin turn in the track, so I just put my right hand out for the nearest tree, grabbed the trunk and used it as a hinge to swing me around the corner. I was running faster than I had in two days. Instead of hearing my watch register a kilo-metre every 8–12 minutes, it was beeping at me every 3–4 minutes. I was absolutely legging it!

Down, down I went. I couldn't look away for a second or I would fall. I saw a couple of runners stack it ahead of me and others who were badly grazed, limping or bleeding. A couple of competitors were running ahead and I linked into them. We were running so quickly, it felt like I wasn't in my body any more – I was a machine among other machines. After a while, I wasn't even worried about slipping. I just let myself go, falling down the side of that mountain.

I ran across the line into Rebecca's arms, finishing in 5:46. When I stopped, my heart was pounding and my body was shaking. I sat down, my eyes skiting all over the place, still trying to find the next rock, the next tree, the last footfall. It was a strange feeling and it took me a while to calm down.

Soon we were on our way again. It was a hot day and as we drove north to Milan, we passed winding rivers where the locals splashed around, trying to cool off. On impulse, Bec pulled the car over and we headed for the cool mountain water, the best substitute I could think of for an ice bath. I lowered myself in over the rocks and sighed as the chill seeped into my legs. In the past week Bec had helped me more than she could ever know. I would miss her.

Two mountain marathons in two days. I was a little bit broken but far from defeated.

Bec drove to Milan while I slept and then shouted us a nice hotel for our last night together. The Westin was by far the ritziest place I'd stayed in on my tour. We ate Japanese and watched Spain win the World Cup.

The following morning I drove Rebecca to Milan's Malpensa Airport. As I dropped her off, we were both quiet.

'I don't much want you to go,' I admitted.

'I know. I don't want to go either. I almost wish . . .'

'Yeah, I know. But you have to get back to your holiday. We'll stay in touch, right?' I was beginning to feel forlorn.

'Of course. You owe me a date when you get back to Melbourne.'

I kissed her, hugging hard. I watched her enter the building and sat for a minute, wondering if I'd ever see her again. *Sure you will, mate.* That week had been one of the sweetest of my life. How lucky I was.

I drove to Nice via Turin and Cuneo. Getting lost in Torino, as the locals call it, I realised how much longer this drive was going to be. It was no fun navigating by myself. I usually don't mind driving solo in foreign countries. It's not that hard – one road connects to another, petrol stations are universal, road rules pretty similar. But now I felt lonely. I sang to myself, but without Rebecca laughing next to me, it sounded hollow, forced.

From Cuneo, I picked my way across the Italian Alps, passing right through Limone, the village where my stepfather was born. Jim was only a year old when my *nonna* (grandmother) took him all the way to Australia to follow my *nonno*. Jim had been back to visit Nonna Netta and his aunty, Zia Franka, a number of times, and after he passed away, I made a pilgrimage to Limone to honour his memory. I loved the tiny ski village and enjoyed meeting my great-grandmother and great-aunt. I came back the following year with Alexis and Mum. That was more than a decade ago and I hadn't been back since.

Even though I was a long way from Nice, and I hadn't planned it, I stopped the car. Walking up the winding streets, searching my memory for the path to my aunty's house, passing ski shops and restaurants, I came to an intersection that I recognised. I looked across the alley and stared at the old stone structure. A painter walked out onto the landing above the steps and looked at me so I was forced to say something; I asked if he knew where Nonna Netta's house was.

'*Questa é casa della Netta? Nonna Netta?*'

The man looked at me strangely.

'Giacomo Nasi . . . I'm his son . . . from Australia.' My Italian sucked, so I gave up.

Then the man's eyes sparked. 'Aha! *Australiano! Nipote di Franka?*'

'*Si, si, Franka!* Where?'

He pointed down the street, but then came down and led me down the road. '*Netta é morto*,' he told me with some hesitation.

I recognised the word, and the look in his eyes said the rest. 'It's okay, I know she is dead.'

I waited while he went to another house and brought my aunty back. She was old, but still looked very lively. She recognised me – a real surprise, as I had given her no warning of my arrival – and hugged me, prattling away in Italian. Before I'd even tried to speak to her, she dragged me down the street to a group of neighbours. Zia Franka spoke as little English as I did Italian, so one of the younger women translated for us. After a bit of banter, she took me by the arm again and we wandered down the old cobbled street.

We caught up on news and she pinched my arm a few times and gave me lovely cherub-cheeked smiles. But I really couldn't stay. I said my goodbyes and she walked me to my car. Zia was still waving as I drove off down the winding mountain road.

Something quite unexpected happened in mid July. I'd all but given up on getting sponsorship for my year. Every time Nick McCormack, my PR friend, or I spoke to the big brands about using my journey as a vehicle to promote shoes and GUs and that sort of thing, they told us they would have got more value from it if they'd been on board at the start. But back in December, they'd told me to come back to them when I was underway, if I was still in one piece.

Lesson learnt. Big brands only want to support assured success. There was nothing sure about the outcome of my journey and I didn't promise any more than I could deliver. That had meant no sponsor dollars for me.

My good friend Matt Jeffers had been living with his girl, Chloe, over in the Cayman Islands. He had been spruiking my escapades to anyone who would listen and one chap took a particular interest. Kenneth Krys, of Krys & Associates (now KRyS Global, a corporate recovery and insolvency company) decided that he should help me. Ken is an ultra runner himself. He's a a powerhouse, not super-fast but unflappable in his determination to conquer a challenge. He has completed the prestigious Marathon des Sables.

We spoke on the phone and realised we had a lot in common. I mentioned the end-of-year Antarctic Ice Marathon and he said he'd be interested in joining me. Finally, Ken committed to a corporate sponsorship of US $10 per race mile for my year, which rounded out to about US $15 000. Even better, he didn't apply any unnecessary restrictions on my style of travel or my behaviour. He basically said: 'Keep doing what you're doing, it's amazing!'

He did ask, though, that I shift my charitable focus to include a group that was important to him, so I included Facing Africa in my fundraising efforts. Facing Africa helps kids suffering from a disfiguring malnourishment disease called NOMA. The disease affects children in third-world countries, particularly in Africa, leaving vicious infections in the bone structure of their faces. Most kids die from the infection. Some live, but they're often so monstrously disfigured that their communities reject them. Facing Africa tries to save these children by aiding in reconstructive surgery and initiatives to train doctors to perform these surgeries.

I had to take the car all the way back to Spain, or I'd be charged $1000 in transfer fees. On the way to Barcelona I had a little break in the French countryside with some old friends: Mohit, Joseph and Florence. It was a real summer holiday, with cheese, wine and laughter. My legs were still toast, but my mind was reset and even though I had a very long road ahead, I felt refreshed. After 10 days in my own set of wheels, I was really going to miss this little Ford. But I had a plane to catch.

30

MONGOLIA SUNRISE TO SUNSET MARATHON

22 July, Lake Hovsgol, Mongolia

12:55.26 (100 kms – second place)

I arrived at Domodedovo Airport with a day to kill in Moscow. That seemed like a great idea until I felt the sweltering heat of a 40°C day kicking in – at 7 a.m.! There's not a lot of air-conditioning in Moscow, as there's rarely a need for it, so when a really hot day comes calling, people just keel over. I caught a train into town, nearly expiring in the heat with the effort of carrying all my bags, and spent six hours in an internet café keeping cool with their air-con, such as it was. So much for seeing Moscow!

I got to Sheremetyevo Airport with plenty of time but the national airline, Aeroflot, not known for its punctuality, kept us waiting for four hours, meaning I'd miss my connecting flight in Ulaanbaatar (UB, capital of Mongolia). I wanted to complain, but I was fairly sure the Russians would sooner lock me up than provide any level of customer service. At least I had a chance to speak to Rebecca while I waited. She was in Croatia, having a lovely time.

Russia to Asia. Another flight, probably the worst one yet. Aeroflot is not my friend.

The flight to Mörön was taking off as we landed. Then more drama – it turned out I didn't have a visa, just a letter of invitation to the marathon, so the customs officials wanted to send me back to Moscow.

I argued and pleaded and contemplated crying, but I was confident this was not the first time a clown like me had shown up without the correct paperwork. I handed over a wad of cash and the problem was suddenly solved.

I teamed up with a group of runners in the same boat as me. A quick trip into town – and another wad of cash – secured us a flight to Mörön, then we wandered around the main strip of UB. I gotta tell ya, it's not a pretty place. After an hour, I was done. We ate, then headed back to the airport for my fourth flight in 36 hours.

Mörön Airport was just a landing strip with a little box for processing people. A small minibus took us to Lake Hovsgol, and I ended up in the front passenger seat, which I thought was a bonus – until we got moving and I realised that this was going to be the most uncomfortable, sickening bus ride ever. For five hours, we bounced along barren dirt tracks. When the sun went down, the lurching drive became even worse. I thought I'd throw up all over the windscreen about a dozen times as old mate driver was never going to stop for me to hurl on the side of the road. It sucked.

Eventually we got off the green desert (the steppe), so at least there were trees around. It was late when we finally arrived. We went to our *gers* (wooden tents) and passed out.

I slept like the dead, but when I woke, I didn't want to get up. I was crushed. I hadn't recovered physically from those two tough alpine marathons. My legs felt bruised on the inside and I hadn't run during the long travel time.

We all descended on the main log pavilion for breakfast. The number of runners had swelled overnight so that there were about 70 people from across the world clustered at the tables, eating a simple breakfast of bread and cakes, and rubbing their eyes. We were all spent from our journeys.

It was a glorious morning so I wandered down to the edge of the lake as the mist burnt away to reveal its huge expanse – 136 kms in length and 36 kms across, in a huge national park. I was about as far from the world I knew as I could possibly get. This was seriously remote.

The Mongolians were friendly in a stoic kind of way. They weren't quick to smile, but any request was given due consideration. Mongolia is really just opening itself up to tourism and the rest of the world, and it seems that the people are fearful of their environment being plundered. As their country is bordered by China and Russia, two well-known heavy consumers of natural resources, that worry is probably justified. Plus American, English and Australian mining companies are trying to tap their reserves. They're an economic target, ripe for the picking. If I were Mongolian, I'd be worried about my country too. The sons and daughters of Genghis Khan had turbulent times ahead of them.

Over the next couple of days, we went walking and running around the nearby forest. The focus of the race is to raise awareness for the lake, reminding us of our duty to protect such wonders. It became apparent that while some people were there to seriously race, most just wanted to soak up the atmosphere. Everyone took advantage of the wild pony rides and a few brave souls even took to the water. If your toe touched the lake, you were guaranteed to shiver uncontrollably. It was the height of summer, but the altitude was very high in an area plagued by bitterly cold winters. Although, the air was warm enough, the lake remained as cold as a ghost's breath.

My phone rang unexpectedly out by the lake – there was a newly installed antenna at the south end of the park – and it was Rebecca, calling me from a beach in Croatia. I missed her a lot right then, yet I was reassured by the fact that she hadn't completely moved on either. I stood by the water skimming stones, wishing I could share this experience with her.

My room-mates were Maurice, the American businessman who lived in Hong Kong, Israel, the American ex-soldier who lived in England; and Ramón, the pharmaceutical salesman from Barcelona. Dinners were fun and the chatter between the runners was exciting once people settled in. No one knew what to expect from the race, even after the organising team ran through the details a few times.

We were all feeling pretty nervy when we were woken at 4 a.m. on Wednesday to get to the start line. I was as ready as I would ever be, with a new backpack full of survival kit. 'Just in case,' they said.

The race itself is called the Sunrise to Sunset Marathon, known as the world's most beautiful 100-km run. Not quite in keeping with the name, they wanted to begin the race before sunrise, so we set off at 5 a.m. We ran through a forest for a while, then north along the edge of the lake, up a few mountains, down to the lake again and back to the camp. That would tick off the marathon distance. Those who were to run the full 100 kms would refresh and run out again, heading south this time.

With head torches glowing, we blundered our way through the forest. It was a dangerous path, and we had to concentrate so as not to fall. When we emerged on the road, I knew I was on track. I steamed along the stony roadway, looking for little lights bobbing ahead, hoping the sunrise was not too far off. I came across the edge of the lake and kept moving, seeing the grey of the horizon. There were a few people ahead and a lot more dots of light following far behind.

Up a muddy road, I charged the first hill. I could see people moving far above, the front runners being led along by a pacer – a white horse. They were already a long way off, so I had no need to worry about them. I was near a couple of the Singaporean runners though, so I settled into a seesaw with them – they'd pass me, then I'd pass them. It was wet and cloudy, with mist engulfing us.

At the top of that first big rise, I looked around to see the lake. Nothing. We had emerged above the clouds that sat right across

Hovsgol, off into the horizon. It was clear where I was standing and clear above, but I could see only clouds below. I ran over the crest, then down the other side, straight back into the blanket of clouds.

I was running alone most of the time, but every so often I would come across another guy trudging along. Ewin, one of the Singaporean guys, seemed to be my main competitor in this race. We rolled along paths and broken roads together, through fields and over logs. Up, up, up, then down and down and down. My feet were sucked into the sludge on the swampy track and I nearly came to a halt. We were only 15 kms into the race and it seemed to have taken a lifetime to get there.

And yet there was worse to come. Ewin and I crossed the side of a mountain, through fields of wild blossoms. We traversed a river and within seconds I lost sight of him. I looked for markers and could barely make out the fluorescent pink splashes of paint on trees and stumps that guided us. At one stage I was following a stream bed that trickled down the side of another mountain, winding through a tangle of trees. I picked up a branch and used it as a walking stick, but it felt futile. I pushed on cresting again and heading down into the pea-soup fog.

I couldn't see more than a couple of metres ahead of me, but I didn't want to slow down too much. Then I took a tumble. I got up, disoriented and confused. All I knew for sure was that I was in a rain cloud, on the side of a mountain, somewhere in Mongolia.

I had no idea where I was going. It was easy to say the lake was a huge landmark, but it was a landmark that I couldn't see. I called out. For a fleeting moment I thought I might well have a use for the waterproof clothing and the survival kit in my backpack. But my room-mate Maurice bounded out of the thick gloom. 'Follow me!' he cried as he powered down the mountain.

With a huge sigh of relief I followed him. It wasn't long before we were out of the cloud and passing Mongolian volunteers once more. They stood by their horses and passed us cups of water. A while later we found a fire track, then a broken road and the main sandy lake road we had run along earlier that morning. I lost Maurice, but my speed on the flat meant I caught up to Ewin again. We were only minutes apart coming into the 42-km marathon finish. Our supporters were all there waiting and clapping. It turned out we were running fourth and fifth, with Simon the Kiwi finishing first, followed by two local lads. Only the Kiwi had pushed on for the 100 kms.

Ewin was gone again in a flash. *Sneaky bugger*, I thought. I changed my wet socks and used some tissues to soak up the water in my shoes, then I was away again, feeling fairly light-footed. As I covered the next 8 kms to halfway, something switched off in my head. I was completely spent. I was walking and struggling to even keep pace doing that. I had a long way to go and no drive to get there, so I was in a bit of a pickle.

'Okay. C'mon. You can't give up now, buddy.' I was pleading with myself. I did a maintenance check of my body and realised it was still fairly willing; I just had to get my head around the fact that it had taken me six hours to get to the halfway point. I swallowed a GU and pulled out my secret weapon. My iPod. I never use it during marathons, but I figured I was allowed to if I was running more than 50 kilometres. The thumping bass of Daft Punk filled my head and silenced the voices that were whining in pain. Waves of power began to pulse down through my legs.

'Okay, dickhead,' I muttered to myself. 'It's about time you showed me what you're really made of. Barry! Wally!' I said fiercely to my two legs, deciding they now needed names. 'You guys are *not* done. You still have a fair bit of work ahead of you and this is no time to be going to sleep. I know you're tired, but I trained you for this. You were built to run like this. You are the pistons of this motor. You are the wheels on the STEAM TRAIN. You are the MACHINE'S LEGS. I AM A MACHINE!'

And, with that, I was running again. I repeated these messages incessantly. I found empowerment in this mantra. I clicked through the kilometres. On one rise ahead, I thought I saw movement. Ewin, perhaps? I would chase him down like a rabbit, I decided. I would not give in till I caught him. When I passed a teepee of broken branches, colourful ribbons tied all around, I circled it twice, believing the tale that these shaman pyres would bestow blessings on those who respected them. As I left the road and hit a trail again, I saw a flash of colour in the distance and I knew my man was in reach.

I ran and marched and ran again. Every so often I would glimpse the rabbit and it would propel me on. The speck became a shape, and then the shape became a man. As we came to the 65-km aid station I caught him. He was still running, slowly and deliberately, barely breaking his stride, but I was faster on the flats. I just needed to stay with him across the next lot of mountains. We seesawed for a while, then I pulled up next to him.

'Hey, buddy. I can't chase you any more. How about we just run together?'

He looked at me with exhaustion clearly written across his face. 'Yeah, man, this racing is too hard. Let's go together.'

It made all the difference. With our forces combined, we made good time. We came out of the hills and back down to the edge of the lake, far south of the camp. It was the best view we'd had all day: the lake shimmered silver under a blue sky, ringed by thick green forest. A herd of yaks munched lazily nearby.

When we got back to the last road, we'd been running for 10 hours. We were both shattered, but I knew I still had speed left in me. Ewin had consistency, though, and he seemed never to need a walking break. I needed them far too often. Eventually I moved away from him, running a kilometre, then walking 100 metres, over and over until I started to see familiar faces from the camp. Rain began to fall, but I was like an ox, muscling my way home. I was told later that I looked unstoppable, but the truth was I was just hell-bent on getting to the damn finish line.

Every time I turned, I expected to see Ewin nearly on top of me again, but I was slowly putting distance between us. I was getting more confident that I would finish second and I let the Daft Punk album *ALIVE 2007* click over to the start, ready to play for the 10th time. Any time I turned off the music, I felt like I would fall flat on my face, but when the ear buds were in and those massive beats punched into my brain, my legs drove into the ground, again and again and again.

When I was within half a click of the finish line, I slowed to a walk. As I crossed the line, 100 kms complete, I gifted the race to Tribal for all their support: 'Second place. All for YOU – BANG!' They were having their annual awards night on Saturday and there was no sweeter way to tell them how much they meant to me.

The full Sunrise to Sunset Marathon took me 12:55, 40 minutes behind the winner and only two minutes ahead of Ewin. The last runners came in well after the 24-hour cut-off.

When I stepped in the lake, I yelped like a child. I knew it was good for me and that I would never enjoy an ice bath in such beautiful surroundings again, but I also valued my manhood and I began to think I wouldn't keep it much longer if I stayed in such freezing temperatures.

We got back to UB in one piece. I had a night in a nice hotel as part of our package and that afternoon we went out to a restaurant for a big meal and a lot of back slapping and congratulations for going the distance.

When I woke the next morning, my stomach was churning. I spent some time on the toilet and hoped the cramps would pass but to no avail. Quite a few of our party were sick – the food we'd eaten the night before seemed fine, but hygiene is not highly regarded in Mongolia, and in our depleted physical states, it was bound to catch up with us.

Sick as I was, it was time to move on, so I got on a train and chugged slowly north, crossing back into Russia.

31

SIBERIAN INTERNATIONAL MARATHON

7 August, Omsk, Russia

3:58.59

On the train I got a whole lot sicker. Maybe it was the none-too-clean toilets. Maybe it was the previous three weeks of beating my body into the ground. I certainly hadn't taken my health seriously enough through the month of July, so I guess I had it coming. Whatever the reason, I was using the toilet at least once an hour.

Siberia is a huge place, so to cross each section of the Trans-Siberian Railway takes between 10 and 20 hours. That first section, from Mongolia into Russia, is actually called the Trans-Mongolian and it brings a lot of Mongolians to Ulan-Ude for work. The carriages then connect with the Trans-Siberian line and continue on along the main east–west route. It was a scenic journey while the sun was out, with the cleared hills and landscape glowing gold in the late-summer sun. I was heading to Irkutsk, on a fellow runner's recommendation.

No one in my carriage spoke much English. I did my best to connect with a few Mongolian lads, but they were more interested in watching movies on my laptop than anything else. I ate simple fibrous food, downing noodles and plenty of fluids, but that just made the cramps worse. My computer died quickly and with no way to power it up again, the time went very slowly.

I spent the next few days negotiating train trips, travelling from Irkutsk to Tomsk, a university city. I'd squeezed in a side trip to Olkon Island, on picturesque Lake Baikal. Even though I was still very ill, it was a phenomenal experience, shared with an Aussie girl, an Italian and a Frenchman. I thought a lot about Rebecca. I wrote to her, a rare handwritten effort, redrafting my letter a few times.

Looking out the window at the vast Taiga forests, seas of thick dark green spread out in every direction, I felt very small in this big wild world. I began to question why the hell I was out here. I guess I wrote to Bec hoping it would also dissipate my loneliness. I had felt very connected during our short time together, but now I was lost. There were not enough good reasons to give up on the journey, but looking at the magnificence of this forest sure made me wish I was sharing it with someone.

There was only one hostel in Tomsk, and I thought I'd meet a few travellers there to share a meal with. I was wrong. The hostel was empty except for me, and at 7 p.m. the receptionist told me she was going home for the night and asked me not to wreck anything while she was gone.

Bugger. Still no one to talk to.

Nonetheless, the more I walked around Tomsk, the more I liked it. The town sits above a winding river, overlooking a long lush valley. The older people looked like they'd all become accustomed to hard times. The youth wandering the streets seemed as carefree as any other kids I'd seen around the world. It made me look at the Russians in a very different light. Their cities, their kids, their attitudes were much in line with the rest of the world, but they just didn't seem that connected to the rest of us. Maybe it's because Russia is such a behemoth of a country, and until you visit, you don't realise that much of the news we see come out of there is filtered and represents State opinion, not the people's view. As elsewhere, the regular Russians just want everyone to get along. They want their children to get an education and to see more of the world. They want opportunities and freedom.

I went on a nice long run the following morning. When I got back, it was train time again. I'd timed it badly, because 12 hours later I got off the train at midnight. I hadn't been able to book a hostel in Omsk, but I figured I'd be fine, and that once I got there I'd find a bed. Maybe I'd even stay in the railway station for a night – I'd heard that the big stations all have beds for travellers.

I walked up the stairs to the top of the old station and wandered into a reception area for a quirky little hostel called the Resting Rooms. I sighed with relief as the guy in front of me was handed a key – they had some beds! I put on my brightest smile, asking for a room.

'*Nyeto*,' the woman said abruptly.

'Nothing?' I replied incredulously.

'*Nyeto*,' she repeated, putting a sign on the desk and crossing her arms. I asked her for some directions, but she made it clear that she didn't speak any English and she wasn't interested in helping me.

I walked downstairs to the station waiting room. I didn't know what to do. While there was fat chance of wi-fi, it probably wouldn't help. I was a fair way out from the city; I thought I'd have to just try going door to door at hostels once I got into town. I'd previously had no luck even finding a map of Omsk, let alone a hotel under $200. It was Thursday night and I was racing on Saturday, so I didn't have a lot of time to get this right.

A Russian guy started speaking to me in passable English. He was waiting for a train and wanted to chat to kill some time. He told me that I was only the second native English speaker he'd ever conversed with. He also told me that it was too dangerous to be walking around outside after dark. I'd get mugged or worse, he said. He encouraged me to just sleep at the station itself for the night. I looked around to see many other people bedded down for the evening, strewn across metal benches. I had nowhere else to go.

I rugged up and got myself horizontal, one hand on my bags and one eye open, for the next five hours, hoping the new day would bring better tidings. When light began to fill the large waiting room, I got myself together again, strapped on my bags and went out to look for a bus or a taxi . . . but to where? I tried to ask some cab drivers where to go and just got shakes of the head. By 6 a.m., all my requests for help seemed too hard so I gave up and walked into town – 6 kms – with bags on my shoulders. Soon my upper body was just pulsing with pain. But I found a dive with a room to rent and put my head down for a few hours.

I stumbled across some race organisers in the central square and slowly everything came together. A couple of phone calls and a quick cab ride and I was at the expo, signing up for the race. I wandered around the streets for a while, trying to appreciate the city a little bit – people were soaking up the sun and looking happy enough, for Siberians anyway. I had a meagre meal that evening.

When I got to the start line the next day, in the big square next to the blue-domed Omsk Dormition Cathedral, I discovered I'd left my GUs back in my room. Not a good sign. The crowd of marathon runners streamed out of the square and headed towards the river. The first half was relatively standard, with a few extra twists and turns. The racers were mostly Russian and I sidled up to one young guy running in his military boots and a blue-and-white striped muscle top. Fifteen kms in, he was still hammering along as though he was in a pair of Nikes.

After halfway we crossed an extremely long bridge, out and back again, and then headed north from the city. By this time the heat had really kicked in, somewhere around 34°C, and I was feeling groggy. It was only my third run since the 100 kms in Mongolia, and I was starting to acknowledge that my recovery wasn't quite complete. I felt sick again, and looked for another toilet. When that business was done, I ran on and found that I had lost my pace, struggling even to run 5.30 per km. I was feeling weaker and weaker, and the sun was a bright spotlight, focused solely on me, and I slowed to a walk, looking for anything that looked like shade. This wasn't turning out the way I'd hoped.

I grabbed at anything I could eat or drink to pump my energy up – flat Coke, wedges of orange. Someone handed me a wedge of lemon, which I thought was a terrible idea, until I bit into it. Unbelievable! It was sweet and refreshing and gave me something to focus on other than my aching body. A little ways later, though, and I was at the side of the road, throwing up all that I had consumed over the past 30 kms. Spectators edged my way, looking at me with dismay. But I lifted myself up, waved weakly and got moving again.

I kept it simple. I looked for the 1-km markers. I focused on what was achievable. If I worried about the finish line, 10 kms away, I would have given up there and then, but I could walk and I could move. I trotted for a few hundred metres at a time, then walked as forcefully as I could muster in the same direction, then stumbled into a run again. Closer and closer I came to the end, 1 km at a time. It was lucky there were so many drink stations on the way back, as it gave me something else to aim for. Another hour passed like that before the end finally came into view. Even with a kilometre to go, I had to walk. It wasn't my day, but at least it was nearly over.

I don't remember finishing, which is strange because I have extremely vivid memories of all my other finishes. I think I was just so happy to be done that I tuned out to the cheering. Maybe it was just too traumatic – 3:58.59 of punishment.

I staggered back to my hotel afterwards and convinced the receptionist to let me lie down for a while before she booted me out. I had a train to catch that evening, but I could barely walk. I sent a text to Bec and she must have sensed my hurt as she gave me a call. I needed that. I needed to hear a kind voice.

I dragged myself onto the train later that night, facing another 36-hour journey. My legs hurt so much that I didn't think I'd sleep, but this time fatigue won and I passed out for nearly 10 hours. I was feeling very unsure of myself on the last leg of my train ride. My legs were toast and when I wasn't throwing up, I was spending far too much time sitting on dirty train toilets.

'If you'll just hold out for another few months,' I told my legs, 'I promise you don't have to obey me any more. You don't have to do anything I say. In fact, I'll totally be your slave and get regular massages and pretty smelling oils rubbed into you. Just 21 more races.'

Man, I thought I was cracking up. I was definitely getting depressed. I'd come off such a huge high in Mongolia, but I was losing my nerve. Sleeping on a bench hadn't helped either. It struck me that I was nearly 60 per cent of the way through my epic marathon around the planet and now I'd hit the proverbial wall. There was bound to be a period of doom and gloom on this trip, although I'd thought it was most likely to be a result of low funds or major injury.

I think part of my depression came from the fact that I had run only 20 kms in the 10 days before the last race. I wasn't running, so I wasn't injecting the endorphins I'd become accustomed to straight into my brain. I couldn't run on the trains, so I was sedentary for huge chunks of time, which wasn't helping my state of mind.

I needed to break this trip down in the same way as I approached a marathon. I needed to find the equivalent of 1-km markers, rather than worrying so much about the 21 marathons ahead of me. If I could just get to the next city, or get on the next plane, I'd be sorted. The Helsinki Marathon was a full week away, so I had time to recover. I just had to get to the start line and the rest would take care of itself. In Helsinki, more people spoke English. And there was real food in the supermarkets – polished apples and fat red tomatoes, not like those grey bloody carrots I'd seen in the Russian grocers, or the cheese-encrusted chicken fillets that looked potentially life-threatening in the current heatwave. Just get to Helsinki and everything will be okay, I told myself.

There was one last thing. I had given myself a mighty gift, a very selfish gift really. I had pretty much tossed in the towel of real life, leaving it all behind to find something different, and maybe find out something more about myself. Not many people are in a position to just drop everything and go. They have mortgages, careers to manage; they have partners and children, siblings or parents who rely on them. Not many people have the opportunity to take on a huge personal challenge like this, or to see the world like I had.

Then there were all the people who were just trying to stay alive. I'd seen them in Egypt and India, in China, Mongolia, Rwanda and Morocco. Even here in Siberia. There were no options for these people. There was no education that might open a few doors. There was just subservience and subsistence. Those kids picking up flotsam from the river in Mumbai. The bones of those children in Rwanda. They would never have the opportunities that I took for granted. Life was decided for them, not by them. I had to make the most of my opportunities, if for no other reason than the fact that I had them in front of me. If I could go on, I should go on.

I had to lift. If this was my wall, I had to find a way to smash through the barrier in my mind. I had to believe I had every right to be here. Not only that, but I had to believe that this was the very moment I'd been waiting for. Just like I did in a marathon, I began to covet the wall, because the wall is the real challenge. When the chips are down and everything in you says stop, you have to find that little voice that says, 'You can do it, man! You're a hero. Just keep going!' If you can find a way to keep going when all else fails, then you will always find the finish line. You will always achieve success in life.

That's the challenge of life itself: to just keep going.

Moscow was 42°C the day I showed up. Fires had been raging around the city and the air was thick with smoke. The little hostel I found had air-con – a massive win. I waited till late afternoon before I went exploring, but it was so hazy outside you couldn't see clearly across the road. I didn't want to breathe in too much of that crap, so I waited till the next day before I took a longer walk. I figured I'd meet a few other backpackers and plan a tour of the city with them, but guess what? I was the only bloody guest again! I love the history of cities like this, but they're also very big, and there was a lot to try to cover in just a couple of days. I kept my journeys to a maximum of two hours in consideration of my health.

A highlight was the Memorial Museum of Astronautics, the Russian space museum. As an Australian, I'd only ever been subjected to the history of space as reported by the United States. I knew plenty about the NASA space program and the first man on the moon, but I knew very little about the first human in space, Yuri Gagarin. He's a national hero to this day and I saw his mug on posters up in restaurants, cafés and hostels right across the country. I even learnt a little about the dogs they sent into space before him, both named Laika, who died a short time into their space flights. I looked at images of Yuri and film of his pre-flight talks and checks and decided he was the most intrepid adventurer I'd ever heard of. Every creature that had gone into space before him had died and yet he willingly entered the space race against the US. Imagine being the very first human to strap yourself to a rocket and go into the great abyss of space. How was he not absolutely peeing in his pants through that whole mission? Brave and ridiculously crazy. I felt like a regular church mouse in comparison.

It was time to go, flying to St Petersburg to get to Helsinki. I was done with trains for a while. The Russian leg of my journey had been memorable in so many ways but mainly for the fact that I now knew if I hit the wall, I'd bounce back.

32

HELSINKI CITY MARATHON

14 August, Helsinki, Finland

3:46.18

On my flight to Helsinki, I still didn't feel well. The scales in the last hostel had said I weighed 64 kg, down from 69 kg. That was distressingly light. I would eat better in Helsinki, surely.

When I got to the hostel, there was a message telling me that a friend from home would be in Finland at the same time as me. Cristina and I agreed to meet at the race expo, the very next day. I picked up my number there and the woman who handed it to me gave me a wide smile and said, 'Ah, your pretty friend was here looking for you!' I found her and I can't tell you how much Cristina's signature gorgeous smile, followed by an enormous hug, meant to me. It was a relief to be with someone who knew me, so I didn't have to explain myself, tell my story again or put on a front. We just wandered around and chatted about her adventures, my adventures, friends back home, all of it.

When I left her, agreeing to catch up later, I felt better than I had for weeks. It was as simple as seeing a friendly face. I just felt connected again. I didn't realise what a positive effect it'd had on me until the next morning, when I woke up with a smile on my face, feeling totally refreshed. And I wasn't sick. I used the toilet and everything seemed okay. I gave myself a little systems check and it felt like I might have come good at last.

That day, I knocked out the marathon. Cristina and her friend Alice came down and cheered for me. The run itself was fun, cruising about the city, then way out of town for a while before coming back.

It was an unusually warm day in Helsinki. I got very hot, and by the end of the race, I was taking walking breaks again, dismayed that even though I felt much better, my body wasn't up to the task of smashing it out. But I did feel good enough to try something new on this race – on the refreshment tables, along with Gatorade, chocolate and lollies, there were cups with strange things sticking out the top. It took me a couple of aid stations to register what I was looking at. They were gherkins! Pickles, sitting in cups of salt. I'd never seen anything like it, but I decided it'd be rude not to get in line with the local traditions. I grabbed one and took a big bite, needing to walk for a second so I didn't choke. It tasted great! I finished with a smile, mainly for my crazy cheerleaders. The girls were jumping and shouting as I came over the line and I really did appreciate their support.

Later that day, I had dinner with some locals followed by a wild night in the different bars around town. We kept downing these disgusting shots called 'Fishermen's Friends'. They were basically vodka mixed with the menthol lolly normally used to clear your sinuses. After five or six, a head cold was the least of your worries!

The following day a local girl I'd met took me on a tour of Helsinki; we took in some history, the popular places to shop and eat, and so on. Then with another group of friends, I got a ferry across to one of the nearby stone islands for a picnic. While we were sitting on these rocks, bathing in the summer sun, chatting about travel and the cooler things in life, I had the most pleasant moment of clarity. I was happy. Really happy. I was okay, had friends with me, old and new, plus now I had 32 marathons under my belt. I was really doing it.

Twenty marathons to go, with some of the greats yet to come. Berlin, New York, Cuba. So much yet to see and yet if time stood still, I was content, proud of how much I'd achieved.

33
REYKJAVIK MARATHON
21 August, Reykjavik, Iceland
3:21.35

Bus, plane, passport check, Oslo. Wait three hours, plane, passport, bus, Reykjavik.

I was excited about going to Iceland. As it's just a bit far out of the way and a lot too expensive, it quite often falls off Australians' radar. This was the furthest I'd be from my home in Melbourne, nearly 17000 kms and a couple of continents away. It was approaching the end of summer in Iceland, and it was bitterly cold. The whole island looked like a huge volcanic rock, with plenty of grassland and pretty mountains on the horizon. Reykjavik seems like a large tourist town, even though it is clearly home to more than just tour operators. The old stone buildings sit on an ancient harbour and there are no end of offers to go whale watching or puffin hunting.

I wanted to see whales if they were out there, so early one morning I paid my money and boarded a large cruiser. Out in the bay, we were directed to the flocks of birds floating around us and told what to look for. Sure enough, when a flock started diving to the surface and milling about in one area, the cruiser powered towards them and we were treated to the sight of a couple of minke whales breaching and feeding. There were no humpbacks, but I felt blessed to be able to tick another box in my life: Whales in the wild = ✓. Judging by the reactions of the captain and crew, it seemed we'd hit the jackpot, with half-a-dozen sightings in all, even though it was the end of the whale season.

Our RunLikeCrazy competition winner, Mel Bushby, joined me from London the following day. Mel was excited to be there and I was *really* excited to have another friendly face to spend time with. The marathon was a couple of days away, and was I taking it easy – I was still a bit shattered from the last race.

Saturday, race day. It was a quiet start in the middle of town, trailing straight out and looping the city a couple of times. I had a very strong run, but the story of this race isn't dramatically different from the others. I ran with a couple of very nice gents but each time I struck up a conversation with someone, I found myself leading them a little, then more, then too much, before I waved and was off. We ran around the bay a couple of times, across the city and through some gardens. It really was a pretty run and the sun kept us company until close to the end. Then, out near the old lighthouse in Seltjarnarnes, the headwind kicked up so powerfully that I thought I might have to walk the rest of the way back.

I got over the line, to Mel jumping about in her Viking helmet, waving the Boxing Kangaroo. I posted a time back near my best – 3:21. My legs were rattled, but I was in good spirits. I felt like my comeback from the brink of disaster was complete.

As it happens, the people of Reykjavik have an annual culture festival on the same day as the marathon – Menningarnótt. It's a big deal in those parts and up to 100 000 people participate in the fun. That's quite a lot for a country of only 320 000-odd people! After the race, Mel and I wandered up and down the main street, checking out the bands and a show of wildly painted Harleys, as well as a few traditional arts displays. It was certainly festive and it was plain to see that the locals were serious about their alcohol consumption, but the wind had picked up and we were chilled to the bone in no time. I didn't have much fun left in me, so we pulled the pin before the rain hit. The music and laughter around us didn't seem to die down till the wee hours though. Nothing was going to stop the Icelanders from tearing up their town!

It was great to have Mel with me to do some of the touristy stuff. We jumped on a bus tour and found ourselves wandering along the visible fault line of the North American and European tectonic plates. It was quite surreal, especially with their recent contribution to the volcanic activity afflicting the world. The rift valley was also the site of one of the original Viking parliaments. We were taken to shimmering waterfalls, gushing volcanic geysers and then to a centre for white-water rafting. Even though we had wetsuits on, it was the most horrifically freezing experience I have ever had, made worse by the fact that they kept throwing us in the drink. Still, more things on my bucket list complete:

Volcanic geyser = ✓

White-water rafting = ✓

Awesome Viking parliament = ✓

The last thing to do in Iceland was make a visit to the famous Blue Lagoon, the geothermal spa with the electric blue-coloured water. All I can say is they're very clever to limit everyone to three beers while in the spa. By the time I'd drunk mine, I was ready to sink under the water and melt into the silvery mud below. It was so relaxing, I thought I'd never be able to leave.

Blue Lagoon = ✓

33 marathons in 33 weeks = ✓

34

STAVANGER MARATHON

28 August, Stavanger, Norway

3:18.25

Another foreign country, another high school buddy. The old school tie had never been so helpful to me as it was in 2010. My story seemed to find my buddies in every nook of the world, so when I arrived in Oslo, I stayed with David Craig, his local bride, Els, and their bright-eyed young son, Aksel.

I'd also agreed to meet Doc John Barnes in Oslo. We'd stayed in touch after Roskilde Music Festival. We all hired bikes and cruised around for hours in the sunshine, visiting the Opera House and the Royal Palace. Dave then took us to his favourite area in Oslo, Frogner Park. He told us that whenever things had been tough for him, living so far from home, he'd come to the park to contemplate. And it was easy to see why. Built during the first half of the 20th century by Gustav Vigeland, the landscape is dominated by 212 bronze and granite statues of men, women and children depicted in all stages of life. Altogether they are said to represent the human condition, and if you look even for a little while, you find a statue that reflects your mood or personality. It's a remarkable place.

The Doc talked me into getting the train from Oslo to Stavanger on the west coast of Norway. I was into the idea, but thought it might take too long. As it turned out, it was worth going the long way around. It was the most spectacular train trip I'd experienced, winding through gorges and mountain passes, alongside fjords and forests. Our great conversation was constantly interrupted by the ever-changing scenery outside – the greenery was so vibrant and the mountains so breathtaking that it was like being in our own IMAX movie.

One of the things the Doc and I discussed was how I would psychologically handle going home. I told him it was the furthest thing from my mind, but as a clinical psychologist, John was interested in how my mental health would be post-2010.

'I noticed something strange when we caught up at Roskilde. After the race, you were babbling like your head was going to explode. Does that happen a lot?' he asked.

'I guess so. I'm always pretty excited after a race. Well, I'm physically shot, but my brain is working at a million miles an hour.'

John hesitated. 'The behaviour I saw is called "forced speech". It just means that your brain is sending more messages than your voice can communicate, so your ideas overlap and tumble out. In extreme cases you become incoherent, but in your case I just wanted to shake you and tell you to slow the hell down and think before you speak!'

'Okay . . . So, it's normal though, right? As a result of the excitement of finishing another marathon?'

'It is,' he continued. 'You're essentially pumping your brain with a tonne of endorphins and other chemicals, like serotonin, adrenaline and dopamine, which work together to make you feel good. That's why they recommend exercise and running as an antidepressant.'

'Yeah, I've read that and I think I've experienced it first-hand. Running pulled me out of a dark place after my divorce. It saved my life!'

'Okay, but I'm wondering what the cumulative effect will be when you return to Australia. Every week you're overloading your brain, which is where the forced speech comes into it. I'm not sure it would be healthy for you to just cut it off. Will you just stop running?'

'I don't think so,' I said slowly, not really worried, but thinking through the ramifications. 'But I'll have to have a rest, man. My body will most likely collapse, if I even make it that far.'

'I'd just suggest you consider what you'll do. I reckon you'll be due for a fairly obvious crash, so be a bit prepared for it.'

'Okay. Thanks, dude.'

'No probs. Hey, look at that ridiculously beautiful fjord, with the hot Norwegian mermaids dancing near those whales over there . . . Man, this is a great train trip!'

I didn't have any massive expectations for Stavanger. As far as I knew, it was just a fishing village. I'd read that the headquarters for a lot of offshore drilling operations were also in Stavanger. What I hadn't realised was that the oil companies were having a conference on the same weekend as the marathon; there was no accommodation under $500 a night for the Doc and me.

Once again, the Aussie network pulled together to help us. A friend from Melbourne hooked us up with her old schoolmate, Emma, and her husband, Joel. It was fantastic to be around Australians – I know that sounds tragic, given that I was trying to expose myself to new experiences and different cultures. But this was a much-needed patch of homegrown quips and humour that kept the demons of homesickness at bay and lifted my spirits. Soon I was the most relaxed man in Scandinavia.

I was going to need to stay relaxed, too, because I had another epic task in front of me. Before I was miserably sick for two weeks, I'd decided I needed to have another race in hand. That plan had served me well in the first six months, giving me that much-needed break in South America, plus the flexibility to go to remote places like Mongolia. So I'd considered a double-marathon weekend while in Scandinavia, as there was a cluster of them at that time of year, but in my later research, a possible hurdle had arisen. I'd phoned Rebecca.

'You remember I mentioned a race I was considering in Bornholm, Denmark? It would be the day after the race in Stavanger.'

'Yep, I remember. It seems you're doing a lot of double marathons this year. Is it really necessary?'

'It is if I want to stay on track. Especially if I want to got to Antarctica at the end of the year. Anyways, it looks like the marathon in Bornholm is actually an ultra-marathon. There is a 42-km option that begins at 1 p.m., or there's a 100-km kicking off at 7 a.m.'

Silence.

'So, it turns out that I could run the marathon in Stavanger, fly to Copenhagen, then get an overnight ferry to Bornholm. There are no direct flights that will get me there in time, but I'd make it by ferry.'

Silence.

'It could be quite exciting.'

Silence broken. 'Exciting? It could be *very* dangerous! It's one thing to run two marathons in two days, but a marathon and an *ultra* in different countries? And you're not getting much rest with all that travel. How will you recover? It just sounds crazy.'

'Yes, it does sound crazy, doesn't it?' That was the reaction I was aiming for. 'That's what's so awesome about it! No one would expect it. Hell, I don't even think I'll make it. But I love the gamble! It's all very RunLikeCrazy!' I was swelling with pride and bravado.

'It sounds like you've already made up your mind.'

'I have now.'

'I'm worried about you . . .' Bec's voice had lowered.

'Don't be.'

'Easier said than done.'

Now, some weeks later, I wasn't so enamoured with the idea, but I'd committed to it. I'd put a couple of kilos back on and was running more consistently again, so maybe I'd be okay.

The race participants met in Stavanger's sports stadium. There were only about 100 of us and it was definitely a low-key race. There was a little bit of cheering as we kicked off, racing around the athletics track once, then out and around the block, passing the entrance one more time; then as if from a sling shot, we took off through a couple of neighbourhoods and into some parkland to get into our race. It was like a scenic tour of Stavanger, showcasing the bays, the gardens, and a nearby forest.

Every so often I'd look at my watch and worry that I was going too quickly. I had plenty of kilometres ahead that weekend, so there was no point in crushing myself just yet. More water, more trees, more water again. Rain began to tumble down, becoming increasingly fierce with every step for about 5 kms, then it abruptly stopped. I was saturated from head to toe, my shoes squishing under me. Within the last 10 kms, I was flagging, but still running, so I tried not to slow too much. The sun burst through the clouds and reflected off the water to my right. It was enough to distract me for a moment as I looked in wonder.

The end came quickly enough. We forged through a few back streets, before emerging onto a main road and descending down towards the harbour at the centre of town. It was a brilliant place to finish, with plenty of supporters there to wave and cheer. I fell over the line. I'd had every intention of sandbagging in that race, saving something for tomorrow, but felt good, so I kept running. I'd knocked it off in 3:18.25.

Emma and Joel took us to a jetty and put me in the water to cool off; it hit me then that I was in one of the loveliest parts of the world I was ever likely to see. Little beach, cool fjord, towering mountains across the water. It was a magical sense of achievement to come to this remote city and soak up this atmosphere, even if it was only for 24 hours.

After a hot shower and another life-affirming meal I was bundled into the car and we gunned it out to the airport.

I was about to be on my own again but I had a packed lunch from Emma to keep me company, a fitting reminder of the excellent Australian hospitality my international network had provided.

35

BORNHOLM MARATHON
29 August, Bornholm, Denmark
10:28.32 (100 kms)

Copenhagen Airport to Copenhagen central. Then a bus or train to Køge to find the overnight ferry to Bornholm Island.

It all sounded simple enough, but I was on a train system I didn't know, going to a port I'd never seen and hoping the boat was there as described. I was also lugging around my life on two very tired legs, having punched out a respectable marathon time that morning. I sometimes wondered if a big part of my training that year came from walking about lost, lugging 25 kilos of baggage. Every time I strapped on those bags I gave a little sigh, either saying goodbye to another temporary home, or mentally preparing myself for another series of experiences in a strange new land.

My shoulders and back now hurt as much as my legs. If you'd slept upright as often as I did, you'd have a crook back too. For eight months now, I'd been twisting my body to get comfortable on planes, trains and buses, let alone various hostel beds. I spent a lot of time in transit lounges trying to stretch out my back, or lift my skull a few millimetres from my spine just to ease the compression. I had a dull ache at the base of my head and found the only relief came from ibuprofen products, like Nurofen or Advil, but these anti-inflammatory drugs are pretty tough on the stomach and work your kidneys a whole lot harder than they should, so I had to steer clear of them as often as possible. I was travelling on a knife edge with my health as it

228

was, so throwing random painkillers in the mix would've been just the nudge I didn't need. Better to suffer in silence and hope my conditioning would eventually supersede the discomfort.

By the time I got to Køge it was all but closed for the night. Instead of traipsing around looking for food, I thought I'd check in on the ferry first. When I'd booked my passage, there weren't any cabins, but now one was available. It was twice the cost, but still only €60, a small price for some privacy and rest.

It was nearing midnight, and I realised the only food I'd get was the cafeteria meals offered on the ferry. I picked up two pasta salads – it wouldn't serve as carbo loading, but nor would it make me too sick. I sat eating, staring into the ink-black night ahead, alone on a boat, one marathon just behind me and a 100-km race up ahead.

I snapped wide awake when the ferry hit the dock and had to work quickly to collect my things. I seemed to be the last person walking off the boat and I found a slightly anxious fellow, Brian, waiting for me outside the terminal. He'd been wondering if I was even on the boat. He was also running the 100 kms and didn't want to be late. We raced across the island. It was 6.15 a.m. and the race was to begin in 45 minutes – we had no time to lose!

We made small talk and I learnt that for centuries this area had been farmland, so it had its own unique heritage, having been swapped between the Danes and the Swedes a couple of times and occupied by the Nazis during World War II. We crossed from the port of Ronne, on the west side of the island, to the northern town of Tejn. It was a chilly morning, though the sun was up, and people were gathering in the registration tent to pin their numbers and stow some gear. There weren't a lot of us. I tried to just smile at all these strangers and get my head in the right space, but I felt like I was still in a dream. Things had happened so quickly since I woke up that I hadn't quite come to grips with my surroundings or situation.

We were off and out of town within minutes and the other runners were chatting among themselves and waving to their friends near the start. Runners are generally quite subdued at the beginning of ultra-marathons, but all the participants here were yabbering like crazy. I liked the atmosphere, but I didn't speak the language and I was still in too much of a haze to try to communicate.

I did finally chat to some nice lads and a big guy named Michael, who schooled me on ultra-marathon ethics, telling me about all the big runs he had done and giving me the history of their running club. The more I heard about them, the more I realised they were all completely nuts! The organisers of this race were responsible for an annual pilgrimage to Athens to take on the famous Spartathlon, a race that dismissed as many as 75 per cent of its runners each year, where completing the 245 kms in just 36 hours proved too gruelling for most. These guys were serious about their running.

The route was pretty, as the road meandered along the northern coast. I was concerned about the heat, but it soon became apparent that I had more pressing issues. My stomach was twisting and cramping, as though I'd eaten an eel. That was a terrible way to start a run, and within 5 kms I was looking for a secluded bush behind which to disappear.

After that near disaster, I couldn't find anyone to fall in step with. But my legs had finally loosened up enough to find a rhythm, rather than just stomping wearily along. Time passed slowly, through rustic little tourist towns. Each drink station was on a 5-km marker, which gave me a perfect target every half-hour. I just kept my head down and trucked along. And the scenery – it was exactly what I'd come to see, as we cruised through fields of golden wheat and passed ancient wind-mills with their sails billowing in the breeze. I'd found a little slice of heaven to run through.

At the 70-km mark, I'd just about had enough. I was passing through

Ronne again, the port I'd seen that morning, and I felt like I was dragging leaden balls along the road. This wasn't going to cut it with 30 kms to go, so with the next GU, I put my iPod on to try to re-energise, as I had in Mongolia. I found myself striding a little better and my mood began to change. I was getting angry again. I would not be defeated by this race. After seven hours of running, the thought of being out here any longer than I had to made me feel sick. It was time to run.

My pace picked up. With each checkpoint, I saw a significant improvement. My walking breaks became fewer and when I was running, my legs felt ready to gallop. I stopped being passed by runners and started getting some of my own back, drifting past marathon and ultra runners alike. People who had glided past me some 50 kms before were now on Struggle Street, just ahead. I came up quickly behind them, giving a little wave on the way past and then looked for the next bunny rabbit. I couldn't believe how much strength was still deep inside my legs. I had honestly limped along for more than 70 kms of the day, following on from 42 clicks the day before, and yet my brain took over as pilot and the machine got back to work. Each kilometre ticked by and now, as I headed east again along the top of the island, I knew I had all but nailed another epic weekend.

I tussled with a wiry-looking woman for a while, but with a last big heave I passed her through a small coastal town and then didn't stop running. When I cleared the 98-km mark, I paused for a photo, then gave my chest a belt with my clenched fist and fired my last salvo, tearing two more kilometres from my weary legs to bring me home in 10 hours and 28 minutes.

I was sore after the finish line, but I wasn't nearly as busted as I thought I'd be. A lot of strong runners sat about, gaunt and withdrawn, but they all looked like heroes. Kim, the race director, had graciously invited me to his home for the night. We shared a few stories over dinner, but it really wasn't long before the cramps kicked in and I was dragging myself up the steep stairs to bed.

36

MONTREAL INTERNATIONAL MARATHON
5 September, Montreal, Canada
3:27.56

I dropped into Paris on the way to Montreal. Clément was working in Luxembourg but had left a key with the neighbour, so I had a bed for the night. I missed my train out to the airport and arrived just in time to be bundled onto the plane as they were shutting the doors. I hated making my heart work unnecessarily during those close calls.

This was my first time in Canada. I'd come from reasonably cool conditions in Paris, so when I walked off the plane into a 30°C day, I was pleasantly surprised that summer hadn't quite left this neck of the woods. I went for a walk and was perturbed by my initial experience of a city that I'd heard so many good things about. Lots of people walking along the main shopping drag were extremely drunk and quite a few seemed under the influence of one drug or another. Apparently it was just a response to the heat, compounded by the fact that I was in the 'loose' part of town, straddling the border of the Latin Quarter and the Gay Village. This area was prone to wild parties, even in the middle of the week.

I floated about on Thursday and checked out a few parks – I needed to be outside. My New York pals Olah and Caz, and Katherine and Dave arrived on Friday, having made the long drive up. Olah was going to run this marathon with me and I can't tell you how happy it made me feel to know I'd be running with a mate.

On Saturday morning we went to the expo and picked up our numbers. I was meeting up with Nathalie, who had been following me online, sharing my story with her young family. She had been encouraged by friends to start running and had already knocked out a couple of half marathons that year. It was a very strange but good experience to have this family asking detailed questions about all my travels.

I met up with the team again. We went to Montreal's Little Italy for dinner, chomping down some very impressive plates of pasta. Montreal was growing on me. The French Canadians are quite a determined lot, maintaining a solid grip on their French ancestry. They seem to feel that they are more European than North American, but I couldn't help noticing that the buildings and the body shapes were a lot more representative of their American neighbours.

Race day rolled around. Olah was really amped, and that kind of energy is infectious. We were soon on a bridge near the Biodome, with a large number of very excited marathoners. Europe's 'The Final Countdown' was pumping out of the stereos and within seconds of arrival, we were trotting across the start line and heading towards the Montreal Grand Prix track. The course was like a long stroll around the city, meandering from island to mainland, through the city and around to the north of town.

The course merges with the half marathon, so after about two hours of running, we went from a slim stream of marathoners to a flood of foot traffic. It's always good to see more people out on the course, but when you hit a large group of runners that aren't moving as quickly as you, it breaks your rhythm.

We ticked along until the spectre of the Olympic Stadium began to loom. Olah was tired, but I'm sure that guy could dish out a cheesy grin even in the most dire of situations. We were on track for a solid sub-3:30 and began to pick up momentum right at the end. We caught sight of Dave, Kath and Caz just as we entered the stadium, but we were too close to home to stop and chat. Olah and I legged it to the line, cheering each other on, but also giving a shout to our dads. It was Father's Day in Australia.

Such a rush. 3:27.56, running side by side with one of the greatest guys I know. I was thrilled to share marathon number 36 with Olah and then to celebrate with friends. We met up later for dinner, and although we had all the best intentions of drinking a truckload of beer in reward for our efforts, a couple sufficed, with a lot of reminiscing about the great moments of the day.

After breakfast on Monday, the team was heading back to NYC. Olah dropped it into conversation that a trip to Cuba in late November was on the cards.

'For real? You could get there at the same time as me?'

'Yeah, that's what we're planning for. Hang with you a couple of days in Havana, then go do our own thing.'

I hadn't relished trooping around a strange place like Cuba completely alone, so the thought of having my good friends there made the prospect a whole lot more exciting. I hugged everyone. I would see them in New York for marathon 45 in early November, only a couple of months away.

Then it was back to the airport, and off to Paris once again. Montreal had been the sweetest surprise.

37

MARATHON DU MÉDOC

11 September, Médoc, France
5:21.36 (blind drunk)

Another night in Paris: I stayed at Clément's and he arrived later that afternoon from work. We'd be running the next race side by side.

The following day, Friday, Clément's son Clovis dropped over and we headed straight to the station to head south to Bordeaux. The TGV, France's fast train service, is one of the best in the world. We powered through to Bordeaux in only three-and-a-half hours, covering nearly 600 kms. I couldn't believe how quick and comfortable the trip was – it sure beat flying. I tried chatting to Clovis, named after the first king of France, but he was a little shy. It's no wonder with this scruffy Australian lad yabbering only in English, a kid would certainly have some reservations.

We stayed with Clément's brother Cedric, his wife, Sophie, and their four kids. I'd been travelling around by myself for the best part of a year and all of a sudden I was in southern France with five wild kids, all telling me jokes in French and trying to play with me. Surreal. Cedric's English was pretty good, so I was able to talk to all of them without too much trouble. He cooked up a barbecue and the kids danced about. It felt just like the summer holidays I'd enjoyed as a child, hanging out with my cousins, throwing water bombs at each other. We ate divine cheese and sipped splendid wine and I wondered yet again how the French had got it so right.

The Marathon du Médoc is a famous race that runs through one of the finest wine regions in the world. It's appealing for a number of reasons, but the two stand-out clinchers for me were:

1. Fancy dress: it's a wild costume party, encouraging everyone to dress up in theme.
2. Fancy wine: instead of water stations they have wine stations!

We got away very early to hit the start line in Pauillac with plenty of time. The dress-up theme for this year's race was 'Cartoon' and I'd picked up a couple of Super Mario Bros. outfits for Clément and me. We looked hilarious, and how was I to know there'd be five other sets of Mario Bros. out there? The array of outfits at the beginning of the race was astonishing, with plenty of obvious superheroes (Superman, Spiderman and Batman) mixed in with costumes from all sorts of kids' cartoons (*Toy Story*, *The Incredibles* and SpongeBob), along with French favourites (Asterix, Obelix and Tintin).

The marathon is designed for everyone to walk or run between famous châteaus, encouraging you to 'taste' all the different wines available and eat plenty of local produce. It's like a roving street party, covering a big chunk of this wonderful wine region. You don't have to dress up and you don't have to drink the wine, but if you do go to this race, it should probably be your intention to make the most of it.

Ninety-five per cent of the participants at the start line were dressed to party. We realised very quickly that our outfit selection was none too wise with the task ahead of us, as the sun was shining in a clear blue day and 30°C heat was only a few hours away. But we were there to have fun, so Clément and I cheered and shouted in the first 5 kms, speaking rubbish in terrible Italian accents. We passed a group of guys in provocative outfits pushing a mock-up bus that was blaring out music from *Priscilla, Queen of the Desert*. The roads were jam-packed with runners and floats, even though only 7000 or so had left the start line, with laughter and singing wafting across the rows of vines. I couldn't stop smiling, watching costumes disintegrate almost immediately as the rigours of running tore them apart.

Within 7 kms, we were sipping our first cups of wine. This early in the race, there were too many hands and not enough servers, so it became a bit of a jostle to get a share, but with a gulp and a hurrah, we were off again in search of more treasure. Clément cautioned me to take it easy: there were some 30 châteaux along the route. But from the 10-km mark onwards, these classic estates were cropping up every couple of kilometres and it felt like a slight to their hospitality to refuse the wine that was handed to me. The French always eat when they drink, so we were handed cheeses and pickles to consume. Some wineries dished out slices of beef and sausage, which is probably the worst thing you could eat while running long distance – but then, drinking a few litres of wine isn't too clever either.

By halfway, my red and blue outfit was soaking up gallons of sweat and I could feel the heaviness of drink throughout my body. Some of the towns along the path had set up their own 'illegal' drink stations, encouraging runners to sip aperitifs like cognac and Ricard. The more robust French runners stopped at these stalls but Clément told me he'd drunk at many of them the year before and had nearly been hospitalised by the end of the run. I gave them a miss.

Every town and garden had a band of some sort playing. I was whooping at Luigi and every time we saw a band, we'd stop and dance for half a minute, before striding on in search of the next glass of red juice or white nectar. Wherever you looked, there was madness. We found runners tossing themselves into estates' garden ponds. Things were getting a little too wild and it wasn't long before Luigi and I were trying to run through a mess of drunken laughter. It was getting harder to keep moving though, as the sugar from the wine overloaded our bodies and we became tired and in need of a pit stop. If I'd had my way, I would have lain down in the grass on the side of the road for a lengthy slumber, but Clément wouldn't abandon his sidekick and he kept jostling me through the kilometres. We ate the local sweet, canelé, shoving the whole cakes into our mouths as we passed 35 kms.

At 39 kms, we tumbled into a tent where they were passing out plates of beef and the last glasses of wine. I was too drunk to even look at the wine, but behind us, the music blared and a few mad runners were up on a podium strumming toy guitars along to AC/DC's 'Thunderstruck'. I wasn't too drunk to get involved in that though, so I jumped up and pulled out some wild air walks and added my voice to the bellowing brothers. In my drunken state, it was a total rock-star moment.

I was laughing maniacally as I stumbled from the tent, chasing Luigi down the road. He had an ice-cream in his hand and was telling me we needed to sort ourselves out before the end. I said something about being sick of running and Clément scolded me for my lack of commitment. We were soon home, though, shuffling back into Pauillac with even more music and cheering. Cedric and Sophie had brought the kids down and they were all wearing little RunLikeCrazy T-shirts. Clément and I were in a somewhat sorry state and I had to mind myself in front of the kids. We were still laughing, but the silliness was passing quickly, replaced with tired bodies and sore heads.

Marathon 37, completed in a rollicking 5:21. It was by far the craziest party I'd ever seen and the most expressive marathon I'd ever attended. This combination of wild characters, beautiful scenery, exquisite food and delicious wine was the best reflection of French culture I could imagine. DrunkLikeCrazy!

A few days after that, Clément and I were on an easy run east along the Paris' Canal Saint-Martin. People were meandering along the river, holding hands and chattering away. Girls were lying about laughing, catching the last of the sun's rays as groups of men played boules on gravel fields. Workers rode home in ones and twos, while some couples lined up at an arts theatre.

Clément had decided to join me in Ljubljana in a month's time. He was in search of a fast marathon time. I was racing in Berlin before that, but I promised I'd have one more crack at it with him if he could meet me in Slovenia.

That was my final visit to Paris. It felt like I wasn't doing so much of this trip by myself any more. I was with different people every other day and their generosity was overwhelming.

38

WACHAU MARATHON

19 September, Wachau, Austria

3:06.16 PB

I was ready to really push myself, and Berlin was going to be the place to do it. So I figured Wachau could be a good training run if I focused on even splits for the whole race. I'd already run a few times that week. Gerhard, who I'd been hooked up with through the trusty grapevine, introduced me to one of the most impressive running parks in Europe, Prater Park in Vienna. It has a 5-km pedestrian boulevard that runs straight through the centre, with markers so you can pace yourself out. Man, you could do some blistering training down that road.

Gerhard drove me 80 kms to the start line on Sunday morning, which meant I felt relaxed from the outset. The race took off from a small town called Emmersdorf by the side of the Danube. The course then wound its way through the Wachau Valley, a picturesque wine region in Austria. That day, the sun was out and I wasn't cold, so it was the perfect place for a Sunday run in September.

Around me, about 700 very fit-looking men and women were preparing to power through this marathon. We kicked off with a shout and ran a few kilometres up river, before turning around for the long run to Krems. It was a wonderful scenic route, with acres of vineyards on one side of the track and the powerful Danube flowing with us on the right.

Anyway, the starters raced away and I did my very best not to get caught up in the excitement. I'm a sucker for a rabbit, so when 50-odd competitors sprint well in front of me, I have to stick a leash on my inner greyhound (his name is Sir Drinksalot) and ease into my own rhythm. I sat for a while on 4.18 per km, but registered that this was a little fast and dropped down to a more comfortable 4.20–23. After all, this was just a strategic training run.

I remembered the Cougar telling me that a guy he knew had been advised to try faster long runs. It's usual practice to run slow on the weekend and sprint in your shorter sessions during the week. That had played on my mind for a while, because this gent had smashed his PB by doing the reverse: easing his weekday mileage up, and running his Sunday session at speed. I'd had trouble fitting in my Monday to Friday runs around all the travel and recovery, so it seemed a logical thing to trial.

So, although the Wachau Marathon wasn't meant to be anything special, I found myself sitting at this pace very comfortably, only five seconds per km off a sub-three-hour target. Somewhere near the 15-km mark, my opportunistic nature got the best of me and I started doing the calculations. If I held this speed through the halfway mark, then I'd be looking at a 93-minute half. And, if I could hold onto that . . .

'It's a training run, dude, let that crap go,' I told myself, but I wasn't really listening.

I ran in a couple of groups for a while. Everyone was chugging along too fast to be chatting, so I didn't try to make it uncomfortable for myself or them by striking up conversations. A number of runners had powered on past me up until the 10-km mark, and as the halfway point cruised by, I saw a few familiar singlets ahead of me. It's rare that I get to run at that kind of pace and not be on the receiving end of the back-half shuffle, but I was still holding my speed and feeling in control.

A few lads that I had passed earlier sat in behind me. Apparently, I was now the pace setter. I didn't change my speed, but they obviously decided to step it up, because at about the 30-km mark, they edged by me and I tucked in behind them. They caught another guy ahead and jumped in step with him, but about a kilometre later I realised that everyone had slowed down, so I took the opportunity to push past.

I had my good kilometres and my bad ones, but I was holding my own and as I came through the 35-km point, I was among a big mix of walkers and runners from the half marathon and the 10-km race, which had used various start points on the same track. I could pick the marathoners, though, and became fixated on passing as many as possible, using consistency to wear them down.

And, against all logic, I calculated once more and saw a PB looming. I figured I had to take the advantage where I found it; with no routine because of the travelling, every day provided barriers to having a good race. In reality, I had no idea what would happen in the lead-up to Berlin, so I decided to make sauce while the tomatoes were ripe. So I downed another GU, and did the only thing an idiot like me is gonna do. I legged it!

Running into town, I got a great reception from the local crowds. I was in the top 50 and crossed the line in a PB of 3:06.16.

I hit the deck not long after and my legs began to spasm. The daggers were back, easing deep into the muscle tissue of my calves. I'd worried about it in the early days, but now I could predict it would last for around 15–20 minutes before I'd be able to walk again.

I texted Cougar to ask him what his Melbourne Marathon time was last year. He's my traditional training partner and friendly rival, so when he messaged me back telling me that I was a bastard and had beaten him by 11 seconds, I knew he was happy for me.

I texted back, reminding him that it had taken me 38 marathons to better his time!

39
BERLIN MARATHON
26 September, Berlin, Germany

3:03.31 PB

By Monday night I was in Berlin. I spent a few glorious autumn days relaxing at the Circus Hostel in old East Berlin. On Tuesday I headed to a nearby running track, where my session was gruelling. A lot of locals were pumping out laps too, making the most of the unseasonably warm weather. I was running as fast as ever, even after Sunday's efforts.

I had plenty to keep me occupied: a pub crawl on Tuesday night, lunch with an old colleague from Google on Wednesday, and then on Thursday my family and the Tribal boys poured into town. It was so nice to meet James, my sister Alexis's fella, who I'd heard many great things about. And Alexis looked relaxed, which just doesn't happen often enough, as she's a bit of a workaholic. My bro, Chris, and his wife, Janette, came as well.

We were all staying in two apartments in two adjoining buildings, but they were at the same height, so we could yell at each other from our windows, kinda like school camp.

To recap the main players in this big adventure:

Kevin Leiberthal (aka Kevlar) was one of the team who'd come to Comrades with me. He's a hell of a runner, conservative but consistent, and always gets the job done. He doubles as a physio and running technician.

Shane McGrath (aka Ooh Aah McGrath) is a bad man with a big

heart. He's had a number of sub-three-hour marathons, and seems to have settled into fatherhood and generally mature behaviour in his thirties. He loves a boys' trip, though, and I was worried about what this might lead to.

Derham Moss (Mossy) was the real danger to everyone's health. He's one of those guys who can balance work and play with equal amounts of over-zealousness, and he's had way too much field experience at creating the ultimate lads' weekend.

David Nanfra (the Nanf, or Toughest Man at Tribal) is a Blockbuster store owner and all-round good guy. Dave's one of those fellas who just adds a bit of happiness to everyone's life. He also has an evil side that only comes out when there's the potential to party all night.

Shane Campbell (Yabby, Yab, the Yabster) had been in Tokyo already with me this year and is one of the fastest runners I know, but he also likes to get loose with the boys. In Berlin he was looking for a 2:55 or better, which would be a cracking PB.

Ali Holmes (aka Allan) was the sole female in the group. She'd been quickly renamed Allan so she could join this boys' trip. She was also a Comrades finisher, but opted out of the Berlin Marathon, content to just drink and party for a couple of days instead.

Then throw my brother into the mix. Chris is a very funny guy and even funnier when he's drunk. We laugh so much that it usually hurts my sides the next day. Other than our hangovers, though, it's all pretty harmless. One day, I'm sure we'll be too old for nonsense, but I'm proud to say that day hasn't come.

Given the players, I had my concerns about staying healthy for the days before running in the Berlin Marathon.

It was Yabby's birthday on the Thursday. We went to Berlin's oldest restaurant, Zur Letzten Instanz, which had apparently been frequented by none other than Napoleon Bonaparte. There, we dined on a lot of meat and sauerkraut. The wonderful thing about eating in Berlin is that you have to be incredibly unlucky to find yourself at an expensive restaurant. It's a city for the people and happens to have a huge number of artists, students and misfits living there, so food and living prices are probably the lowest in Western Europe. After dinner, the Tribal crew bailed, choosing to conserve their energy for the big race on Sunday.

My sister Alexis could also have bailed, but she listened to my brother's and my arguments that we should have just a couple of drinks at a nearby bar before finishing up. So James, Alexis, Chris, Janette and I found a trashy bar pumping out drinks by the dozen, where we downed a range of shots and cocktails, including Jager bombs, tequila and mojitos. By the time we left there and headed to Week End, a club where famed house DJ Steve Lawler was to play, it was after 12 and we were pretty drunk. The club was busy, but not packed, the views across Berlin at night were wonderful and the tunes were cranking! It wasn't long before I decided I was the world's coolest disco dancer, and my brother was strutting about, flapping his wings and crowing like an eagle. Janette was ordering more tequila shots, James was hugging strangers and Alexis was tired but still dancing.

I got home at about 5.30 a.m. I woke to find everyone had left for the day, but I pulled myself together and met the guys at a café near the Berlin Wall at 11 a.m. The questions started to fly immediately: 'You did what?' 'How late?' 'How many drinks?' The boys were incredulous as to how I could have such a big night a couple of days out from a marathon. Truth was, I looked fine, but I might have still been a little drunk.

Maybe I shouldn't have gone drinking before races. Maybe I shouldn't have eaten rich local food, or gone dancing, or walked for kilometres as a tourist, or slept in cheap hostel dorms, or flown every few days. Maybe I should have just stayed home. But the trip had been about breaking down the barriers we set in front of ourselves. There is no doubt that these barriers are there to guide us, but sometimes you just have to do all the fun stuff too. Chris was only going to be there until Saturday, so it was the only opportunity we would have to celebrate together on the far side of the world. It was too good an opportunity to miss.

But then there was the reality of a massive hangover two days before a big race. Not ideal, and I don't recommend it, especially when you go sightseeing and want to throw up over the side of the open-topped double-decker bus.

Saturday was a bit slow. We got up early and went to a pub to watch the Aussie Rules Grand Final. Collingwood slogged it out against St Kilda and it resulted in the first draw since 1977. Any other code in the world would have added 10 minutes, but the archaic laws of AFL forced a replay the following week. I didn't really care about the result, it was just fun to be around so many Aussies.

Back at the apartment, the team pulled out a few items they'd brought me from home. There was a commemorative jacket, some new Nikes, a big blow-up kangaroo named K-Bone, and an Aussie flag signed by all my friends at Tribal back home. I was taken aback by their generosity and support.

It was time to get race-ready. We hit a thrift store up the road and I purchased the most exciting piece of clothing I was ever likely to own – a purple ski suit with crazy orange panels, circa 1983. It was two sizes too small, which added to my runner's butt accentuation. At €12 it was definitely worth it even if I would only have it for 12 hours.

Race day arrived. The boys were all pretty serious but I was just happy to line up with my good mates in one of the biggest races in the world. Berlin is hallowed turf. It was here my hero Haile Gebrselassie laid down an astonishing 2:03.59 in 2008 to beat his '07 time by 27 seconds. In 2008, Haile held the top-three fastest times in history, and until 2011 he still held the top two – both from Berlin.

Although I wasn't fazed about the start of a race any more, I felt a little tingle when jumping into our start group. We'd all managed to wangle the same corral, so it was pretty exciting to have the countdown with the boys. It had been an extremely stormy night, so everything was wet around us. I ditched my sexy purple jumpsuit and looked a little emaciated compared to the bubble body I was rocking with the suit on. When the gun went off, people all around tried to bolt from the gates. I could feel we were all going to scatter. We said our goodbyes and the race began.

My Garmin wouldn't pick up a signal at the start and I had to fiddle with it a little. I caught McGrath and Mossy further along and sat in with them. But before I could get comfortable, I realised that they were settling into a pace slower than I wanted to go. If I really wanted it to happen that day, then I needed to haul ass. To run with my friends or run fast, but alone? It's the eternal question.

'Good luck, fellas,' I called out as I got a move on.

'Go well, mate,' was the response.

People were in a hurry as we raced through puddles away from Brandenburg Gate, down through the Tiergarten. A lot of runners, looking for dry patches, were stepping into the path of other competitors, which felt like it would soon end in catastrophe. I'm guessing Haile never had to deal with such shenanigans when he set his records.

The rain wasn't heavy, but it was frustrating. The great thing about running in the wet is that your muscles stay relatively cool. The bad thing is that your shoes get saturated and although I wouldn't class them as heavy, it definitely changes the dynamic of your footfall as your foot slides within the shoe. This obviously creates blisters, but also makes your feet swell with the water. Not very comfy.

By 30 kms I was flagging. I still held a pretty good pace, but having passed the halfway mark at 1:28, I knew I was motoring but also that I probably couldn't hold it. I didn't need to walk just yet, so I kept trying to hold my kilometres under 4.30. It didn't work too well, as each split bounced between 4.25 and 4.55. But the overall result had me as close as ever to that magical three-hour marker.

Dietmar, the barefoot runner from Bad Füssing and Rome, came up beside me at about 34 kms. 'Tristan!' he shouted. He told me he'd seen my logo on some guys earlier and that he'd kept an eye out for me. 'Come with me, my friend, we go under three hours!' The guy's excitement was infectious, but I was out of gas and now just hanging on till the end. He took off and I could only shake my head in disbelief as his bare feet slapped against the ground.

I cruised closer to the Tiergarten and found myself passing more and more runners as they fell apart just minutes before the end. I saw K-Bone, the blow-up kangaroo, bobbing up at me and gave the support crew a grimace and a little wave. I couldn't pull a sub-three, but a new PB was on the board and it would be my most impressive effort to date. I pushed and pulled my body along, every inch of me screaming now.

A kilometre from the end, my body went numb to the pain. I didn't hurt any more and I could feel the finish looming. One last turn had me facing the Brandenburg Gate. Just past the gate, the finish line beckoned. People lined the streets in thick rain jackets and cheered us on. I dug as deep as I could, looking for anything my body had left to dish up. There was something in there, after all – and so I ran faster.

What a rush! I wouldn't call it my favourite race in the world, but it has to be one of my best performances. I finished . . . staggered a little . . . righted myself . . . then decided I was fine and wandered off to find my friends. The first person I found was Dietmar.

'Tristan! How are you? I wanted to run with you!' Dietmar seemed like he was on happy pills, but actually he's just an effervescent character who wants the world to run and be happy.

'I'm pretty tired, Dietmar. How about you?'

'I got 2:59,' he chortled. 'I had so much fun!' I looked down at his feet, then I looked at him, then down at his feet again and slowly shook my head. He hugged me.

'It's the natural way, Tristan, I keep telling you!' I hugged him back.

He'd been doing this for 11 years and his record for 24 hours barefoot was 160 kms. His record for 12 hours was an astonishing 116 kms. Unbelievable.

I waited at the meeting point. Everyone showed up slowly, smiles and hugs all round as we shared our times.

Kevlar – 3:27.44

McGrath – 3:08.43

Mossy – 3:12.11 PB

Nanfra – 3:33.20

Yabby – 2:54.37 PB

T-Bone – 3:03.31 PB

Three personal bests! What an extraordinary day on the track.

The next couple of days were spent exploring as much of Berlin's nightlife as we could fit in. The boys went out till all hours on Sunday, Monday and Tuesday nights. I was falling apart by that last night.

Kev and I spent some time in the Jewish Museum, a memorial of sorts, focusing on the history of Jewish culture through Europe, up until the persecution by the Nazis in the '30s and '40s. It was hard to get my head around the enormity of what occurred during that period. I was left wondering how the Jewish people coped, and how they managed to forgive the atrocities inflicted on them. I'd now seen persecuted groups in South Africa, Rwanda and South America and I wondered why humanity is constantly looking for scapegoats to further their political misdeeds. It was a sobering visit.

By the time I got on the plane come Wednesday, I was a complete mess. I'd really taken the challenge to a whole new level and it had left me drained, busted up and with a couple of very sore big toes.

In London, I left my almost-full passport at the Australian Embassy;

there was a chance I'd soon run out of pages. Better to get a new one, and forget about it for a few more years.

It's always nerve-racking leaving your passport in the hands of others in a foreign country. I was heading to the Loch Ness Marathon for the weekend and I'd been told I didn't need my passport to fly to Scotland (which made sense), but I would need it on Monday before heading to Chicago on Tuesday. *Hmmm.*

I was extremely fatigued after my blow-out week in Berlin. I'd only just recovered from the madness in Médoc, then smashed myself in Austria and finally celebrated too hard in Berlin. I was lucky that the magic of Vijay was on hand at the Happiness Centre to work through my shoulders and my legs, to reduce the tension that had been building up.

So far, with 39 marathons in the bag, and two PBs in two weeks, it felt like I'd had an astonishingly lucky year.

40

LOCH NESS MARATHON
3 October, Loch Ness, Scotland
3:25.13

I landed in Inverness on a Saturday morning and met up with the mighty Deano, the friend I'd made at the Great Wall Marathon. He'd given me his race number – 52 – and we'd stayed in touch.

I'd been to the southern part of Loch Ness with an old buddy back in 2007 during the rugby World Cup. I remembered that I was struggling personally at that time of my life. The place was magical, but I was stressed by what'd been going on back home, and I distinctly recall standing by the loch in Fort Augustus wondering what on earth life had in store for me. If anyone had told me then that three years later I'd be running up the far side of this mystical body of water, towards Inverness, I wouldn't have believed I had it in me.

On the day of the race, the local school supplied a marching band with bagpipes and there was plenty of highland spirit among the throngs of runners. In true Socttish style it was cold and misty, and as the coaches arrived to take us to the start line, the rain began to tumble down. There was no escape, so I just stood there getting wet, trying not to shiver.

The racers took off with a hoot and I sat with Deano for the first few kilometres. The rain continued for half an hour, then it abruptly stopped. The weather might have improved but my strength didn't. My shoes were soaked through and my feet were already a little sore.

Deano was looking very strong. I'd be no help to him in this race, just a hindrance. He eased ahead. I was still sweeping along at a fairly steady pace, though, and the views of Loch Ness shimmering in the morning sun were inspiring. My feet hurt and my body strained, but every turn gave us a different view. It was so vibrantly green, like a luminescent painting.

'So this is where I get to run today.'

The warmth of the sun was wonderful and dried me quickly, but the next shower drenched me again and my shoes continued to slosh.

By the final 10 kms, I was taking walking breaks. The race had flown by, but my feet were sending staves of pain up my legs with each step. Something was really wrong now, but I couldn't stop till I got to the end. I picked up a couple of runners who wanted to walk but listened when I told them the finish line wouldn't get much closer if they inched along that way. We ran together, pacing into the city, passing Inverness Castle and crossing a bridge to float back down to the athletics fields and finish line. I ended strongly, knocking the run off in 3:25.13.

The finish area was a sea of mud, so Deano and I vacated quickly. My feet were on fire and I just wanted to get back to the hostel. When I finally removed my shoes, I discovered the problem: both big toes were infected. They were bulbous and red, hurting just to touch, pulsing with excessive blood. 'Hmmmm,' was all I could muster. 'That can't be good.' Both of the toenails were stubbornly hanging on even though they were blackened with dried blood caked underneath.

I'd run the last three races in wet conditions. It had showered a little in Wachau, then bucketed down in Berlin, so after a solid rinse in Inverness it was certainly time for my feet to revolt. Skin that has been sitting in pots (or shoes) of water for three hours at a time has no defence against infection.

After doing what I could to help my poor toes, I headed over to a pub with Deano to celebrate the race. He'd punched out a solid 3:10, a little off his best, but still a time to be proud of. He was taking us to meet up with some people from an online runners network, of which he was a member. We traded stories and I told them how I was aiming to be home for Christmas. One of the guys told me to check out a You-Tube video of an Australian comedian, Tim Minchin.

I looked it up back at the hostel. Tim sings a song called 'White Wine in the Sun', which begins quite comically, taking the mickey out of Christmas. As the song progresses, you realise it is an anthem for every Australian who is thousands of miles from home, while their families cook up the Chrissie lunch on the barbie, sipping chilled white wine, missing their children. By the end of the song, my heart was constricted with homesickness and I had tears rolling down my cheeks. All I wanted was to make it home in one piece.

Forty marathons down. Forty marathons down. You'll get there, champ.

The following day I was on a long train ride south, heading back to London. The train had been half the price of a plane trip and I had little enough money to splurge on comfort as it was, so I took the slow option. It was a brilliant surprise to find that the railway line snaked its way through some picture-perfect countryside.

I went straight to see Dr Johannes, on Alexis's recommendation. He looked at my toes and shook his head, but gave me a prescription for two rounds of antibiotics and a couple of hypodermic needles to bore holes in what was left of my toenails, to release puss and pressure. It was an ugly sight, but the good doctor thought I'd caught it just in time. He insisted, though, that I should rest as much a possible over the next few weeks. I told him I only had six days before my next marathon in Chicago, to which Dr Johannes shrugged and said, 'Well, you'd better start praying instead!'

I collected my new passport the following day. Sixty-four pages of blank canvas. A world of potential in the hands of a madman!

41

CHICAGO MARATHON

10 October, Chicago, USA

3:30.57

I hopped off the plane to a warm day in Chicago. By rights, this time of year should have been chilly, but a last-minute heatwave had chosen to pound the city as I arrived. I wasn't going to complain, I much preferred a little heat to a lot of cold.

A close friend of my sister Rebecca was there to greet me. Wendy had lived all over the world as a consultant, but had settled in Chicago some years before. In my sorry state, I really needed another slice of home, so when Wendy ordered take-out and we cracked open an Asahi, I relaxed immediately. It wasn't long before I'd passed out on her couch. I didn't wake up till the sun was rising, so clearly this was one sleep that needed to happen.

We had a great couple of days, kicking around town with Matt and Chloe, who had put me in touch with my sponsor Ken Krys. I got myself out to yet another huge expo and stopped in to see Dean Karnazes do his talk again. He greeted me warmly when I queued up for his autograph. I heard people in the line discussing his achievements and it made me wonder where I'd fit in.

I often found myself wondering what I would be doing in 2011. People kept bugging me about it, trying to create a sense of urgency to consider my options, but I could only reply that I was taking this year one week at a time, so 2011 was still a lifetime away. But the months were flying past, and I had no idea what I was going to do next. My grand plan had only included 12 months of insanity.

I was late getting to the start, so bade my farewells and entered the race near the back of the throng.

I don't have a lot of good memories about the Chicago Marathon. It was my fourth Major marathon and certainly the crowds around me were exhilarated, but I think the last few races had taken some of the wind out of my sails. I wasn't feeling too good about my chances of having a smooth run, with the inflammation of my toes only just beginning to abate, but I still took off with some good energy.

The course zigzags through the wide eastern streets of the city for a while, before heading steadily north. Wendy, Matt and Chloe were shouting and waving each time we came over the same cross street, but when we moved out of town, I was running alone. I found myself in that annoying position of passing people for the entire race, having started too far back in the pack. It was my own fault, but because my pace was quicker, I wasn't falling in step with any runners looking at the same time as mine. This was a huge marathon and the support along the sides of the road was up there with the Berlin and London marathons, but I wished I had someone to savour it with, but I just grinned at some of the raucous Americans waving flags and banners and kept on nutting out the kilometres.

People all around me were huffing and puffing, working towards their 10-km target, their halfway goal, or the inevitable 30-km wall. I'd be passing all the same benchmarks, but without any anxiety or distress. I'd be tired, that was certain, but I knew how my race would turn out. It had happened 40 times that year already, one foot after the other until the finish line eventually showed itself. Without speaking to someone in a spectacular race like this, I was little more than a voyeur. I was detached.

The course switched back towards the city and the friendly people of Chi Town did their darnedest to pump up every runner. After halfway, we edged out towards the south-western part of town. The heat of the sun went to work and the runners around me began to flag. I struggled too. Some of the course weaved through an industrial zone and I lost my mojo, but others were breaking, so I had nothing to complain about. At 35 kms I was elated to see my team with the Boxing Kangaroo. I slowed to a walk, though, shaking my head. 'Too hot,' I complained to my friends.

'Not far, though – you can do it!' The enthusiasm lifted my spirits for one last push.

I didn't have to run much further south before the final kilometres up Michigan Avenue delivered us into the city again. As I passed the 25.2-mile mark (the final mile), a girl slapped face first into the concrete to my right. The heat was taking its toll. Supporters jumped onto the track to help her, and all I could do was look for the last turn into Columbus Drive. I crossed the finish line in Grant Park at 3:30.57. It had been a difficult run but I'd made it.

42

ISTANBUL EURASIA MARATHON

17 October, Istanbul, Turkey

3:29.29

I bounced back through London yet again. I was only there half a day, but still managed to fit in a Happiness Centre massage. Then it was on to Istanbul.

I'd never been there, despite many people having spruiked the place to me over the years. It was wet when I arrived, but even then, the city was active and vibrant. Its history is as magnificent as any European or Arabian city, largely because it is the gateway between the two regions. My friends Kris and Kate were living in a nice part of town, and from their apartment we could see the striking minarets around Aya Sofya, with each hill seemingly crowned with a mosque or palace.

Kris had challenged me to include this race in my itinerary: it was the only course that allowed you to run from the Asian continent to continental Europe. It was an appealing idea.

My first couple of days there were pretty low-key. Kris and Kate took me to a few of their favourite cafés and bars and to a classic Turkish football match, between the giants of the league, Galatasaray and Ankaragücü. When Galatasaray lost, the crazy fans started setting off flares and throwing chairs at the players on the field. It was awesome! Between teaching shifts, Kate was the perfect tour guide, taking me to the Blue Mosque and the Basilica Cistern. There's nothing like walking through a super-old water tank with a friend to share it with.

Kate and Kris had both trained for the half marathon, and they knew we needed to get to the start early. Apart from the marathon and half marathon, the race offered the locals a chance to join a bridge walk that took them into the local Inönü Stadium. Around 100 000 people took part each year, in a great celebration of this remarkable city.

The weather had completely cleared by the Sunday and we were treated with a day that was like so many I'd raced in recently – perfect to start with, but ending up far too hot for a marathon. The three of us ran together for the first few kilometres, crossing the mighty Bosphorus as a group. We lost Kate after that, but Kris and I stuck together till around 5 kms. I was hanging on to a paddle with a picture on it. Lynton Tideman had sponsored me with over $400 back in Australia, on the promise that I would run one marathon wearing a mask of his face – a race face! It was getting late in the year, and it was time to come through for him. But it's hard enough to breathe in a marathon without a mask, so I put Lynton's head on a stick instead and got pictures and videos of 'him' running across the bridge and through the city. It was as close as I'll ever come to carrying a mate through a marathon. My only complaint was that my pal's neck gave me splinters.

All sorts of local runners were out attacking the course, along with plenty of European and American tourists. I had the chance to converse with a few runners this time, unlike my previous couple of runs. I watched one local guy run over to his mates on the side of the road and grab a cigarette out of their hand, puffing for a minute, before firing back onto the track and stampeding straight past me! I was aghast, but I guess old habits die hard.

The course crossed over to the west bank and took us out to the Eyüp. It doubles back a couple of times and somehow along the way I started talking to a Norwegian guy who I'd run with in Stavanger. We finally skirted back along the port, past the Royal Palace and up the hill to the Blue Mosque and Aya Sofya. Those last kilometres were hot and hard, but I stuck to my race plan and got it done.

I'd love to say I nailed that race, but the reality is I just held a pace I could sustain. My time was 3:29.29. Each week I was feeling more and more physically vulnerable. I couldn't control the conditions in which I was running, and I just had to hope a hot day wouldn't cause a serious strain. So with a potentially fast race the following week with Clément, I was happy to consider this a significant long run in one of the world's most exotic cities.

Forty-two down. Only 10 to go.

On Monday, I took a bus tour down to Anzac Cove. It was a long day, but I was glad I made the effort. We walked the shores of Gallipoli and visited the sites of each major battle, learning of the heroics of our Australian–Kiwi contingent and the young Turks. The Turks spoke of our boys with such reverence, and then put it to us that we had been the enemy, with no right to invade their homeland. It was a confronting conversation, because it wasn't an accusation, just a fact. And they were right, but strangely the conflict galvanised three nations in its wake – New Zealand, Australia and Turkey.

In the eight-month siege back in 1915, nearly 400 000 dead and wounded were recorded on both sides, and close to 60 per cent of those casualties were on the Turkish side. Yet the Turks still care for the memorials and graves of our lads as if they were their own sons. After touring this space, you cannot help but hold the Turkish people in high regard, if not embrace them as brothers.

Following the fight, the Father of the Turks – Atatürk – rose up the ranks from hero to major general, leading the people of his country to form an independent Turkey from the ashes of the beleaguered Ottoman Empire. As the first president, Atatürk modernised Turkey, presenting it with a new sense of self-worth and a belief in its abilities as a potential independent nation, rather than a subject state of the victorious Allies. He instituted new health and education programs that changed the direction of the country's economy and future.

On the flip side, the Australians and Kiwis went home with a collective bloodied nose, but an air of self-respect and an appreciation for the power of 'mateship', which remains an enduring cornerstone of our culture.

From blood and ashes, nations are born.

The young boys from my home town had come overseas looking for adventure, just as I had. They'd answered the call of duty, but some of the lads were only 15 and 16, too young to get caught up in the madness of war. Even so, they'd all become heroes. There aren't many conflicts where the defeated side still holds their fighting men up as the victors, but such was the power of the simple tragedy lived out on this tiny coastline. It defined young men in Australia, for evermore.

I wasn't putting my life on the line as they had. Perhaps my health, but certainly not my life. I was just having an adventure, testing my mettle and experiencing all that the world had to offer. These lads had sailed around the globeand found themselves on a beach with bullets and bombs to welcome them to a new land. You couldn't help but look quietly around and imagine the horrors that played out here. I clearly could still learn a thing or two about heroics.

43
LJUBLJANA MARATHON
25 October, Ljubljana, Slovenia
3:04.09

I flew to Slovenia on a Thursday. Clément was coming in later that afternoon and Claes (I runner I'd met in Oslo) on the Saturday, so I spent the first day just wandering around, trying to get a feeling for Ljubljana. I found an athletics track on the far side of town, empty and a little grown over, but perfect for me to stretch out my legs. I powered through sets of 2000 metres, feeling as quick as I ever had. I had a good shot at finally breaking three hours on Sunday.

The city is truly beautiful. Slovenia has long been a powerhouse economy in that part of the world, largely propping up the Yugoslav Union until it claimed its independence in 1990. Ljubljana had been reasonably well looked after throughout the Communist period and has become increasingly popular with tourists, enjoying a renaissance over the past decade. The children of Slovenia are comfortably European and the cafés and restaurants charge to match the cost of living of its Western European neighbours. With a castle perched right above Old Town, a spectacular river cutting through its centre, and bridges adorned with gargoyles and goddesses, it's a fairly hard city to beat for a rich classical atmosphere.

When Clément arrived, we went out for an excellent meal and he told me this was one of the most romantic cities he'd visited in Europe. What a shame we were wasting it on one another. It was brisk at night, but bright and warm during the day. I got one more run in on Friday

261

and felt as ready as I was ever going to be for our next assault. Clément and I hired a car and cruised down the coast to visit a client of his in Piran, a tiny town on a promontory that juts out from the sliver of coast the Slovenians hold between Italy and Croatia. It seemed that everyone in Piran was living in a little piece of heaven, a spider web of cobbled streets and lanes. We were treated to a sumptuous lunch with Slovenian produce and wine, a pure local experience.

We drove back to Ljubljana and found Claes at the hostel. He was excited to be there, and as he and Clément got to know each other over dinner, I reflected on how lucky I was to have two great new friends from different countries come to meet me all the way down here in Slovenia, just to run a marathon.

The next morning we were out early and I was lot more anxious than usual. We walked to the starting area and found that Old Town had come alive, the streets buzzing with anticipation. The three of us wore RunLikeCrazy singlets, featuring the raging red bull, so I felt like I was part of a real race team. A few runners came over and patted our backs, having seen us on the local news.

We got a quick start, pitching away from the line, immediately in front of the three-hour pacer. The course is a double loop, taking runners westwards away from the city and looping up to the north through a forest and some outlying suburbs, before delivering them straight back into town. All three of us were holding a solid pace through the first 15 kms, but already I could feel Clément pulling away. We were way ahead of pace, so Claes and I let him go and stuck to our plan, holding solid 4.08s through the first half.

The Slovenians waved flags of all nations at different points on the course. The forest we tracked through was gorgeous, offering cooler air that reinvigorated our lungs. In all, it was a stunning route and we were perfectly provided for. All was set for a record-breaking run.

Claes and I were still together through the halfway mark and I really felt I had the legs to go all the way. But I'd underestimated the distance plenty of times before, so I sucked down another GU and kept on pace, checking my watch at 1:27 for 21 kms. But by the time I made it back to the forest, the wheels were coming off. I coasted through the 30-km mark more or less on pace, but I was beginning to slip to 4.20s per km. I'd left Claes behind, though he was well on track for a PB, and I couldn't see Clément out in front any more. I was back in the alone zone, arguing with myself to keep pushing to the finish line. There weren't too many runners around me, but the supporters were generous, yelling encouragement in Slovene.

I knew I was cactus when I slowed to a walk in a drink station at 35 kms and couldn't get running for another 100 metres. When I finally got moving again, I couldn't find the pace to go close to the three-hour mark. I'd lost seven minutes in the back half and could only muster a 3:04.09 – a mere 38 seconds off my personal best.

Clément had rocked another PB of 2:56, getting stronger and faster with each passing year. Claes finished on 3:08, also smashing his personal best. What an outing for the RunLikeCrazy crew!

44

ATHENS CLASSIC MARATHON

31 October, Athens, Greece

3:29.45

I'd been to Athens three times in my life, but I hadn't ever taken the time to appreciate it. I would have six days here this time around, and it'd be my final stop in Europe.

The Athenian train drivers were all on strike. And once I got into the centre of town after a very long bus ride, we were further delayed by the marching train drivers. The Greeks love a protest. I was a wreck by the time I made it to the hostel and fell asleep for an entire day. By night I was wide awake and took in the spectacular views of the Acropolis from the rooftop of my city hostel.

I wandered the streets in the following days. I was tired and trying to ignite my passion for exploration. Athens is the home of the marathon and I wanted to make the most of my final European experience. The sun was still shining in these parts, clinging to the forgotten days of summer. I caught up with the brother of a Greek friend from Melbourne, who took me for a cool tour of the city and out to the hills east of Athens on the back of his scooter.

Back down in the city, I wandered over to the expo, a celebration of Greece's biggest marathon and the 2500th anniversary of the battle that gave birth to the idea. It was being held at the Zappeion, a conference building in the National Gardens, not far from the Panathenaic Stadium – the original Olympic stadium – where the race would finish. Around the circular atrium in the centre of the building, the stories of

Greek battles and formation of its empire were displayed on walls and in installations.

The Greeks themselves were extremely excited by this year's race. There were 13 000 competitors in the various distances, up from around 8000 the year before. Everyone wanted to be part of the celebrations and people from right across the globe had made the journey to Athens for this once-in-a-lifetime event. The expo was bursting at the seams, with participants buying anything they could get their hands on that represented the anniversary race. I was caught up in the hype too, buying a key ring and a couple of wall hangings. What the hell was I going to do with wall hangings when I didn't have a wall?

I stumbled across a machine that shot electrodes through your body, to determine your body fat or if you had enough 'body water'. The woman at the display explained that my body water should be sitting at around 60 per cent. It returned a reading of 40 per cent and a fat percentage of 13.

'What does that mean?' I asked, mildly alarmed.

'Either you're too fat or you're not hydrated enough,' she informed me bluntly.

'Oh. I don't think I'm too fat. I only weigh 69 kilos.'

'Well, then, you must be thirsty. Go buy some water.'

Very scientific, I thought, walking away.

I had certainly been told before that I had issues with hydration: my nutritionist had pointed out numerous times that I don't sweat very much because I don't maintain a sufficient store of water in my body. I'd tried to increase my water and electrolyte intake, but it just eventuated in an overloaded and somewhat uncontrollable bladder, so I gave up that approach early on. If I was thirsty, I'd drink. If I wasn't, I wouldn't. Call me old-fashioned, but I liked to listen to my body.

Some friends had arrived at this race. The mighty Deano, my old Roadrunners Reading mate, was in town. He was looking to enjoy this race as more of a fun run, which was great, because I had zero intention of running fast in this race. Clément's friend Bertrand connected with me and so did a Canadian mate called Zac. Together we had quite a race team.

It was a huge bus trip out to the site where the Battle of Marathon was fought in 490 BC. It was the obvious starting line for the run. I almost missed the bus to get out there, but luckily the Greeks are not strict with their schedules. It was a warm morning and just being in the area made me feel like I had completed my pilgrimage. I guess it's like going to the Vatican for the Catholics, or Mecca for the Muslims, except that when you get to Marathon, you soon turn around and run away as quickly as you can, all the way to Athens!

And that's exactly what we did. For the first half of the race, Deano, Bertrand and I stuck together. It was far too hot to get comfortable in the initial 10 kms, but once we began to rise from the beach to tackle the mountain range that separates Marathon from Athens, the air cooled significantly. Unfortunately, the course was a whole lot harder as the steep incline took its toll on tired legs.

But the Greeks were out in force, cheering us up the mountain. One older lady yelled to us, 'Welcome to Athens – thank you for coming!' I felt very welcomed too, as did most people around me, with everyone's faces showing a mixture of strain and euphoria while we followed, loosely, in the footsteps of Pheidippides. And there were plenty of runners dressed up as the legend himself, donning leather armour and wielding swords instead of drink bottles. The drink stations were well distributed and the volunteers overflowed with encouragement. The Greeks have a long history of being fantastic hosts, and, in this instance, the whole fabled city of Athens seemed to have opened its doors wide and cheered for this conquering army of runners.

'*Bravo, bravo!*' they shouted. '*Singariteeria* (congratulations)!'

I was grinning, even through gritted teeth. I lost touch with Deano as he steamed ahead on fresh legs. I didn't have much left in me but heart. That was the one thing I had clung to when the chips were down throughout the year. If I still had heart, the rest would take care of itself. And if your heart doesn't lift at the idea of running from Marathon to Athens a mere 2500 years after a young wounded soldier carried a message along this route, then I would challenge whether you have a heart at all. Mine was right up in my throat. I was swept along in a dream, fulfilling the extraordinary plan that had come to me in 2009. It was coming to fruition under my very feet. I was doing it all.

Buoyed by enthusiasm to see the task through, I battled over the mountain and descended into Athens. The road switched and turned, taking us ever closer to the cliffs of the Acropolis, adorned by the pillars of the Parthenon, emblazoned against a blue sky. One more turn and I rolled quickly down a hill, and across to the old arena.

The stairs of the stadium were packed with supporters, singing along to 'Zorba the Greek'. I was hot and flustered – it had been one of the hottest races to date, with one too many hills, but such is life.

A great dinner followed. We all had stories to tell and all wore our medals proudly. After necking two beers I was wiped out. I decided I deserved a lamb gyros, then I decided I deserved two.

Back to London. I'd passed through the city 13 times throughout the year, mostly managing to get into the Happiness Centre for sisterly support from Alexis and a massage from Vijay or Tim. It was sad to stop in there knowing it would be the last time for a while. I wouldn't get to see any of these friends again anytime soon. I only had time to stop by and catch a few zzz's at Alexis and James's place, before shipping off to the airport for my trip to New York City.

London had been a great base, the perfect stopover during my mad journey around the globe. I'd never had a lot of love for London as a city, but in 2010 she earnt my undying appreciation.

45

NEW YORK CITY MARATHON

7 November, New York City, USA

3:22.26

New York City. You just want to sing those words. I'd been waiting for this one all year long, particularly after visiting back in April. It was freezing when I got off the plane from London, but I didn't let it get to me. This was going to be an all-guns-blazing week and I couldn't let a little thing like impending winter get me down.

I lobbed up to Olah's and got myself settled. So many friends were coming, as well as my eldest sister, Rebecca, with my mum, Cherry-ann. I was there a few days ahead of the crew, so I had time to get my head right and relax a little.

Koya and Gareth from Tribal were coming to smash another marathon. Koya had faithfully supported me all year long and laid the groundwork for the final marathon in Melbourne. One of my closest friends and old schoolmate, Haydn Tomlinson, was flying over with his buddy Jason, to run his first marathon too. Chris and Paul had won a RunLikeCrazy–Compeed (blister bandaid) competition to join us. Lisa and her mother, Susan (from the Great Wall Marathon), and Kate were coming to the party as well. So many people! It'd be a huge task just to see everyone, let alone have a crack at the world's biggest marathon event!

I got to meet Australia's reigning wheelchair marathon champion, Kurt Fearnley, who was there to defend his crown as the four-time winner in his division of the NYC Marathon. He took some time out of his busy media schedule to have a chat to me. Kurt has won numerous Paralympic and World Championship gold medals. He even crawled along the Kokoda trail, a feat barely achievable on two legs! Kurt's an Order of Australia holder and a goddamn national treasure. And he wanted to hear about *my* adventures? Kurt had a whole host of buddies with him to cheer him in the marathon, before heading to New Orleans for his own bucks party.

Koya and I took a nice leisurely trot around Central Park, just to get fired up for Sunday. We were cruising past a gent I thought I recognised and just as we had passed him, Koya shouted out, 'Hey, Deek!'

Rob de Castella MBE was the second Australian national icon I met that day. He's a former marathon world-record holder, with a 2:08.18 in 1981, Australia's first ever Track and Field World Champion in 1983. He won the Boston Marathon with a time of 2:07.51 in '86. He was superbly dominant through the '80s, being voted World's Best Marathoner in that decade. And here he was, going for a walk around Central Park.

Deek stopped and had a chat with us. He was looking after a crew of Aboriginal fellas who he'd brought over as part of a new initiative to find Australia's next world champion. It also exposed people from remote communities to the joy and discipline of distance running, giving different opportunities to disaffected youths. I gushed about how we were looking forward to his breakfast talk the following morning. Then Koya told him about my adventure and he gave me a wide smile, saying, 'Ah, you're that guy. I've heard about you!'

We let him go, but as we walked away, I was laughing to Koya: 'Deek knows who I am!'

'I know,' she giggled. 'But I still can't believe I shouted at him like that!' It was all very surreal.

My year was made when I had a teary reunion with Mum and

Rebecca that same day in Manhattan. I hugged them both and made a bit of a scene.

The following morning, I attended Deek's breakfast talk. While we were waiting for him to start, he came over to ask if I'd share a little piece of my story after his talk. You don't say no to a national hero, so I got up and told my tale and ended up signing autographs with him at the end.

I'd been invited to give a talk at Google's New York office, which was a strange twist after having lost my job through office closure over a year before. But Olah still worked there and he wanted me to fire up the troops. I jumped at the opportunity.

A few of us hit the biggest expo I'd seen yet. There was so much security around bib collection, with all sorts of people trying to get a free ride onto the course. Every booth sold garments emblazoned with NYC Marathon motifs. This was big business.

Race day hit before I knew it. I was to meet up with a Paris Marathon buddy, Big Jay, in the morning, following his lead to get to the race start. A few of us headed to his house and we cabbed it to the Staten Island Ferry Terminal, where there were hundreds of people waiting to get the ferry across. It was freezing cold there, but the sun was shining, so it was promising to be a brilliant day.

The journey across the harbour was the most exhilarating ferry trip I'd ever had. We passed the Statue of Liberty and every foreign runner clung to the rails, grinning at the sight. We were all abuzz with anxiety to get there on time and not lose each other, but as soon as we were near the start line, we got divided according to our race groups. I managed to stay with Big Jay and his friend Dan, but I lost Haydn, Koya and the others.

We moved up onto the foot of the Verrazano-Narrows Bridge, where the MCs and dignitaries stood on double-decker buses, revving everyone up and counting down the final minutes to lift off. A wave of runners had already departed, so we were now in the second wave, which only meant that I wouldn't be winning the race that day.

There was a huge cheer as we got moving, pushing onto the long suspension bridge, on both the top and bottom levels. I stuck with Dan and Big Jay, and we collected various other runners. Once we finally got into Brooklyn and found a rhythm, four of us were sitting on a rock-solid pace, looking at around 3:15.

The first 10 kms took us all the way through Brooklyn, and even this early, locals were extremely vocal in their support. Americans are very good at telling you how they feel – which is pretty exciting when what they feel is a whole lotta love for you! They were shouting the house down and there seemed to be rock bands and DJs every kilometre, so you always had something to sing along to or have a look at. I was laughing my butt off at the crowd's antics. There were parts of the run where I couldn't even breathe, the madness of the race and the screaming support stealing my usual composure.

We came through Williamsburg, where Olah and Dave (from Montreal) had been hiding out, waiting for us to cruise through. The boys were styled up in RunLikeCrazy gear. Olah ran onto the course, flying the Boxing Kangaroo flag above his head. I was trying to control my laughter, but this celebration was just getting the best of me. I stopped to hug my buddy.

We pushed on through Greenpoint and punched our way through Queens. We'd all quietened down a fair bit when we got onto the Queensboro Bridge, about 25 kms into the race. There was no more brass bands, just the laboured breathing of runners, pushing through their walls. Heading to the end of the bridge, you could hear a low rumble, which got deeper and louder the closer we came. We corkscrewed around a bend and rolled onto First Avenue, where the crowds were six deep on both sides of the road, and flags of every nation were fluttering about. People were going off their dials at us, screaming in support, and the noise was both deafening and exhilarating. The adrenaline that kicked through my body right then could have sent me sprintingt6 the final 15 kms to the finish line. All I could think was, *this* is why you run the New York City Marathon. Right then, I knew I'd be back.

We swept north, and the crowd numbers didn't abate until we crossed into the Bronx. There were still tonnes of people out, but First Avenue had been electric. Olah found us again and ran along for a while, vowing to run the marathon with me the following year. When we kicked back across the last bridge and headed onto Fifth Avenue, I knew we were all but home. It was just Jay and me now, keeping in step, looking out for our loved ones.

I was about to give up on seeing Rebecca and my mum, when Bek jumped out of the crowd and grabbed me. I was so relieved to see her, as they'd come all this way, but when I asked where Mum was, Bek pointed over to her chatting to some guy at the side of the road.

'MUM!' Rebecca and I yelled in unison. She looked embarrassed, but happy to see me. We all hugged and grabbed a quick photo, celebrating race 45 in style.

'I love you guys!' I said. 'I'm so happy you made it.'

'We're proud of you!' Bek told me and right there I just wanted to have a little cry.

But there was still some work to do, so Jay and I locked on for the final 5 kms through Central Park. The supporters were bulging onto the track, shouting and blowing horns. The sun was shining and we rolled through the last section of the course, lapping up the atmosphere and feeling jubilant. At the south end of the park, bands were rocking and I was singing along, laughing and puffing, cheering and huffing.

We finished in an extremely respectable 3:22.26. It was an epic run and I thanked Jay for sharing the journey with me. It was the greatest marathon experience of my life.

All my friends got over the line eventually. Haydn ran 4:11.45, Chris and Paul knocked it out in 5:55.43. Koya smashed it again with 4:13.19 and Gareth pushed through his for 3:34.32. Kate powered through for 4:29, even with an injury, and Susan and Lisa, going for their first effort at anything like this distance, took 8 hours and 14 minutes to complete their race, and they were more sore and rightfully, extremely proud.

We got drunk that night. I was out till late at various bars and clubs. I don't know how Koya mustered those dance moves on tired legs, but, man, she was definitely Best on Ground!

We did some touristy stuff over the next couple of days, but eventually it was time for everyone to move on again, including me. I had some huge final weeks ahead of me, but I believed I could make it now. Only logistics could fail me; my legs were tough as iron. It didn't stop Mum from worrying, but she believed in me and that was enough.

Forty-five marathons, 45 weeks, six continents. Not long to go.

46

SAN ANTONIO ROCK 'N' ROLL MARATHON

14 November, San Antonio, Texas, USA

3:25.00

It was all the Cougar's idea. He said he'd only come over to meet me again if I went to Vegas with him. It was likely to go terribly wrong, but I did want to race with him, so I committed. It was a big weekend but, as they say, 'What happens in Vegas, stays in Vegas.'

We flew from there to Austin via Dallas. I diverted from my plan a little to take the opportunity to visit my good friend Christian Hawkins in his new home. It was another long day of flights and I wasn't feeling very well. Not very well at all.

It was hot when we arrived, but Hawkins told us this was cool in comparison to the recent balmy weather they'd had. We dumped our bags and headed to the bar he managed. Everyone was up for some banter and it made for a really fun atmosphere. Except that I still wasn't feeling right. One beer and I was out, heading back to an air mattress on Hawkins' floor. It seemed that a huge week in New York, followed by Vegas, had knocked me from my perch. I slept badly and woke up feeling just as sorry for myself.

I had to run another marathon that weekend, so I'd found one in nearby San Antonio. I was forcing Cougar to run the marathon with me too. I came to Vegas; he ran the marathon – that was the deal. It would be his third for the year, having punched out Tokyo with me in February, then the Melbourne Marathon (in a blistering 3:05) in October.

We hired a car and drove down on Saturday afternoon. We picked up our registration for the San Antonio Rock 'n' Roll Marathon, got a late entry for Gareth who was flying in to join us, and found a San Antonio Spurs match being played that night against the Philadelphia 76s. I'm not a big basketball fan, but I do love the atmosphere of any American sporting event. Whether it's supporting a marathon, watching football or seeing an NBA team in action, Americans just seem to lose their flipping minds!

After a terrible meal at a diner and a restless sleep in a small motel on the edge of the city, we were on the start line again. I must admit, this was right up there with the worst lead-ups to a race I'd had. Except maybe that 100-km race in Bornholm – that was really messy. I just wasn't quite 'in it' for this one. But the weather wasn't too bad and thousands of very excited runners had clustered in the starting area. It wasn't long before I got that tingle of anxiety – another marathon about to get started.

San Antonio had never been on my list of must-visit places, yet I found myself admiring the pretty CBD. It's the home of the Alamo, the famous battle between the Texans claiming independence and the Mexican army of General Santa Anna, fought in 1836. Jim Bowie, Davie Crockett and a band of doomed volunteers went down all guns blazing, against huge odds, sacrificing their lives for a chance at freedom. Moments like that define the Texan legend.

There was not much to tell about the race. We ran as a trio, switching left and right through the north side of town. Gareth, Cougar and I were trucking along at a pretty good pace, but we were never going to set the world on fire. The highlight was the plethora of bands dotting the streets. It was the Rock 'n' Roll Marathon after all, part of a large race series that was gathering momentum in the US.

The course rolls around town for a while, then heads down south past trailer parks and parklands. The Texans were out in reasonable force to support the runners but I'd been spoilt by the NYC Marathon crowds just the week before. It was great to be sharing the race with my old running buddy, Cougar, though. We'd racked up countless kilometres in training back home and this was our fourth international marathon together. Cougar is a human steam train. He's never had the thin marathon runner physique, but, man, set that guy a solid pace and he'll stick to it till the week after next. He's all heart.

We pushed on through and finished back on the east side of town at the aptly named Alamodome. There was fanfare and by this stage I was getting towed along by the Cougar. He was looking tired, but he just powered on home. I was just tired.

Marathon 46 in 3:25.00.

That was once a race time I would have worked extremely hard for. Now it was just a default time when I wasn't feeling well or the heat was up. I don't remember when that goal became easy to attain, but it was now the norm. I couldn't help but think that I should start that sort of planning for 3:00 to feel that way too. If my conditioning to hold a 3:25 came from running that fast every week, then it stood to reason that all I had to do was run faster every week.

The key had to be in the conditioning. I was not physically stronger than anyone else. I would argue that I was more fatigued than most people for a variety of reasons. I believed that carrying the backpack contributed to conditioning, but regular running at speed was paying dividends in the back end of the year. My legs were getting stronger, even if my brain and the rest of my body were ready to pack it in and go home.

The highlight of this part of the trip was being treated to the Salt Lick barbecue in Driftwood on our journey back to Austin. Brisket, a cut of beef around the chest area of a cow, is big in Texas. Hell, everything is big in Texas. It's rubbed with spices and marinated until it's singing to itself. Then it's smoked slowly on a big open barbecue, creating the most succulent meat you've ever tasted in your life. And because it tastes so wonderful, you think you need five times more than a normal portion, so you just keep ordering. Then your body realises it's fallen into the classic Texan trap of biting off far more than it can chew. But your brain keeps saying yes and your mouth keeps chewing; and you can't swallow because you're full of brisket, but everyone's doing it because it's Texas and no one's willing to back down – so instead your eyes bulge and your heart starts to race.

Suffice to say, nobody choked, but by rights we all should have died.

We went back to Austin. It's easy to get drunk in Austin and we really made the most of it, even on a Sunday night. I don't know how we made our flight. I just know we had a hell of a time.

47

MARABANA MARATHON

21 November, Havana, Cuba

3:54.10

I landed in Miami after a stop in Dallas. I was about to get exceedingly friendly with Miami International Airport, with five stopovers the following month. It's the largest hub between North America, Latin America and the Caribbean, which is where I would be spending almost all of the remaining weeks of my journey. First, I bounced down to the Cayman Islands and went to stay with Scott and Sarah, friends of my local connections – Matt and Chloe.

I had managed one important task in Austin. I spent $2500 on a variety of thermal layers, jackets and boots in preparation for what would be my biggest test of the year: the Antarctic run. I realised I wouldn't be able to find appropriate gear in the Caribbean or Costa Rica, so I decided to get all my purchases done early and leave everything in Cayman to pick up in three weeks' time.

I met Jane Wareham, my local contact for Facing Africa, who was organising to get me from Jamaica to the Cayman Islands in a couple of weeks. She was training as a helicopter pilot and had arranged a flight for Saturday 4 December, picking me up in Montego Bay, a couple of hours after my estimated race finish. It was going to be a very tight schedule, but I thought I could run fast enough to stay on time. I thanked her and promised I'd be on schedule.

I stopped in to see my sponsors too. Ken from Krys & Associates had saved me from financial failure in the last few months, keeping me running when I would otherwise have been busking with a set of panpipes. On top of this, both his personal assistant and marketing manager had aided me in all sorts of ways in those final weeks, making sure I had everything I needed. They also organised a fundraising night for Facing Africa.

Ken was ready to come down to Antarctica and race there with me. It was difficult to train for snow running in the humid conditions of Cayman, but once we'd spoken, I realised this guy could take on just about any challenge.

I only got a night in there before I was off to Havana. You generally need to fly out of the US to get to Cuba, hence the roundabout trip to Cayman. It was a Wednesday when I flew across the short strait to Cuba and, I must admit, I was a little nervous about going there. But, as with any place you've never been, your worries are rarely justified. Most of the fear-mongering is American hype used to justify the embargoes they have on the Communist country a stone's throw from their shoreline. Some of it, the strict military rule and social constraints, might have been a problem in the past, but I didn't see any sign of it as I entered the country or throughout my week on the island.

Havana is a complex city. You can see the wealth that they once had in the style of buildings through the centre of town and out along the harbour between Old Havana and Central Havana. La Habana Vieja has actually been listed as a UNESCO World Heritage site, so despite the crumbling buildings and brightly coloured antique cabs, you can also feel a city and a country in recovery.

I was there for two days by myself before Olah and Caz flew in. I took a couple of crappy tours around town, checking out cigar factories and a rum house. The centre of town was the most intriguing, teeming with foreigners, including loads of Americans who were supposedly restricted from travelling here by their government. People were queueing up for absolutely everything, whether it was to withdraw money from a bank, use a slow internet connection, or buy some basic groceries. The stores had plenty of shelf space, with very little stock on any of them. It seemed that everything was in short supply, except for pizza and rum.

I was over the moon when Caz and Olah came. I didn't want to crowd them on their holiday, but it's not too much fun walking around these cities by yourself. We ate out and explored a few bars, drinking mojitos at La Bodeguita del Medio and Cuba Libres in La Floridita, bars where Ernest Hemingway drank in the bad old days before the Communists tore into town and cleaned up the joints. We did some wandering together, but I gave my friends some space too.

Olah came to the race with me. It was a two-lap course – no surprise if you're organising a running event on a budget. It ran from the El Capitolio building in Habana Vieja, down to the forts along the harbour, then sent us all the way out along the boulevard past Centro Habana. Soon enough we swung down south and wound around near an athletics stadium and a big baseball stadium, before returning downtown via the Plaza de la Revolución, where Fidel gave all his wild speeches. There were huge murals of Che Guevara and Fidel on the buildings too.

I had a great run with Olah, but when we dropped him back in front of the El Capitolio, I found myself getting very hot very quickly entering the second half of the race. It rapidly turned into a massive battle to keep going. For a few kilometres I'd run well, then I'd capitulate and walk for a while, then I'd run again for 20 minutes, followed by cramp-afflicted walking breaks. Basically I overheated and the second half of the race went to hell in a hand basket.

But I finished. It sucked, but I finished in 3:54.10. Just too hot.

Not so smart any more, are you, champ? Can run all day, can you? Your default is 3:25, is it?

Never underestimate the marathon.

We spent the rest of the day in Havana, but then decided to share a car across to Viñales. I wanted to see something other than the capital and the two lovebirds wanted to get the hell away from me so they could continue their canoodling in peace. They dropped me in Viñales and then drove on to get a boat across to the Cayo Levisa, a beach resort off the nearby coast. The Viñales Valley is also on the UNESCO heritage list, such is the beauty of the farmland and the strange-looking Mogotes, island-like hills that stick out of the valley floor. It's a popular place to go horse-back riding, rock climbing and hiking. A tour guide took me up through the cave system and I was stunned by the vistas that spread from the mouth of each cavern.

I rolled my own cigar, crushed my own coffee and drank the farmer's homemade rum. It was certainly an experience and one of the absolute highlights of my year. I was at peace in this area. Another slice of heaven, and cheaper than chips. I befriended the Dutch girls starying in the little B&B next door and we took a bus trip out to a beach, Cayo Jutias, and just hung out for a few hours. It was the first time in my entire tour that I had just got up, put on some shorts and went to the beach for the day. I needed it.

That night we hit the local salsa club. Man, can those Cubans dance. I'm from Belgrave, just outside of Melbourne. No, I cannot dance. But it was a year of firsts and I tried my hand at salsa. I tried to keep up with the girl who took my hand, but I'm quite sure she wanted to get rid of me and grab a local.

Getting back to Havana was a nightmare, and I was just in time for my flight. I learnt my favourite Spanish phrase from the taxi driver who got me to the airport on time: 'Tranquilo, amigo!' (Relax, my friend!) She was right. I had no money and no time, but everything was going to turn out okay.

Back to Cayman for another night, then I'd be off again, this time to Costa Rica.

48

MARATHON PUEBLA

28 November, Puebla, Mexico

3:45.56

To get to my next stop I had to fly up to Miami. Then I had a cheap fare on Copa Airlines that would take me first to Panama, then back up to San José, the capital of Costa Rica. I had a few hours' delay in Panama and sat in the airport lounge, skimming through emails and notes using an expensive internet connection.

I looked for the race information I'd need to pick up my registration in San José the next day. No confirmation email. Okay, not unusual. I looked on the marathon web guides and everything looked okay, but there wasn't any registration information there either. I checked out their website, and although it was all in Spanish, it looked a bit different to other marathons' websites pre-race. Alarm bells started to ring. I kept looking for info, using Google Translate, but the only thing I could determine was that there were now two dates listed for the San José International Marathon.

I didn't like this at all, but I couldn't figure out which information was correct, and by this time I was ready to board the plane. I put a message on Facebook:

'I have a sneaking suspicion that the marathon I'm going to run in Costa Rica doesn't actually exist. I was using two websites for my timing, but it seems both of them are guides and not actually the official site. The main one is in Spanish and says the marathon is this weekend, but has no other info, now that I'm looking more closely.

This could be a big problem as I will be there in seven hours . . .'

By the time I got off the flight in Costa Rica and found the well-hidden hostel, I got this in return:

'Mate, the marathon has been moved to 27 March.'

Damn. There was plenty of other advice, but most of it was that I should take a week off, or fly to another continent to run, but it was Thursday and I needed a quick solution. My Rosario buddy Ivan and Alejandro from Mexico, who had been following me online, suggested I head to Puebla, near Mexico City, where there was a race on Sunday morning. I checked the flights: I was going to be out of pocket a further $1000 to divert to Puebla and get back on track.

Alejandro said he'd meet me at the airport and help me get to Puebla. He had recently returned to Mexico City from living in Australia for a few years. Mexico it was, then.

I got a quick three-hour flight to Mexico City on Saturday morning. Alejandro's suggestion was that we hire a car and drive to Puebla to register for the race by 4 p.m. He'd have a place for us to stay with his aunty. It sounded like a pretty solid idea and I didn't have too many other options by this time, so I hired the car and handed him the keys. I didn't know Alejandro and I didn't know anything about Puebla, but I figured I'd had pretty darn good luck up till now, and Alex had no reason to steer me wrong.

So here we were, driving to Puebla. I was in Mexico, my first time, in a year of firsts. There were young guys riding pushbikes up the highway, dinking Virgin Mary statues strapped to their backs and heads. Apparently they ride all the way from Mexico City to Puebla, as a sort of cleansing pilgrimage.

Alex had enlisted his cousin Sandra to pick up our race registrations. We met Sandra in town, with her mother and little son. Puebla is a very pretty little city and the centre of town is absolutely beautiful.

It's peaceful and the town square is surrounded by cafés, a cathedral and wonderful old buildings. We sat down for some lunch, cramming in some pasta, and then went back to Sandra's place to meet her husband, Julio. Alex and I stayed at Aunt Lucía's overnight, in a townhouse just outside of the city, then Julio picked us up early in the morning and dropped us into the town square to find the start line.

Distance running has long had a place in Mexican culture, and the country produced some amazing marathoners in the '90s, like Germán Silva and Salvador García, both NYC Marathon winners. Whatever might be in the blood of the Mexicans, they sure are a passionate people and I found myself in a very happy place at the start line of the Puebla Marathon.

We all ran through the main square and took off out of town fairly quickly. The course is a single loop that skirts the city before delivering runners back to the centre of town. There were loads of bands and tonnes of drink stations, but better than that, I was running alongside a great new friend in a very interesting new place. We pounded the streets of Puebla, soaking up the sun on an increasingly warm day, but it was still cool enough to keep a steady pace.

Puebla is actually at high altitude (around 2100 metres), so the air was noticeably thinner. I'd like to use that as part of my excuse for getting tired and bombing out by the end of the run, but that would be a cop-out. With my messy lead-up and all the travel, I'd never had much chance of attacking the hills around Puebla, so I took finishing the race in one piece as a win.

Alejandro was great company and he put together a really special race. He'd been training for a 10-km race a few weeks down the track, so to just toss this marathon in without much warning was a testament to his courage and fortitude. We smashed it out together and were both wheezing badly by the end.

Marathon 48 – 3:45.56.

We went back to Aunt Lucía's, had a shower and a quick bite to eat, then said our goodbyes to his wonderful family.

By early Sunday evening we were already back in Mexico City. It was Alex's girlfriend's name day, so we headed over to Andrea's home for a real Mexican feast. A few of us ended up watching football in a bar that evening.

The next day, my friends Sean and Hangatu met up with us in town. Sean and I had worked together in Google's Melbourne office. We'd lost our jobs in the same way and taken different paths afterwards. Yet here we were, more than a year later, having adventures. Losing your job isn't always so bad!

'Only four to go,' Sean said to me.

'Yeah, but with 48 marathons in my legs, it doesn't sound so easy.'

Alex took me to the airport the morning after that. On the way he made me buy a Mexican wrestling mask, which is a very popular keepsake in that part of the world. I pledged to wear it in Antarctica, in honour of him, his help and his friendship. I apologised for not making the time to have a tequila with him and his eyes went wide.

'Man, seriously, we didn't have tequila! Your trip to Mexico is incomplete!'

'It's okay, mate, it's 10 a.m. We can do it next time.'

'No way. We can do it now. Come with me.'

He was so insistent, I dared not say no. I followed him through the airport to a bar and he ordered us a round of tequilas. It was early, but I downed the shots. They were goooood.

I sat on the plane and thought about the speed at which the last few days had rushed by, throwing up all sorts of unexpected moments and adventures. Then I realised that November was over and I only had December to go. My big year was nearly complete.

49

REGGAE MARATHON

4 December, Negril, Jamaica

3:31.56

Back at Miami airport, I'd found myself up against another hurdle. The change in schedule meant I was heading to Jamaica a night earlier than anticipated with no accommodation booked. It soon became apparent that there were no cheap hotels or hostels available in Kingston. I'd always intended to head straight out to Montego Bay and Negril on landing, but I would definitely need a bed for the first night.

I turned to Facebook again, hoping the goodwill I'd accumulated might pay out one more time. And it did. Dionne, a friend of a friend, came to pick me up at the airport, even though I didn't get out to the arrivals lounge till after 10 p.m. The immigration people didn't like my story about a local connection waiting outside, nor did they believe I was here to run my 49th marathon. Toss in the fact that I didn't have an exit flight booked – only an estimated time of my helicopter pick-up on Saturday morning – and the authorities decided I was just another stoner here to toke up in Bob Marley's homeland.

I argued for a while and I think they just gave up when they realised it was getting too late to put me back on a flight to Miami. My story hadn't changed and I gave them everything except the specific address of where I was sleeping. Risky, but I got through.

Dionne took me to her home in town. Her husband had fallen asleep on the couch in the lounge and her two little kids were passed out across her bed. I was given a room and a welcome, more than enough. I was a wreck and was out in a heartbeat.

Next morning, Dionne drove me about, helping me exchange some money and buy a bus ticket to Montego Bay. She also dropped me at Bob Marley's estate, to pay homage to the reggae master. It was worth a visit, but didn't have me fall in love with Rasta culture and nobody rolled me a spliff. Then I was on a bus, taking the long, winding road across the mountains of Jamaica, to the north coast of the island at Montego Bay.

Another Facebook friend met me on arrival. Navin was a real stats man. He seemed to know everything about races around the world, but had not quite bumped the four-hour mark in his recent marathon journey. He was aiming to knock it off on Saturday at the Negril race. I was rapt to have already met a fellow runner and even more excited when he offered to have me stay the night at his brother's place. I jumped at the chance, as I was almost bankrupt and it was a much nicer proposition than staying in a crumby hostel.

A bus and a dicey taxicab took me to Negril, where I was hoping to relax. On the bus I was jammed in with half-a-dozen people, then they tried to double our number by loading in schoolkids along the way. If this was any indication of driving in Jamaica, I'd stick to walking. But we got there in one piece and I ended up in a cheap hotel.

The beach nearby was a little manky and Negril was full of Jamaicans who kept harassing me to buy stuff. Not really anything, just tourist junk from their stores, girls from a restaurant nearby, or 'high grade' from their car boot. I wasn't interested and this wasn't the beach paradise I'd been expecting.

Dionne had bestowed one more gift on me. She'd organised a day pass to Sandals Resort, further up the beach. On Friday I woke up with a big toenail giving up the fight to stay attached and a throat so sore, I would have sworn I'd had that very toenail stuck in my neck all night! I was getting the flu.

I pulled myself together and tore the rest of the nail off as gently as possible, trying to avoid infection. I picked up my registration from one of the resorts and then headed on to Sandals. I walked in to discover the paradise I'd been dreaming about, with expansive pools, beautiful girls lounging about in bikinis, and free food – a *lot* of free food. I had a big meal, carb loading as best I could, and then I went and sat on the perfectly manicured beach. I watched guests take sailing lessons, rev up jet skis and, well, girls lounge about in bikinis. This was how the other half lived. The people with money. I didn't have any money, so this was way outside my general experience for the year.

I felt a bit lecherous, so I moved into the pool and took up a bar stool. I met a member of the Jamaican bobsled team, a travel agent making the most of the resort she normally recommends, and finally her husband, a high-school teacher. We punctuated our great discussion with rum and tequila shots and by the end, I couldn't feel my sore throat any more and I could barely feel my legs, but I'd had a hell of a time. I wandered onto the beach to capture the world's most exquisite sunset.

I met up with Navin and some of his friends at the pasta party back at Swept Away Resort. I went to the press conference too, but I was still kinda drunk, so I'm glad no one asked me any questions. Back at the lodge, I was kept up for most of the night by a huge street party raging down in the main square of Negril. It was supposedly part of the marathon celebration, but I really couldn't believe that any marathoners would be out partying at 1 a.m. the night before they were set to run.

I got up at 4 a.m. and made my way to the bus stop. I was even more sick than the morning before, so things were not looking good for the the next two races. But I was here and I could move, so I joined Navin on the start line. I'd encouraged him to aim a little faster with his pacing, anticipating that he would need to be ahead of his target time to allow for fatigue and heat in the final 10 kms. I explained that he didn't want to feel like he was failing if he was just a few seconds off the pace at halfway – he'd need to be in the right mental state leading into the second half. He seemed nervous about the adjustment, even though it was only about 20 seconds a mile, but agreed to give it a go.

The race kicked off, but it was still ridiculously early. We were running by 5.15 a.m. so as to reduce the amount of time spent in the sun. Even at 5 a.m. it felt like 25°C, so God knew how hot it was going to become. There was a big 'Hurrah!' as 1500 people took off up the road, with 500 runners in each of the distances. The support was excellent, even at this time of the morning, with cars pulled up along the side of the course, blaring Bob Marley tunes and beating out island rhythms on calypso drums. We go a lot of 'Ya, mun' too, which I thought was hilarious even the 500th time I heard it.

In my current situation, Bob Marley's 'Three Little Birds' seemed quite appropriate, with its 'Don't worry' refrain. So I kept singing along, hoping that I would reach the end before the sun decided to use its death rays to melt me. I found the outer end of the course eventually, although I wasn't getting any faster. But I wasn't done yet either, so even when the sun cascaded down above the jungle, denying me any more shadows in which to hide, I knew I was going to get home in one piece.

It wasn't easy, yet when I came closer to the resort area, the level of support began to lift. I was coughing up a lung by the end, my chest stressed from the flu. I made it through the 49th marathon in scorching heat in 3:31.56.

Navin clocked 3:57.30 and, boy, did he look happy.

I split fast, grabbing my backpack and tossing my gear in a local guy's car. I had very little cash left and even less time, so I offered everything I had to get me to Montego Bay helipad. The fella obliged, but could only take me halfway, where he'd deliver me to some buddies who could drive me the rest of the way. If I wasn't in a rush, I would have reconsidered this approach, but I had to rely on fate to deliver me safely. Fate and the driving skills of Jamaican madmen.

It was the scariest car ride I've ever endured. These guys swung left and right, along winding roads, overtaking buses and trucks on this spindly mountain pass. I thought I was going to die fifteen times in the first half-hour, then I just stopped looking ahead, putting my faith in the locals. Seeing a truck that had recently rolled into a ditch didn't help my nerves, but the lads kept saying, 'S'alright, mun. Be cool.' *I'll give you 'be cool' in a bloody minute*, I thought, but I bit my lip and waited for it to be over.

We got there and Jane (from Facing Africa)was waiting with Jerome, owner of Cayman Islands Helicopters. Ten minutes later we were in the air. I'd never been in a helicopter before but, I tell you, if I was going to splurge in the future, this was the way to do it. We floated above the sapphire-blue waters of the Caribbean, island hopping in the most impressive fashion. It was breathtaking scenery and I was filled with belief again that my adventure would succeed. With this many people now behind me and so many adventures under my belt, how could I possibly trip up in the final steps towards the finish line?

50

CAYMAN ISLANDS MARATHON

5 December, George Town, Grand Cayman

3:33.58

I stayed with Scotty and Sarah again. As part of my race preparation I devoured a couple of massive bowls of delicious spaghetti bolognaise. I was definitely exhausted, and Sarah winced when I coughed and gave me a Lemsip drink to try to soothe my throat. But apart from that, I felt no worse than I had before any of the other recent runs.

The start time was 5 a.m. There were truckloads of people milling about near the port area and I got that little taste of pre-race excitement once again. I had a number of people introduce themselves and pump me up for the day's run, so I tried to look less fatigued and more like a running hero.

I had no idea how this run would turn out, so I just switched into gear and tried to pull out the same strategy I had the day before – run 4.45s until I couldn't any more. I was running with Canadian Zac for the first 5 kms or so, but his legs were still shaky after his romp in Athens. I connected with a couple of other local runners, including my saviour Ken Krys, who was doing some extra training for Antarctica.

The sun came up as we reached the first 10-km turning point of this two-lap course and I was well on track. By the time we'd snuck back into town, though, the sun was beginning to blaze and my legs were feeling extremely heavy. We passed some beaches and many residents came out early to clap everyone along. Everyone seemed to know each other on Cayman, so it felt like a really nice community race – the Reggae run felt like a tourist attraction in comparison.

I looped back through the centre of town, as many other runners were finishing off their half marathons. I wasn't too far off my pace and tried to hold strong through to the line, so when the MCs saw me and recognised me as 'that guy', they commented that I seemed strong, not even breaking a sweat. The opposite was true. I was hurting like hell but because I rarely sweat, I looked nice even when I wanted to collapse.

After another 5 kms, I was cooked. I came to a walk, just as a car pulled up by me.

'C'mon, mate, you can do it!' Scotty yelled. 'It's not far now, so if you run you'll get there faster!' He was out of the race with an injury but knew what I was going through.

Though I was spent, I managed to grin back at him. 'I know, mate; I've got this.'

Sarah and Scotty kept me company for a while, driving a little distance ahead. I welcomed the distraction and used their car as a moving goal line, just chasing it down the road.

'C'mon, champ,' I said to myself. 'You know how this is going to turn out. It can only end one way, with you crossing that line.' I addressed my legs. 'C'mon, Wally and Barry, you boys know how it's done. You gotta run to get to the end; you want this over, but it's up to you to keep moving.'

At the 30-km turnaround I got a lot of shout-outs from runners who saw me coming the other way. 'Well done, Tristan, keep it up, mate.' 'Looking good, Tristan, fantastic work!'

I truly appreciated how this community had embraced me. It was a lovely way to finish my final big international run. The next would be a lonely one in Antarctica, then it was off home.

I persisted through the heat. By the end, I was coughing and wheezing, but my legs were still skipping along, covering the kilometres.

So that was it. I rolled across the line in 3:33.58, just two minutes shy of my Jamaican time the day before. The magic number 50 was done. Only two to go.

I had a couple of great days in Cayman after that, being well looked after by my hosts. Ken's people were great again, sorting out some final arrangements to send some of my gear home and get me down to Punta Arenas in Chile with Ken. The fundraiser they'd organised with Jane went smoothly, raising quite a bit of money for Facing Africa and generally celebrating athletics in Cayman. My throat was a complete mess, but I scratched out a short thank-you speech.

And then I was gone again. Back on a plane, heading to Miami. I had a whole new pack, full of completely different arctic wear, and one more truly insane adventure ahead of me. I plugged in my iPod and clicked play, listening to Paul Kalkbrenner's 'Sky and Sand' for the 100th time.

I was on my way to Antarctica; it really did feel like the world had no end.

51

ANTARCTIC ICE MARATHON

12 December, Patriot Hills, Antarctica

4:59.08

I had the cheap seats again. Cayman to Miami, to Lima, to Santiago and on to Punta Arenas via Puerto Montt. I was not feeling quite as recovered as I'd have liked, but I was still looking forward to getting all the way to the bottom of South America.

Ken and I were on a couple of the same flights, but he was taking a more direct route. There's no easy way to get to Punta Arenas, though, just a lot of flying with a few pit stops on the way. We landed at 3 p.m. on Wednesday 8 December and met a few other likely runners in Santiago and then Punta Arenas. Everyone had a weary look in their eyes but seemed like fit gents. We cabbed it to Hotel Diego de Almagro, which would be the main base for the our crew before we set forth on our grand adventure.

I'd found myself a nice little hostel about 10 minutes' walk away. Where Almagro was stinging for $90 per night, I had my bed for only $10. I was still on struggle street with the dinero and the organiser, Richard Donovan, couldn't tell us how many days it would be before we flew to Antarctica. We were dependent on the weather.

To be fair, it wasn't Richard's call. He was our booking agent, if you will, but also the tour operator for the Ice Marathon. The people calling the shots were Adventure Network International (ANI). They were updating Richard on a twice-daily basis, looking for a clear patch in the weather that would give them long enough to land a plane, unload us and our supplies, then reload all the people waiting to leave. These windows only had to be five or six hours long, but unfortunately they're elusive little chaps, so for the next few days, we were left waiting by the phone.

I was in good company. There were runners from Ireland, the US, Hungary, Canada, Norway, England, Germany, Hong Kong, India, Brazil and everywhere else in between. Everyone had great stories about what had brought them to the point in their lives where they had decided a little jog at the bottom of the world would be a splendid idea.

Most people were there alone, so everyone had a reason to get to know each other. I spent most of my time hanging out with Greg Swan, a guy from Brisbane, and a Norwegian fella, Stephan, who was working as a diplomat in Venezuela. We took a few walks, nailed a couple of training runs, and I had heaps of work to catch up on. On Friday, the wind speed around Union Glacier was exceeding the maximum 30 knots acceptable for landing on the ice. No plane. We went to see penguins on Magdalena Island, but after an hour of choppy seas, the boat turned around. It wasn't good – six-and-a-half hours in a leaky boat, with only a Britney Spears concert to watch on DVD and everyone puking. No penguins. We sat around twiddling our thumbs.

The next night we were still stuck at the bottom of chilly old Chile. That was three wasted days and my emotions fluctuated between being pissed off about it and anxious about the run – if we were ever going to get the chance to do it.

Sunday went to dust as well. The cloud cover was too low for us to land around Union Glacier. N.O.T. C.O.O.L. Apparently it was all very normal but I started looking at back-up races just in case we didn't make it.

On Monday, the skies were clear in Antarctica, and we were just waiting for the winds to abate. Finally we were off. I was on my way to my 51st marathon at the bottom of the world.

I've flown to a lot of places around the globe, but that trip down to the seventh continent was a truly wild experience. We were strapped into an old Russian Ilyushin jet, with rows of old passenger-plane seating bolted onto the hull. The plane only had a few small peephole windows and plenty of room left open at the back for the palettes of supplies. I don't know how old that plane was, but it felt like a flying tank.

As soon as we were over ice, everyone began to take turns peering out the little windows. There were just massive chunks of white below and with every kilometre, they clustered closer together until it was a connected mass. It took around five hours to get to our destination. We flew to Union Glacier, where the ANI team had carved a runway out of the ice pack. The glacier is also not too far from Mount Vinson, the highest peak in Antarctica and therefore the seventh summit, making it a great launching pad for these expeditions.

Exiting the plane was like stepping onto another planet. We all rugged up, pulling on gloves and hoods, but as I stepped out and climbed down the ladder, I realised I was fairly ill-equipped to be in a crazy place like this. I should've had a space suit on. The wind was blowing down the glacier and striking through us as we plodded across to the reception portable. A couple of big orange snow trucks dropped off the passengers who were heading home and then loaded us in, to ferry us across to the station.

The Union Glacier Station sits in a protected dip in the lee of a mountain at the edge of the glacier. It's essentially set up as a hotel. A hotel manager and staff were there to make sure all guests were suitably safe and comfortable. The rooms were a series of dome tents with a few larger tent structures, more like small hangars, for the recreation rooms and mess tents. A couple of other portables housed the toilets and communications facilities. The season only lasted from early November to the start of February, but could be shorter. It was completely weather dependent.

Nearby, a smaller airfield catered for a Basler aircraft, which looked like a DC-3, and a de Havil and Twin Otter, both aided by skis. These planes were used to ferry passengers to the different sections of Antarctica, whether your final destination was Mount Vinson or the South Pole Station.

All sorts of groups were passing through, some scientific, but mostly recreational. We met climbers and teachers who were there to carry out some experiments on behalf of an education program. Others were simply en route to the South Pole to take a look at the 'true' bottom of the world.

A number of adventurers had come to do the 'last degree', which saw them dropped at a latitude of 89° south, and from there they would cross-country ski to the South Pole. Apparently the air is much thinner within the arctic circles, so it's hard to process enough oxygen. Not only that, but if you think of Antarctica as an island, then it rises quite high above sea level in its centre, around 3300 metres, where it levels out to a wide plane; in the middle of the icy plain is the South Pole. These adventurers ski across the plain, following a bloke who is guided by his compass alone. It takes around four days, even though the distance is just 111 kms. Such is the fatigue incurred from exertion near the pole, they can only manage 25–30 kms a day.

Other expeditions were trying to cross the continent, by truck or by foot. One gent we met, a Norwegian named Christian Eide, was attempting to ski from the coast to the South Pole. His was a completely unsupported mission, so he had to drag a sled with all his supplies. I later found out that Christian smashed the previous record, completing the trip in 24 days, 1 hour and 13 minutes. How's that for endurance?!

We had a marathon to run and everyone wanted to know when it was going to happen. The weather had been quite patchy, so all that Richard could tell us was that it wouldn't be tomorrow, but it could be the next day. At that time of year, the sun never sets, instead it just cuts laps around the sky, so it was hard to know when tomorrow was, or whether we should go to bed.

The tents were heated 24/7 by the sun, so they were effectively like saunas. It was only cold outside the tent, but you could comfortably sit in your underwear inside. The thick goose-down sleeping bags were actually too much. And with a few other sweaty guys in the tent, it became a place only for sleeping.

I kept standing outside my tent for as long as possible, looking around at the snow being blown around, at the jagged white peaks nearby, at the constantly changing array of clouds in the sky. I was in Antarctica. I was really there. Who'd have ever thought this would be something I'd experience?

We sat about in the mess tents and talked, went for short walks (because it was far too cold for long ones). If you were outside more than five minutes, you began to feel the cold deep within your bones. The food served up at breakfast, lunch and dinner was spectacular – we had roast lamb on the first night and pasta on another night. Or day. Whenever.

We ate extremely well, but inevitably you needed to use the loo and this was an adventure in itself. The toilets were set up so you'd urinate and defecate separately. I'm only explaining this because I was impressed by ANI's determination to leave a neutral human imprint on this magnificent landscape. It's part of their charter, but they do take it very seriously. The effluent is regularly transferred into a tank that sits away from the camp, waiting for an opportunity to load it back on the same Ilyushin jet that brought us down from Chile. Nothing gets left behind.

A day after our arrival, Richard encouraged us to go for a training run, to acclimatise to our surroundings. It took me around 20 minutes just to cover a few kilometres, and when I turned to head back, I was absolutely crushed with fatigue. Each step was tentative, looking for solid ice, but with one footfall I'd step in soft snow, and the next back onto ice. It was like going to the beach and running from sand to concrete and back onto sand again. It was extremely difficult to get a rhythm going.

Back in the mess tent, we were discussing the difficulty of running on this surface and without as much oxygen, when Richard turned up with the all-clear: we'd be running the next day. I was excited but it would be close to 24 hours before we started out, so I didn't get too carried away. Everyone retired early and got as much rest as possible.

I was nervous. I slept badly and woke up early to prepare. I've never worn so much clothing in my life, let alone to run a marathon, putting on two layers of pants, two pairs of socks, three layers on top including a Marmot soft-shell jacket, a balaclava and goggles. I had my Salomon Gore-Tex trail shoes, hoping they'd keep out the snow, plus a little utility belt that housed my camera. Everyone was looking rather serious in their different race get-ups. No one wanted to freeze.

There were 36 participants, of all shapes, sizes and ages. A couple of the Union station crew were joining in, one of whom, Marc, had won for the previous two years. One Californian girl, Sarah, was running with her dad, attempting to be the youngest person to run a marathon on all continents, plus the North Pole, at only 16 years of age.

We spread out quite quickly, the faster runners trying to find a rhythm and stick with the experienced guys at the front. I stayed with them for a little while, but they were too quick for me. The course would take us on two long loops, one 25 kms and the next 17 kms. There were two portable tents waiting at reasonable intervals, so you'd see them twice each throughout the race. The tents were for anyone who was feeling the cold too intensely. In front of them were volunteers serving warm water and electrolytes.

Once we disengaged with each other along the course, there was no one nearby. Just cold breath and bright white. The sound was eerie, and I focused on my breathing and footfalls to fill the void.

I worked systematically to get from one little orange flag to the next. I was reasonably steady, even though it was hard to put a good series of footsteps together. By the time I got through the first loop, I was feeling kind of cactus, so I pulled up and got a couple of drinks into me. Apparently I was somewhere in the top 10. I wanted to hold on to that for a solid ending.

I seemed to lift on the second lap, cruising past a few runners. They were specks in the distance, then forms, then people struggling along, and finally forms behind me. I could have stopped to encourage people, but I was desperately trying to keep moving myself. At one stage, I looked up and out to my left, away from the loop and towards the white wilderness. It was difficult to get any perspective on what I was seeing, because it was just plains of snow, edged by mountains and hills, that were in turn covered in white. I was inspired by the view, by the magnificent ocean of white around me, but that kind of desolation also makes you afraid. It's not what you can see in a place like that – rather it's not knowing what's beyond those mountains: it seems as if there's *absolutely nothing* out there.

I focused on the job at hand. I was finding it hard to breathe through my balaclava, so I kept pulling it down. Then my face would begin to freeze, so I'd pull it up. The ski goggles were uncomfortable, but without them I could feel my eyes working extremely hard to process the terrain through the brightness. I'd get a run on, then just hit soft snow and be dragged to a near halt again. By the time I passed the last medico tent, I was flagging and a couple of runners caught me again.

I stumbled, walked and ran through those last couple of kilometres. I got my camera out when I passed the final 25-mile marker and babbled, 'Nearly there, then I'm coming home. Aw, I'm coming home.'

My 51st marathon was completed in 4:59.08.

Everyone finished eventually. The race was won by Brazil's Bernardo, and I came in sixth. I'd take that any day of the week.

I had nothing left.

I had considered running the 100-km version of the race, which would follow in a few days, but when we were informed that a plane would be leaving the following day, I canned that idea on the spot. We were warned that we could be there till Christmas if we didn't take this plane. Having seen the ever-changing weather here, I wasn't about to argue. I couldn't afford a flexible fare, so if I missed my return flight to Australia, I'd have to buy another ticket. I'd been too lucky for too long, so it was time to get the hell out of Dodge.

We celebrated our achievements by drinking beer and any other alcohol that had been smuggled down. Somebody suggested a 100-metre topless dash and within minutes we were all back out on the ice, charging towards the finish line, skin glistening with sweat turning to frost. I donned my Mexican wrestling mask in honour of Alejandro and within metres of running took a spill onto the cold, cold ground.

Then we were gone. The big Ilyushin took off and I was awake for about five minutes during the entire flight. We'd only been down there for four days and three nights, but it had felt like two weeks. I was completely exhausted when we returned, and I wasted half a day sleeping.

We were back in Punta Arenas earlier than anticipated, so a few of us went on a bus tour to the glacial area of Torres del Paine, at the base of Chilean Patagonia. This was the last touristy thing I'd do on my world adventure. If you only visited this place in Chile, you'd be awe-struck by its magnificence. But I'd just come from Antarctica and I was struggling to stay awake.

I headed to the airport one more time. From here, I would be in planes and airports for two-and-a-half days.

But I'd be home for Christmas.

52

MELBOURNE MARATHON

27 December, Melbourne, Australia

3:43.20

Punta Arenas–Santiago–Guayaquil–Miami. Nineteen hours of flying. It was 4.15 a.m. at my favourite airport – Miami International – with all my friends. My flight wasn't till 1.30 p.m. so I lay on a bench, begging for sleep until the tellers opened.

'Any chance I could get an earlier flight to LA?'

'Sure, let me see. That'll be $600.'

'Oh, okay. Actually I quite like it here; I think I'll stay a while.'

I emailed, Facebooked and killed enough time to get to the gate. Then my flight to Washington was delayed. When I finally got to frosty DC, it seemed that every flight in the northern hemisphere was cancelled. Storms were raging from New York to London and right across Europe. My flight took off eventually, but it didn't leave much wiggle room for my connection in LA.

I listened to music on the flight, too tired to write and too emotionally drained to watch a rom-com. But I stupidly listened to all the songs that had encapsulated my year, reminiscing about the highlights and the lowlights. When I played Tim Minchin's 'White Wine in the Sun' again, I started to weep.

I told myself I'd made it. I should be delighted. But I was done. I'd used everything I had to come this far. *Please, please, don't miss the connection.*

I walked off the flight, up the ramp into the terminal and took a sharp left, just in time for final boarding for the flight Sydney. Phew.

I wished the world farewell. Thanking it for looking out for me on my epic journey. It'd let me be successful, when it could have just as easily doomed me to fail. I believe that good things happen to good people, but it was more than that this time. Something magic had been in the air during 2010, a type of divinity that only comes along once in a lifetime.

I went from LA to Sydney, crossing the shores of the northern beaches on a bright December morning. One more change, one more coffee, and then a short trip to Melbourne and home.

I'd made it.

I felt like a shell of a man, but I still had my emotions welling up. My heart skipped a beat when we touched down at Tullamarine, more than 60 hours after I'd left Punta Arenas. No more cheap seats. Never again, I vowed. This was the last of 113 flights I'd taken during the year.

I stepped off the plane and moved quickly through immigration. For all the stamps in my passport, I just got a nod from the immigration clerk. I planted my bags on a trolley and wheeled it towards those big sliding doors, passing through them with a sigh of relief.

Throughout the year, I'd watched strangers hugging after each flight. Friends embracing, families reuniting, lovers kissing. I'd rarely had anyone to meet me and always felt a pang of jealousy or loneliness as I wandered to the bus station. This time it was different. A whole host of people waited, wearing RunLikeCrazy T-shirts, clapping and cheering. My friends, my family, my mum. She was about to cry. I grinned, my heart lifting with one last flutter to see them all. There were hugs, high fives, pats on the back. I felt like I'd come back from the Olympics with a gold medal around my neck.

Bec was there too. She'd kept me company by Skype for much of the last five months. Nothing crazy, just chatting. She was someone with whom I'd shared my little stories, my fears and my triumphs. She kissed me.

'You made it!'

Yeah. We made it.

Koya and Bec had been working frantically over the last few months to make the last race happen. They'd rustled up volunteers from our friendship groups and complete strangers. They'd got sponsorship money from Schepisi Communications, National Australia Bank and even Krys & Associates. There was more to do in the days leading up to the race on 27 December, but first there was Christmas.

Christmas dinner was with Mum, my sister Rebecca and her soon-to-be-husband Michael, Alexis (all the way over from London) and Bec. I'd met most of Bec's family earlier that day too, and was treated as if they'd known me forever. But sitting there with my mum serving up roast lamb, making bad jokes with my sisters, and looking over at Bec, I felt a huge pang of guilty happiness. I'd done everything in just one year, seen so many people in disadvantaged situations, been gifted hospitality by people who had nothing else to give, and here I was with a table full of food and a roomful of loved ones. Man, was I lucky.

Traditionally I get one leg of lamb and my family gets another because I'm the youngest and therefore the favourite. It was bliss. And then I had a white wine in my hand – I thought of the Tim Minchin song and got emotional again.

Two days later a crowd of people descended on Albert Park Lake. There were hundreds of people! I knew a lot of the participants, but plenty were complete strangers, yet they sure seemed to know me. These were the people who'd carried me on with their words of support for a whole year.

The race got going. It was two, four or eight laps of the lake, giving people the chance to do 10 kms, a half or full marathon. I'd thanked everyone for coming down on the megaphone before we set off, but now I was introducing myself or chatting to people I knew, putting faces to names. Each drink station had a theme and those manning it were dressed wildly, cheering us as we went past.

One lap, two laps, the crowd began to thin. Four hundred people decided to join the race, some people running 10 kms for the first time, some running their first marathon. They kept telling me how inspired they were. As the 10-km runners finished, the crowd swelled around the finish line, waiting for the rest of us to come in. A band was belting out tunes, pumping everyone up, and with every lap I'd see more of my friends appear. The Sultan was there, all the way from Dubai. Opray and Kim appeared from out of nowhere, on a surprise visit home from London. There was even Teash from the run in Egypt! Dee and little Jac, who'd lost Damon that year. My new nephew Eli and my godson, Atticus. Lisa's boys, Cooper and Bailey, running along next next to me. Will and Leila! Kids everywhere, some who'd just been born when I left, others who'd been introduced to the world while I was gone. I'd missed so much.

I ran and ran, laughing at my old companion, Dazzler, covered in red body paint, running his first full! I felt like I was going to cry with happiness. I was running with friends, not strangers in a foreign land. My friends, in my home.

I knew I'd definitely made it now.

So many people pushed through their first, fifth or fifteenth race, all celebrating the joy of running. As I came around to cross that line for one last time, my heart was in my throat. The applause lifted to a crescendo and I ran myself right into history.

Marathon 52 complete. A lazy 3:43.20.

AFTERWORD

I've never read about anyone else running so many marathons in so many parts of the world. Maybe it had happened before but, believe me, I looked. I'd run in 42 countries and on all seven continents in just 52 weeks, covering around 320 000 kms by plane, train, boat, bus and car. I ran just over 2300 race kilometres, plus a tonne of training kilometres in the middle. I wore out seven pairs of running shoes.

I ran with bulls, danced at festivals, strode atop the Great Wall of China and crawled beneath the Great Pyramids. I tried to hug a yak, rode like crazy on a Mongolian pony and peed my pants in front of a mountain gorilla. I made my way to the remotest islands with huge stone heads, the hottest deserts with oceans of sand and the coldest of climates with acres of nothing. I was robbed, got injured, got sick and depressed. I learnt great lessons: that you can't carry someone through life, let alone for 42 kilometres; that you can prepare with others, but come race day, it's a solo mission. I was gifted friendship, warmth, camaraderie and mountains of laughter. And I found love.

It was the greatest year of my life. I'll never have another one like it, and if I had all the money in the world, I could not have made it better. It was an idea that became an adventure. An adventure that became a common cause. A cause that became an accomplishment. A success that was as much about the selflessness and generosity of people around the globe as it was about my effort.

I missed a lot of important moments in my friends' and family's lives while I was away. I think I felt it more acutely because I missed them all so much. I've seen Dee and Jacqueline a few times – they miss Damon like crazy, but they're doing okay. My mum number two, Gay, has recovered from her breast cancer treatment and she's doing fine too, which is a huge relief. She's even doing public speaking to raise awareness around breast cancer! She's incredible.

Before I'd even finished my year, people asked me, 'So what's next?' I was so engrossed in the big adventure that it seemed a ridiculous question – the only 'plan' I had was to run the Marathon des Sables. Truth was, 2011 seemed a lifetime away.

When I came back I knew I wanted to take on new challenges, but I didn't want to spend the rest of my life trying to come up with year-long adventure runs, just to outdo myself. After 2010, I have little else to prove. As for a job, I feel like I'm near unemployable now, in a good way. I just don't see how I could report to a boss about the uplift in sales, or how I'm tracking towards my stretch targets. I'm not knocking the jobs I had; I certainly wouldn't be where I am today without those experiences in premier sales teams. I'm just out of the game.

My life has changed immeasurably as a result of RunLikeCrazy, but not necessarily in the ways I anticipated. I knew I wanted a new life at the other end. I wanted to be different, with a new outlook on my future. That happened, but instead of becoming a wild adventure man, thriving on thrills, spills and massive hills, I've mellowed quite dramatically. There was no doubt that I was going to need a slow year in 2011 to recover from the beating I'd given myself, so I didn't plan too many specific adventures. Yet by the year's end, I'd spent time on six of the seven continents again, only missing another trip to Antarctica. I ran in the deserts of the Sahara, ticked off four major Aussie marathons and went back for one more crack at New York's biggest road race. With holidays in France, Vietnam, the USA, Bali and Brazil, life has been pretty damn good to me.

'How can you afford that without a job?' I hear you ask.

When I got back, people told me I had a great story to tell, and I was soon given the opportunity to see if I was any good at telling it. I gave a talk to a corporate group and felt confident; I enjoyed it. Soon, every booking was leading to another one. So now I get to relive the adventure over and over, showing a few videos and generally taking the piss out of myself. I now have a pseudo career.

I will have more adventures, though, and I hope I can find a way to raise more money and awareness for good causes. In the end, I only raised a little over $17 000 for UNICEF and Facing Africa, which left me feeling proud but somewhat uncomfortable. I thought I would raise a fortune for them, but it seems press in every language doesn't automatically turn into dollars, especially when people in many of these countries are struggling themselves. I spent approximately $120 000 on my year, so you could argue that I'm a selfish bastard. If I were a better man, I would have given the whole lot to UNICEF in the first place. Well, I hope I've inspired a few people to keep giving generously to causes they believe in. Better still, get out there and do something about it!

And the fairytale ending? My relationship with Rebecca Sherwill blossomed throughout 2011 and I proposed to her in Brazil, at the magnificent Iguazu Falls in January 2012. My luck held out – she said yes. I think I'm much better at relationships now that I believe in myself.

I do want to keep testing myself and dancing on the edge. Something that occurred to me a few times recently is the Freudian idea of Thanatos, the so-called 'death drive'. It's common to us all in some form or another – we instinctively wonder what it would be like to slice our finger on a blade, or jump from a plane, all in the search of the thrill of life. I put myself in so many positions of potential failure in 2010 and there was even a bit of self-sabotage – running with the bulls, running too fast, doubling up marathons, running

100 kms off the back of a marathon. I sought out situations that would push me closer to the edge, to see if I'd capitulate or conquer the fear. I can't explain why I did that, except to say that I have never felt so wonderfully mortal, so wickedly alive as I did throughout 2010. I was emotionally distraught as often as I was deliriously happy, and I wouldn't change a thing about the way I approached it all. I don't want to live quite so maniacally in the future, but I truly believe we need to test our desire for life, even our mental stability, to really appreciate the moments that follow.

I appreciate everything I have now. I take nothing for granted and still speak to my legs like they're my comrades. I'm a little bit crazy and a lot happy. I'm a hero . . . even if it's just to myself. I'd like nothing more than to share the rest of my adventures with the world, if the world will continue to support me as it has.

For just one time in my life, I wanted to be more than I thought I could be. As big as I would be. As bold as I should be.

Just once, I wanted to utterly believe in myself.

And now I do.

I'm not special. I'm a guy who loves to run and likes to have fun. But I'm living proof that 'impossible' is simply a barrier you've set in front of yourself, waiting to be hurdled. You just have to want what's on the other side. A better you. A happier life. But you do have to want it – really *want* it – before you can set out to take it.

Change is the challenge. Believing you can change is actually harder than implementing it. Once you believe, you give yourself permission to find the start line and begin your journey. However that plays out, you'll learn a lot about yourself. You might even become a hero too. Whatever the outcome, remember to do it for yourself. Your opinion of yourself is what matters most. Be your own hero.

Everyone deserves at least one great adventure in their lives. This one was mine.

ACKNOWLEDGEMENTS

I have many people to thank. I'll start with family:

Thanks to my beautiful little mum, Cherryann, for building me. Gay Black, my wonderful Mum #2, along with my inspirational dad, Bob Miller. My big brother, Chris, and his gorgeous wife, Janette, who crossed the world to see me. Loving Little Sister #1, Rebecca, and her fantastic husband, Michael. Gorgeous Little Sister #2, Alexis, who saved me from disaster so many times.

And friends:

Darren, aka Daz, the Dazzler, I couldn't have done it without you, buddy. You'll always be my brother from another mother. Matt Opray, for filling the void and making me laugh so hard. Nick McCormack, for doing an outstanding job, persisting for the whole year to keep the exposure coming. Clément Thevenet – part French, part superhero! –thanks for everything, my friend. And thanks to the entire Thevenet family, for helping me immeasurably. Andrew and Caroline Olah and Jackie Rogowski, for being there throughout my year. All the Tribal guys who came to visit – Andrew 'Chippa' Wood, Sian Wood, Nicolas 'the Cougar' Marie, Kevin 'Kevlar' Lieberthal, Shane 'Yabby' Campbell, Derham 'Mossy' Moss, Ali Holmes, Gareth Bowen, Koya Marney, Dave Nanfra. Thanks to Coach Andy and Pete Lockyer for their huge support, too. I'm grateful to all the smiling people at the Happiness Centre in Shepherd's Bush, London – thanks especially go to the magic hands of Tim Howard and Vijay Netto. Big thanks to Kenneth Krys of KRyS Global (my sponsors), Raymond from MyLAPS, Steve O'Farrell and Sputnick, Johnson and Johnson, the team at Areeba, and Jason Bennett and the team at ESPN. For inspiration in 2010 – Robbie and Frank, Haile Gebrselassie, Damon, Dionni and Jacqueline, Akinori Kusuda.

And a special thank you to Rebecca Anne Sherwill. For everything about you, my love.

I'm also grateful for those who helped along the way. In every country, during every marathon, I met wonderful people. They all contributed to my extraordinary experiences, so I want to thank them here. If I missed you, I apologise, but as you can imagine, the year was full of chance encounters and new friendships. Those named here have my sincere thanks and great appreciation. That sentiment goes out to all who read this and have supported me, or just made me laugh along the way.

Zurich: Roger Kaufmann. Tiberias: Vig and Saul, Roy, Jaynee, Avraham, Yossi, Ofer, Eyal, David, Max and Duby, Danny the Love Guru. **Mumbai:** Laura, Monty, Shobha, Kiwi Kerry. Dubai: Leanne and Hannah, Nick and Renata. **Canary Islands:** Bridget, Marcos, Edoardo, Rebeca, Juan, Tati, Bruno, Omar, Carlos, Fiorentina, Jaimie, Anne. **Marrakech:** Maria, Jamie and Julie, Alessandro, Thierry and Wendy, Maxi and Hamish. **Bad Füssing:** Dave, Nina and Asa. Jürgen Knaus, Günter and Barbara, Johannes Zwick, Helmut Karg, Carlos and Mareya, Amy and Ulrika, the really nice Swedish girls. **Luxor:** The Americans in Luxor, Cam and Teash in Dahab. **Verona:** Elisa and Laurence. **Tokyo:** Brendan and Emma Carey, AJ and Maiko, Fukuyo Nakamori, Sian, Toi, Akinori Kusuda, Alan Williams. **Napa Valley:** Jackie Rogowski, Nicholas Gross, Jessica and Colin, CJ Leedy and Julie, Stuart Sauvarin, Ed Wilkinson. **Cyprus:** Ironman Steve and the team, Tristan Andrews and family, Jes Walker. **Rome:** Dietmar, Massimiliano Monteforte, Nico Pannevis and Blanca. Samantha. **Bratislava:** Sharky, Steve Edwards, Brian Lang, Jozef Pukalovic. **Cape Town:** Vickie Francis, Joe, Deana, Camilla, Kempe, Sharon, Christina, Juli, Ryan, Hansie, Paula and Abby, Mike and Judes, Becky and Jo, Maria and James. Paris: Eric Heine, Chyrisse, Josh, Elisa and Laurence, Aussie Jay and Camilla, Rebecca, Mick and Westo, Narelle Bruhn, Donny and Dingo Davies, Billy, Tim Gruzca, Judy and Hanna. **Boston:** The Di Domenico family (Teyah, Troy, Millie and Georgie) and their Bostonian friends, Ben, Marielle and Megan, Paul Kehoe. **London:** Danielle and Hilton, Crystal, Lyn, Chris, Hamish and Phil, Natalie and Victor, Dave and Nina, Steve Edwards, Raf and Suzanne and Lulu, Tammie, Michael, Keith. **Belfast:** Willem, Kirsten, Philip, Harriet. Prague: Greg, Barjan, Garren and Nuala, Aileen, Per, James, Claire, Jen and Danielle, Lauren and Megan. **Great Wall:** Sharon, Susan and Lisa, Tony, Kate, Jo, Matt and Avril, Jan, Ben and Hanna, Anthony, Malaika and Joe, Cindy, Big Dan, Pete and Kat, Emma and Alyssa, Roberto and Carla, Arne and Gaech, Arthur, Ben and Hanna, the lovely Kiwi trio of ladies, the happy Mexicans and the Latvians (okay, I've forgotten some names), Dan, Anthony and Cindy, the mighty Deano. **Kigali:** Candice and Phillip. Keszthely: Lauren Backenstose and Canadian Chris. **Easter Island:** the owner of La Casa Roja whose name I've forgotten, Tanya, Jorge, Cecilia and her husband, Lyndsay and Pancho. **Rosario:** Royce, Clint and Nick, Milena, Vanessa, Neil, Paddy, Jacka, Scuddsy, Adsy and Ollie, Helen and Lilliput, Iván and Augustina, Tristan Pirouz. **St Petersburg:** Nikita and friends at the Atmos Hostel, Marush and Anna, Alya and Anastasia, the Italian lads. **Kristianopel:** Dr John Barnes, Roskilde Festival friends, Team Blekinge. **Zermatt:** Sophie Cosier for the nipple cream. **Busana:** The Ventasso EcoMaratona organisers. **Lake Hovsgol:** Wayne and Nolene, Maurice, Israel, Ramon and Ewin, along with all the organisers and competitors. **Siberia:** Oksana, Trish, Adrien and Marco. Helsinki: Cristina and Alice, Lauri, Jacob, Lassi and Nelli, Ossi, Anna and their friend, Salla. **Reykjavik:** Mel Bushby. **Stavanger:** David Craig, Els and Aksel, Dave's mates, Dr John, Emma and Joel, Jacqui and Erik. **Montreal:** Katherine and Dave, Maxime Boilard and Emmanuelle, Nathalie, Hugo and the boys, Allison McLerran. **Médoc:** Cedric, Sophie and the kids – Audric, Yvain, Laudine and Elvire, Amandine, Little Clovis. Wachau: Gerhard and Jennifer. Berlin: Jackie, James, Jeanette, the Tribal Boys (including Ali), Dietmar and Vijay. **Loch Ness:** Deano, Mike, Dave and Alan, Dr Johannes. **Chicago:** Chloe and Matt, the Wonderful Wendy. **Istanbul:** Kris and Kate, Helen. **Ljubljana:** Claes Holmberg and Clément, Goran and Branka. **Athens:** Izzy and Stelios, Deano and Zac, Bertrand, Marie and Sophie, Andy and Gordon Fuller, and back in London with Matt, Kim, Jackie Ro and Danielle. **New York:** Lisa and Susan, Koya, Haydn, Jason, Dan, Big Jay, Paul, Chris and Gareth, Trent Blackett, Breana from Lululemon. **San Antonio:** Cougar, Christian Hawkins, Hannah, Chris and all their friends. **Havana:** Antonio, along with the gorgeous Dutch girls, Ellie and Margreet. **Puebla:** Alejandro and Andrea, Fernanda, Sandra, Julio, Aunt Lucia and little Santi, Sean and Hangatu, Linda Birta. **Negril:** Sue McLaurin, Dionne, Navin, Vijay, Payal and Hiren, Cyndi and Mark Rose. **George Town:** Sarah and Scotty, Zac Watts, Dee, Conrad, Jason, Jane Wareham and Jerome, Ken Krys, Helen and Lori. Antarctica: Richard, Brent, Greg, Stephan and literally everyone I was down on the ice with amazing people all. **Melbourne:** Schepisi Communications, Bulla Yoghurt, Tribal, Powerbar, 2XU, National Australia Bank and Krys & Associates and all who turned up to celebrate my final marathon of the year.